SEXUAL ATTRACTION

SEXUAL ATTRACTION

By

MARK COOK and ROBERT McHENRY

PERGAMON PRESS

OXFORD · NEW YORK · TORONTO · SYDNEY · PARIS · FRANKFURT

U. K.	Pergamon Press Ltd., Headington Hill Hall, Oxford OX3 0BW, England
U. S. A.	Pergamon Press Inc., Maxwell House, Fairview Park, Elmsford, New York 10523, U.S.A.
C A N A D A	Pergamon of Canada Ltd., 75 The East Mall, Toronto, Ontario, Canada
A U S T R A L I A	Pergamon Press (Aust.) Pty. Ltd., 19a Boundary Street, Rushcutters Bay, N.S.W. 2011, Australia
F R A N C E	Pergamon Press SARL, 24 rue des Ecoles, 75240 Paris, Cedex 05, France
FEDERAL REPUBLIC OF GERMANY	Pergamon Press GmbH, 6242 Kronberg-Taunus, Pferdstrasse 1, Federal Republic of Germany

First edition 1978

British Library Cataloguing in Publication Data

Cook, Mark
Sexual attraction.
1. Interpersonal attraction 2. Sex
I. Title II. McHenry, Robert
155.3   HQ21   77–30391
ISBN 0–08–022231–5 h.c.
          0–08–022230–7 flexi

Printed in Great Britain by William Clowes & Sons, Limited London, Beccles and Colchester

CONTENTS

PREFACE

This book explores different sides of an activity that preoccupies many people during a large part of their lives. The point of that activity is to appear attractive to one or several other people. There is no need to emphasize its importance for the amount of time or money spent on it provides an index of that. Nor is there any need to emphasize the high regard in which is held one case of attraction — mutual attraction between sexes — for this provides the theme for the great majority of popular songs and the pulp for drama, films, and novels.

A lot is already known about attraction and in view of its importance in human social intercourse it would be surprising if this were not the case. For example, almost everyone knows what type of behaviour or appearance is admired by the majority in our society; almost everyone can describe the feelings of becoming strongly attached to someone or of falling in love. On the other hand, some of our knowledge about the subject may be mistaken. We are often so romantic and attach such value to an individual's freedom of choice in the selection of friends or of a marriage partner that we are blinded by roles played by social conventions as well as chance and arbitrary factors in the circumstance of choice. We have fixed ideas about the behaviour of both sexes in courtship because we believe these ideas have some biological basis. These are two examples of points of view that will be examined closely later in this book. Some attention, too, will be given to aspects of attraction about which little is generally known. Why are individuals attracted to some people and not others who may themselves be generally well liked? How is mutual attraction communicated to both people in a social encounter?

As well as trying to answer such questions, the book has certain major themes. One of these is to argue for the existence of a strong but often disregarded prejudice against those who are physically unattractive. The evidence to be cited in Chapter 2 seems to establish clearly that disfavour towards this group has all the trappings of racial and religious prejudices with which everyone is more familiar.

Reference has already been made to the romantic ideal that many people have about sexual attraction. It is often believed that many marriages happen after an exhaustive search by both partners to find someone who is compatible with their personality. In fact, the research reported in the later chapters suggests that romantic choices are made from a small sample of possible partners who are left after social influences have acted to rule out, in practice, the majority of those whom we could, in theory, have married. Nor does attraction depend only on the qualities, physical, social, or temperamental, of the individual, for chance plays a big part in the early stages of an encounter. Indeed, it is entirely a matter of chance, in the form where they happen to live or work, that brings couples together at all. When they meet or when they seek to strike up a relationship, the outcome will depend to some extent on things most people would not think relevant or, indeed, would indignantly deny had influenced them.

Finally, this book is an attempt to discuss sexual attraction with reference to empirical evidence where possible. Over the past decade more and more psychologists have become interested in this field and they have performed a number of studies and experiments — some of them very ingenious — to test expectations about attraction. Hopefully, all such experiments are performed in such a way that all factors extraneous to a certain effect are ruled out and only one plausible explanation of a result remains. Unfortunately, this state of affairs is rarely attained and often it is possible to see the result in more than one way. However, it is firmly believed by the present authors that only by carrying out experiments will it be possible to arrive at valid conclusions about attraction. Alternative explanations of studies will be put forward in later chapters when it is felt these are required, and certain experiments will be criticized for the lack of care taken in their execution. In the end, it is hoped that the main conclusions of this book will be seen as resting more or less firmly on an empirical base rather than being founded in socially conditioned 'commonsense' beliefs or on single-case anecdotes.

One of the comments consistently made by the five women who read the manuscript was 'It's male-oriented'. Up to a point this doesn't worry us because we wouldn't presume to write a female-oriented book; being men we naturally see things from a male point of view. Women who feel very strongly that our account is biased are free to write their view of sexual attraction. Nevertheless, our critics have a very good point because much of the research we rely on is male-oriented. Most of it was done by men, most of it takes the view that men take the initiative while women wait for it to be taken. Much of it, research being cumulative, was done some time ago, before attitudes changed; we include this research because it's there, but more particularly because it's likely to reflect opinion and behaviour still current in many parts of the world.

We would like to thank Janette Cook, Sally Lloyd-Bostock, Heulwen Ebsworth, Carole Stimson, and Beverley Hone for reading the manuscript and commenting on it.

Chapter 1

BEAUTY AND THE BEAST

*As the most basic form of sexual attraction is straightforward sexual
arousal, the book begins by examining what sexual arousal is in humans.
It has become fashionable, once again through writers such as Desmond
Morris, to see arousal as an automatic and instinctive response to the
sight or touch of another person's body. This leads to sexual contact and
ultimately to propagation of the human species. Such obvious parallels
with animal (particularly primate) behaviour are attacked in this chapter.
It is pointed out that although men and women are aroused by each
others' bodies, they come to this point only after a long period of
learning which produces a wide range of individual differences in
preferences for body types and not a few aberrations. Other evidence
against the automatic nature of human sexual arousal may be found by
examining the physiology of human arousal quoted here in simple form.
For example, it is surprising to find that in men the three processes of
arousal — feeling aroused, erection, and ejaculation — which are normally
assumed to be inextricably linked, are independent and controlled
individually by the higher brain centres. Finally, the chapter looks at the
idea that, as in most primate mating combinations, the human male is
the aggressive, easily aroused partner, while the female is passive and
slower to respond. This myth is debunked by reference to recent German
evidence and flaws in the famous Kinsey report, which have done much to
perpetuate the active/passive male–female sexual role idea, are pointed out.*

In insects, reptiles, fish, birds, and the lower mammals, sexual
behaviour is very largely instinctive. In monkeys, sexual behaviour is still
largely 'programmed'; the female does not have to learn to 'present'

herself nor does the male monkey have to learn what that signifies. Is the same true for humans? Do women instinctively make buttock presentations (or modified forms of them) while men instinctively respond? If you believe they do you would expect female genitals, buttocks, breasts, knees, or nudity in general to be automatically arousing to men. Actually, people's reactions to naked bodies depend a lot on their age, their experience, and on the customs and outlook of the society they live in. This first chapter will demonstrate how small the traces of instinct in human sexual attraction are.

Children in all societies are slow to develop shyness about their own bodies and are equally slow to develop more than a mild curiosity in other people's bodies and sexual organs. In many societies small children go about more or less naked. Even in colder or more prudish societies like ours, children are not very interested in bodily differences, and do not always find out very early what is concealed by the other sex's clothes. An ingenious American study [1] involved getting pre-school children to link upper and lower halves of nude and clothed bodies in a jig-saw puzzle type of task. The youngest children's responses make it clear that they recognised sex differences by hair style and clothing, and that they made many mistakes in genital recognition. As the age of children studied increased, fewer genital recognition errors were made, but just under 50% of 5-year-olds still made such errors. Interestingly enough, most children aged 8 still seemed unaware of the significance of the breasts as a female characteristic. This is not a unique observation, for other studies [2] have reported that about half of 7-year-old children were unable to distinguish between the sexes on the basis of genitals alone, whereas a higher proportion of 9-year-olds could. Only at age 11 do most children become aware that genitals are the essential distinguishing characteristic. Furthermore, children's reactions to seeing the genitals of the opposite sex show no hint of being erotic. One psychologist [3] interviewed children aged 5–13 years who were attending a paediatric clinic and asked those who had had the opportunity of seeing the genitals of the opposite sex how they had felt and responded at the sight. Most children accepted the genital differences as natural, although some were surprised and several thought the differences odd or funny. About half of the children believed that the girls had once had a penis but had lost it in some way.

Of course children may be a special case; perhaps the 'instinctive' reaction to nudity only appears after puberty, or perhaps Freud was right, and children aged 4–5 *are* very conscious of genital differences, but the fear of castration in boys, or the consciousness of it actually happening in girls, is so threatening that they repress all knowledge of sexual differences. But this is an unnecessarily elaborate theory. There must be a simpler explanation.

It is more likely that when adolescents experience their first sexual feeling they become fascinated by physical features of the opposite sex and associate them with their desires. The first sexual experience a boy or girl has is likely to have a big impact on him or her, generally pleasant but sometimes disagreeable. One theory about homosexuality argues that homosexuals are not so much attracted to their own sex as afraid of or disgusted by the other sex because of some disastrous experience in the past. This suggests that human sexuality appears in adolescence as a force lacking specific direction. It needs to be nudged along acceptable routes by socializing forces. When it meets resistance along these routes, it might well become diverted into less well-approved channels. Occasionally, some adolescents happen to take wrong or unusual directions with their new-found sexuality before learning the correct or more usual ones. Thus they have crushes on schoolfriends or teachers of the same sex, and it is very common as Kinsey *et al.* [4] discovered, for boys to have brief covert homosexual relationships. (Just as grown men will often resort to homosexual 'outlet' — to use Kinsey's phrase — when they are in prison or otherwise denied access to women.) Some of these adolescent associations are not extinguished early, and may form the basis for more lasting 'deviant' sexual behaviours. Occasionally sexual interest becomes focused on very odd things: not naked bodies, but ones wearing furs; not the genitals, breasts, buttocks, etc., but the feet; not physical contact or intercourse, but watching elaborate displays and rituals.

A recent theory [5] suggests that the direction given to someone's sexual interests by their first experience is confirmed or even refined by a programme of fantasy rehearsal of sexual behaviour and self-reinforcement — masturbation in other words. The boy or girl will think about that first experience while masturbating, which, being a pleasant experience, will increase their interest in whatever excited them initially.

Over time, however, the exact type of person, or activity, or setting for the activity, will 'drift' from the original, perhaps in the direction of becoming more bizarre and elaborate, as different elements in the fantasy first arouse fresh interest, then gradually lose their appeal. This is a plausible and ingenious theory, not least because it explains puzzling facts, such as how people can learn an interest in very odd sexual targets or activities — leather fetishes, for example — that they are unlikely to be able to perform in reality very often, if ever, and why people maintain such interests, despite the contempt, disgust, or even legal sanctions they tend to attract.

Any behaviour that is strongly 'reinforced' or rewarded — by masturbation to orgasm — several times a week obviously will tend to last. The author of the theory also suggests that the fact — reported by Kinsey and his colleague — that women report less homosexual experience and appear to have less interest in bizarre deviations follows from the fact — also reported by Kinsey — that they masturbate less than men. A dedicated instinct theorist could no doubt explain such rare deviations as mutations, or freaks, or the exceptions that prove the rule, but recent developments in psychiatry present further problems. If someone's sexual interest has become attached to something unusual it is often possible to transfer it to more usual targets by rewards, punishments, or both. A famous instance [6] is of a transvestite male whose sexual interest in dressing in women's clothes was eliminated by giving him electric shocks whenever he cross-dressed. If the target of sexual interest can be relearned fairly easily it is reasonable to suppose it was learned in the first place, especially given the wide variety of physiques, parts of the body, and adornments of the body that different people, in different societies, find sexually arousing. For example, it is often said that American men can be divided into three categories for sexual preference, coarsely referred to as 'breast men', 'buttock men', and 'leg men', according to the part of the female body they like most; these ideas were tested experimentally [7] using 95 college men and 15 silhouettes of female figures in which size of breasts, buttocks, and of legs were all varied. The men saw pairs of silhouettes — every possible paired combination in fact — and said which they preferred. The men did, indeed, divide into breast men, leg men, and buttock men, although it turned out there were two sorts of leg men — the ones who liked large thighs and calves, and the ones who preferred slim legs. More interestingly, the authors of the study found the different types of men had different personalities and different outlooks and interests. The 'breast men' tended to be *Playboy* readers and to be extrovert and masculine in their interests, whereas the men who liked small-breasted women were introverted and submissive, drank little alcohol, and held fundamentalist religious beliefs. Men who liked large buttocks were characterized by a need for order and neatness, whereas those who preferred small buttocks were wrapped up in their work and uninterested in sport. The most striking characteristics of those who preferred large legs was that they did not drink much and were more inhibited in social situations. Men who preferred small legs did not drink much either, but they did smoke and read sports magazines rather than *Playboy*. Overall differences revealed that preference for large women was linked to a desire to achieve — ambition in other words — and a high consumption of alcohol, whereas men who preferred smaller women were persevering and tended to be more upper class.

The first 'silhouette' study has been followed by two more [8,9] in which women chose male silhouettes, seen side-on or from the front. Both found that American women prefer men of average build, but if the man's physique is to deviate it should be bigger above the waist rather than below; as one author put it: 'Women have a very reliable preference for V's rather than pears'. Each study contains a long list of personality correlates, mostly so slight as to be insignificant, in the literal rather than the statistical sense. For example, women's preference for large men is correlated with an interest in competitive sport, with the women's own build (but in the less obvious direction of smaller women preferring larger men) and even with being raised in a fatherless home (and so choosing an idealized masculine man). Rejection of the muscle man, on the other hand, goes with drinking alcohol, smoking marijuana, and rejecting conventional values.

Some of these American findings have been confirmed by a study [10] in Britain, which showed that extrovert men prefer women with large buttocks and breasts, whereas introverts like their women a bit smaller. The introvert men also preferred women who had some clothes on, whereas the extroverts favoured nude women. The authors of the study suggested that the introvert men feel overwhelmed by naked and well-developed women and feel more at ease with thinner women. Another recent British study [11] used real pin-ups to examine men's preferences instead of the black-and-white silhouettes used in earlier research, and found marked individual preferences which seem good evidence of learned sexual attraction. Men of widely differing back-grounds — psychiatrists, psychologists, college porters, maintenance men, and soldiers — were shown 50 colour photos of women taken from magazines, all full length, one-third fully dressed, one-third in bikinis, and one-third naked. The men were asked to rate the girls, expressing their opinion of her as a marriage partner and as a short-term sexual partner. The results of this experiment are typical of the many studies of men rating women for attractiveness (not to mention the rather smaller number of studies in which women rate men). Some of the women in the photos had a more or less universal appeal regardless of the age, social class, or marital status of the men; not surprisingly, perhaps, these were mostly the nude or bikini-dressed girls. However, some interesting systematic differences emerged as well. The porters and soldiers preferred photos of large-breasted nudes in 'bedroom poses' or being sexy, whereas the psychologists liked young, predominantly dressed girls, who were 'unconventional' or 'provocative', and who were 'displaying arms and legs' — a group the porters and soldiers did not like much. All men, regardless of occupation, tended to choose attractive and conventionally dressed women when they were nominating possible wives, and avoided sexy and provocative poses. What a man finds attractive in a woman is not biologically determined but depends on his age, his social class, his personality, and — for want of a nicer way of putting it — what he wants the woman for.

When the author repeated his experiment, using photographs of men being rated by women, he again got a social-class difference, but this time a much larger one. The 30 nurses and cleaning staff tended to like 'muscle men' — taken oddly enough from magazines catering mainly for male homosexuals — whereas the professional women, psychiatrists and psychologists, found the 'Charles Atlas' types not merely unattractive but positively repulsive. Like their male colleagues, they preferred unconventional, mostly dressed, men, who were slim, dark, and sensitive looking. Very similar results emerged from a survey done by a New York newspaper. Men thought women liked a muscular hairy chest, broad shoulders, and a large penis, but were quite wrong, because the women actually liked small buttocks and a tall, slim physique, and many said they were repelled by the features men thought they admired. If British and American women had all liked muscle men, this might have gladdened the heart of instinct theorists, for would not such a man be the best mate, able to protect his woman, breed strong children, hunt successfully, and generally play Tarzan to her Jane? Unfortunately, women chose differently.

Looking further afield, to non-Western societies, the reports of anthropologists make it plain that there are few universal standards for the body beautiful. There are societies where tall and powerfully built women are preferred, others like thin women; very many like women to have a broad pelvis and wide hips, but at least one society specifically dislikes these features. Most other societies are not as 'breast-conscious' as ours, but those that are have again widely differing ideas about the right size and shape, some preferring long, pendulous breasts, others upright well-rounded ones, others going simply for size. Some cultures emphasize parts of the body that Western society pays little attention to, such as the lower leg, and value especially small ankles or shapely, fleshy calves. (It is interesting to recall that the Victorians greatly admired a well-turned ankle, perhaps because they were not allowed to see much more.) The anthropological reports say little about women's preferences for men's bodies, which might be significant.

Another very obvious difference between us and monkeys is that we wear clothes, not just for warmth but because we must keep genitals, as well as breasts in women, covered up. Morris and others regard this as evidence for their point of view, and argue that the sight of the genitals is such a powerful stimulus that they have to be hidden; otherwise men and women would be unable to resist the temptation to have intercourse, which would upset family ties, disturb the social structure of the tribe, and so on. The anthropological evidence appears in fact very compelling. Most societies require men to cover their genitals although there are quite a few exceptions, but nearly all societies recorded in the anthropological literature require sexually mature women to cover the vagina. Even in the few exceptions where women go entirely naked, some modesty is required, so that men are not supposed to look, or else women are taught to sit so that their vagina is covered perhaps by a foot. In fact none of this is really evidence that we instinctively respond to the sight of the opposite sex genitals, but can be very simply explained as an effect of learning or experience; once the man or woman 'has learned the facts of life', the significance of the vagina or penis dawns, and interest in it will remain strong. (To prove that humans do know 'instinctively' that the vagina or penis is sexually significant would be almost impossible. One would require to confront a sexually mature boy or girl with a naked person of the opposite sex, having ensured that he or she had never met one before, or been told about sex, and observe their reactions.)

Clothes can do more than simply conceal the bits of the body we are not allowed to show off, but can be used to change the shape of the body — the brassiere being the most obvious example, not forgetting the corset, girdle, backside padding, and the rest. Less obvious is the way many women try to alter the apparent position of their waist, usually to make their legs look longer, by putting the waist band of their skirt or the belt of their dress higher than its natural place. High heels — popular at the time of writing in 'clumpy' form — are also used by many short girls to make their legs look longer. It is standard advice to fat women not to wear horizontal stripes which make them look fatter, nor to wear tight clothes, which give a 'bulging' effect. Horizontal stripes *are* recommended to emphasize a small bust, or a large one for that matter. Clothes can change a man's figure in much the same way with perhaps more emphasis on height. High heels are now acceptable wear for men, which has probably meant hard times for the makers of built-up shoes. Shoulder padding is occasionally found, and enjoyed some popularity in the Teddy Boy suits of the 1950s. It is worth noting that Teddy Boy suits were definitely a lower-class fashion, confirming the surveys showing that middle-class girls do not admire a beefy torso. Hats, which can add quite a lot to a man's apparent height, as the British police helmet demonstrates, have gone right out of fashion. At one time some men wore cod-pieces — padded penis sheaths, that made it look as if the wearer had an enormous penis, and it has been said that some men wear very tight jeans to try to achieve the same effect. If it *were* fashionable to emphasize the penis — and it is doubtful that women would be favourably impressed — breeches as worn in the early nineteenth century would be much more effective.

Fashion really seems to be a conflict between two opposing interests — the young and attractive, on the one hand, who would like to show off their bodies, and, on the other, the older and less attractive who prefer to use clothes to cover up or improve their figures. Obviously the young and attractive will go for tight jeans, short skirts, tee-shirts without bra, or (for men) open-neck shirts, whereas the latter will prefer loose and flowing clothes, or at least — for women and a few men — clothes that can be worn with 'foundation garments', corsets and the like. Since the turn of the century the battle has been going steadily in the favour of the young as more and more of the leg especially has been revealed by shortening skirts and tightening trousers. In the past, fashion has been legally controlled by 'sumptuary laws'; for example, in Ancient Greece only upper-class women were allowed to wear dresses that exposed their breasts. The most striking and restrictive example of the control of dress is the Arab's flowing floor-length robes, supplemented by the veil for women, all of which make it virtually impossible to see anything of the wearer's figure.

A person's choice of clothes also, of course, tells other people a lot about him or her, and forms part of what sociologists call the 'self-presentation'. A recent study [12] in the north of England gave some idea how large the effect and of the range of messages people convey about themselves by their choice of clothes. In this study 15- and 16-year-old girls were given photographs of widely differing female outfits and asked what they thought about the sort of person likely to wear each. It is not surprising that they agreed on ratings of 'snobbishness', 'rebelliousness', 'shyness', and the like, but what was rather striking was the number of quite specific predictions they were prepared to make — that the wearer of one outfit smoked, the wearer of another drank, while the wearer of third had loose sexual morals and a lot of boy friends.

It is fairly obvious to anyone who has owned a dog or cat that smell features more extensively in their social and sexual lives than it appears to do in ours. The males of both species 'advertise' for a female by urinating on upright surfaces and also rely on their noses to determine whether a female is in heat or not. Monkeys also sniff and lick the female's genitals before mounting, while the sexual odours — or 'pheromones' — of moths can be detected by other moths literally miles away. At first sight it would appear that nothing of the sort happens in human sexual behaviour because we go to a lot of trouble to destroy or mask our natural body odours. Surveys in women's magazines have shown that virtually none — 2% to be precise — of their readership would admit to not using deodorants, while an experiment [13] in Britain showed that smelling of sweat was considered quite unacceptable behaviour in men and women. (A lot of people break the rule all the same as anyone with a sensitive nose will testify.) Many non-Western societies also use scents of various sorts, including flowers in the hair, aromatic herbs, or oils rubbed into the skin; according to one authoritative review of courtship [14], dirtiness is one of the few things that is universally off-putting.

Recently, however, the comparative argument has taken a new turn and it has been said that we use and react to natural body odours. The argument takes several forms. One is 'psycho-dynamic' and says that we must really be aware of sexual odours because why else would we go to such great lengths to suppress them, except that we are afraid of their great potency, unacceptable in our repressed society? This type of argument is highly suspect, reminding one of the old joke about the man who scatters powder everywhere to keep away elephants and says he knows it works because he has never seen an elephant. It is also historically inaccurate; the rise in the use of deodorants and the like has paralleled increasing freedom of sexual behaviour and outlook, whereas the highly repressed Victorians probably offended the nose rather by modern standards. Another argument for supposing the existence of human pheromones is comparative and anatomical; most animals use pheromones, while humans have a 'virtually complete set of organs which are traditionally regarded as non-functional, but which if seen in any other mammal would be recognized as part of a pheromone system', namely armpit hair, the male foreskin, and the female vaginal labia. It is further argued that the practice of circumcision reflects an unconscious realization of the role of sexual odour.

However, recently more direct evidence has come to light suggesting that pheromones exist in humans [15]. For example, steroid sex hormones emitted by women are said to be identifiable by dogs and mosquitoes. It is also believed that most women secrete a powerful and pleasant odour from their armpits which indicates their presence in a room; it is not a specifically sexual odour but is specifically female. Furthermore, children aged around 3 have a marked awareness of the sexual odours of adults and may even have a distaste for the smell of the same sex parent. It has also been established that women's ability to smell musk varies with the menstrual cycle. What is needed now, to settle the question, is research showing humans can detect sexual odours, and that one sex or the other is more attracted to partners who give off sexual odours than to ones who do not, together with some explanation of our apparent distaste for natural odours.

In animals sexual arousal and readiness can often be perceived relatively easily. For example, in monkeys the females of some species have a 'sex skin' on and around the vagina that changes colour when the female is in heat. In the female guinea-pig the vagina actually closes up when the animal is out of season. Sexual readiness in humans is rather harder to perceive. It is important to distinguish between 'general arousal' and sexual arousal. General arousal refers to a state of the nervous system usually characterized by mild palpitations of the heart, slight sweating, faster breathing, and the like. However, the effects of arousal may not always be as noticeable as this and may only appear as a slight enlargement of the pupils or a slight flush on the face. They are often so subtle that specialized electronic equipment is needed to measure — the so-called 'lie-detector' is an example of this. It is very difficult often to distinguish specifically sexual arousal [16] from forms of 'general arousal', including emotions of fear, surprise, and anger. If sexual arousal could be measured easily by monitoring body functions like breathing, then certain interesting studies could be carried out very easily. It would be simple to tell, for example, how sexually attractive a person was merely by measuring the physiological reactions of others to him or her. Equally it would be possible to find out just how arousing pornography is or to discover what sort of person is most aroused by it. However, at present such measures are difficult because the physical changes in the body can be easily misunderstood. For example, dilation of the pupil of the eye can be a sign of mild sexual arousal, but can also occur when we are thinking hard, are making a physical effort, or when we are surprised or startled.

It is in fact very difficult to know for sure that someone is sexually excited in the early stages of a sexual or would-be sexual encounter.

Masters and Johnson [17] distinguish four phases of sexual arousal — excitement, plateau, orgasm, and resolution. They conclude, after very detailed studies, that there are few if any visible signs of the first 'excitement' phase, and the ones there are appear only in some people. Thus sweating as a reaction to 'excitement' is only observed in 30 — 40% of men and women, and in fact the only specific signs of sexual arousal in this phase are erection in the men and vaginal lubrication and possible nipple erection in the female. A 'sex-tension flush' is seen in a minority of women (25%) appearing late in the 'excitement' phase first on the stomach then spreading rapidly over the breasts. These signs by their very nature do not communicate much about the other's sexual readiness that is not already obvious, with the possible exception of the male erection. By the time the man is in position to see a sex-tension flush on a women's stomach, or observe vaginal lubrication, he already knows that she is sexually excited. There are not any reliable long-distance early warning signs the man can use, and the only one — erection — the woman may be able to notice. These findings may surprise readers who distinctly recall the 'heavy breathing' and grunting and groaning some men and women go in for in the early stages of necking and petting. The point is that these are not part of the specifically sexual arousal pattern described by Masters and Johnson but are more likely to be a bit of showmanship in which a man and woman try to impress each other with how passionate and sexy they are feeling. Some misleading claims have been made by authors who either fail to realize the unreliability or non-specificity of such signs, or who perhaps confuse the preliminary 'excitement' phase with the three later phases which all occur after intercourse has started. Thus Desmond Morris in his *Intimate Behaviour* [18] claims that blushing and sweating are sure signs of sexual arousal, saying, for example 'the most important signal is the blush or reddening of the skin caused by vaso-constriction' and noting that pin-ups of either sex often show the body looking wet or shining in some way, simulating sweat. Blushing and sweating only occur in the later stages — plateau, orgasm, and resolution — and not invariably then, so cannot be used as any sort of clue to a person's intentions.

The male sexual arousal system has been studied in greater detail than the female one and several facts have emerged that cannot easily be explained. For example, the three main aspects of male sexual activity —

arousal, erection, and ejaculation — although linked are controlled by essentially independent systems of nerves and brain-centres. Thus it is possible for a man to be aroused without having an erection, to have an erection without being sexually aroused (as in fear or during non-erotic dreaming), and to ejaculate without having an erection. This last point is perhaps the oddest of all, but is clearly illustrated by a piece of research [19] on infertility involving 40 schizophrenic and normal males. A vibrating cup was applied with gentle pressure to the glans penis, and although full ejaculation was eventually induced in all 40 men, 'no full erection was ever observed' although in some instances 'a partial very soft erection was observed at the time of ejaculation.' Only five of the men reported erotic fantasies or orgasmic feelings in the period leading up to the ejaculation, which demonstrates that it is quite possible to have orgasm without arousal.

For men at least mild sexual arousal seems to have a pleasurable effect which remains with them after the events which led to the arousal. One investigator [20] demonstrated this by giving men the opportunity (or so they thought) to deliver electric shocks to other men who were with them in a psychological laboratory. Before taking part in this study, some of the men who were to deliver the shocks were shown pictures of scenery, furniture and abstract art. Others were shown nudes from *Playboy*. As expected, those who saw nudes delivered shocks of significantly shorter duration than the other men, which might be interpreted to mean that being only mildly sexually aroused can put men in a good mood.

Sexual arousal in women is less well understood. The ovaries in women do not seem to be crucial for sexual arousability as it appears they only generate the hormone necessary for vaginal lubrication. However, there is very tentative evidence to suggest that women at the time of ovulation are more easily aroused sexually than at other times. There are two studies which show this [21]. In one 48 female college students were assigned either to a pre-menstrual or ovulatory group depending on the time of menstrual cycles. All the individuals in both groups were asked to describe their mood at the time of the study and to state their sexual reaction as they watched colour slides of men taken from magazine advertisements. The findings indicated that the girl's general feelings of well being and her sexual arousability were higher at ovulation than at menstruation. Another study [22] examined the rates of sexual intercourse and orgasm that women reported on throughout their menstrual cycles and found that the highest rates of intercourse and orgasm occur at about the time when ovulation is happening.

Hormones such as androgen are known to affect a woman's arousability. Many women who receive androgen replacement therapy report increased sexual desire and this is partly because one of the effects of this hormone is to sensitize the clitoris. However, a woman's sexual arousal is not just dependent on her producing large amounts of androgen. It has been shown that beyond a certain level additional supplies of hormone may not make such a difference. From all this it may be seen that male and female sexual arousal (what we often call the 'sex drive') is far from being a simple and mechanical reaction to a sexual stimulus. It is a subtle and complicated process involving individual differences in responses and it is largely under the control of the higher brain-centres.

Because there are almost no other measures by which sexual arousal and attraction may be measured, most studies of sexual (as opposed to physical) attraction monitor changes in the penis or vagina of volunteer subjects. For men, the technique is to measure changes in the volume of the penis and this is sometimes accomplished by inserting it through a flat, soft, sponge rubber ring and an inner plastic tube made from a contraceptive, into a glass cylinder. Changes in the volume of air caused by any erection — full or partial — of the penis in the glass cylinder can then be monitored. There are many demonstrations of the effectiveness of this technique. In one, [23] 58 male homosexuals and 65 male heterosexuals to whom the apparatus had been fitted were shown a series of pictures of men and women. Erections to the pictures, as measured by the apparatus, correctly identified 48 out of the 58 homosexuals and all 65 of the heterosexuals. Equivalent measures of women's sexual attraction and arousal have not been so easy to devise, but the most successful method used to date is a thermal flow meter designed to measure changes of blood flow in the vaginal wall [24]. This device is mounted in a vaginal diaphragm with the centre cut out, which is inserted in the usual way. A device for measuring vaginal contractions, the control of which is taught in some forms of sex therapy, has also been described recently; [25] it consists of a flexible rubber chamber inserted in the vagina and connected to a pressure gauge. Techniques like these allow reliable research on the differences between what males and females find attractive, and on individual differences within both sexes.

One important difference between men and women is claimed to be that they are 'turned on' at different speeds and by different things. For example, when choosing a sexual partner women are said to be impressed by personality and character, whereas men tend to go for good looks. This can be illustrated by a study [26] of dating carried out in an American university. Men and women of about the same age were introduced to each other for the first time and asked to go and drink a 'coke' together for half an hour. Before the introduction some of the couples were told individually that the person they were about to meet was 'similar' to them, whereas others were told that they were dissimilar. (Both statements were quite untrue.) It was found after this brief date that the suggestion that they were similar influenced couples liking for each other but actual follow-up dating by the couples only occurred when they were allegedly similar *and* highly attractive. When couples who had continued dating were interviewed, the men generally said that it was the girl's appearance that had attracted them, whereas the girls tended to say it was similarity of outlook.

The view might be taken that a basic biological difference between men and women is being illustrated here. Some might even say, mistakenly, that in man as well as in other animals, it is the male who must take the initiative and follow the dominant role in courtship and mating. This ensures that only men with a certain amount of dominance and aggression will father children, which will in evolutionary terms be an advantage. It follows that the male of the species is pre-programmed for nearly immediate feelings of excitement in sexual encounters and that is why he is so easily excited by physical appearance. On the other hand, one could argue that all these findings are merely evidence of the sex roles our society teaches men and women. It *is* true that many men say that they choose their partners on the basis of looks, while many women say they pay more attention to personality, and it may equally be true that they actually do choose their partners on these differing criteria, but none of this actually proves there is an instinctive biological basis to mate selection.

The theory of sex differences in attraction gained a lot of support

from the Kinsey report, [27] which made three important points that
have tended to be taken as gospel ever since:

(1)   men are more easily aroused than women by the *sight* of a
       sexual stimulus, e.g. pin-ups;
(2)   men are more easily aroused than women by *reading* about sex;
(3)   the main method by which a woman can be aroused is close
       physical contact and by *touch* in general.

Kinsey and his co-workers reached these conclusions by a sort of opinion
poll. The standard question was: Does it arouse you sexually to see (or
read) sexual themes? The problem is that the phrase 'arouse you
sexually' is ambiguous and could easily be taken to mean Do you
experience other than a mild feeling of pleasure? For the poorly
educated who might not understand the question, interviewers were
allowed to rephrase it: Do you get all hot and bothered? Again this
suggests the idea of passion rather than titillation, and is doubly
unsuitable because it does not make it clear that sexual excitement, as
opposed to embarrassment or indignation, is meant. Only those who
grasped the idea that any degree of response might suffice would reply
appropriately. All this ambiguity almost certainly affected the replies
given by women more than those given by men, because men are almost
certainly less inhibited in admitting sexual impulses in such stark terms.
This all adds up to suspicion that Kinsey's data and conclusions about
visual stimuli and sexual arousal in women might be untrustworthy.

Just recently some more research has been done that incidentally
throws quite a lot of light on the topic, although it was meant to study
the effects of pornography. In a study [28] in Germany, men and
women were brought into a laboratory where they were shown a series
of 72 slides, ranging from one showing a person of the opposite sex in a
one-piece bathing costume to a naked couple in coitus face-to-face, man
above, showing genitals. The most 'hard core' picture in the series was
described by the authors as showing a couple in coitus in 'a position
other than from the rear or face-to-face'. Before they saw the pictures
the men and women were asked to give information about their work,
social and political attitudes, and their sexual history. Twenty-four hours

after they had seen the slides the men and women were asked whether it had had any effect on their feelings (e.g. making them feel aroused or sexually excited) or on their behaviour (e.g. petting, intercourse, masturbation). Only small changes were reported and the main difference between the sexes was that more men than women had been induced to masturbate. Otherwise the women's reports of their responses to the slides showed they felt much the same — and felt it just as strongly — as the men; women also said they liked what they had seen as much as the men.

There are several possible explanations for the difference between Kinsey's data and those of the German study. The German sample were young and college-educated, whereas Kinsey's sample included some from poorer backgrounds, with less education (but even so had a disproportionate number of college-educated women in it). It is more likely that women have actually changed over the 20 years between the two studies, and had become less inhibited. There is after all now at least one magazine — *Playgirl* — that includes full-frontal male nudes, and is intended for women rather than homosexuals. Yet another possible explanation is that the German respondents made their reports just a day after seeing the pictures, whereas Kinsey's respondents had to remember how they had felt when they had seen erotic pictures at some unspecified time in the past. Erotic material was hard to come by in the late forties and early fifties, especially for women, who were not supposed to like that sort of thing anyway. Finally, it is worth noting that the German study has been repeated in the United States with essentially similar results. [29]

If Kinsey was mistaken about women's reactions to what they see, perhaps he was similarly mistaken about their reactions to what they read. In fact there is new evidence [30,31] which bears on this question, also done in Germany, at the Institute for Sexual Research at the University of Hamburg. One hundred and twenty male and 120 female students volunteered, mostly single, sexually experienced, Protestant, and in their early twenties. Two stories were prepared for them to read, both dealing with sexual themes. In the first, sexual experience between a young couple was described in some detail, covering flirting, petting, foreplay, including oral-genital stimulation, intercourse in various positions, orgasm, and post-coital behaviour. In both stories the man and the woman took the initiative equally often, were equally active, and enjoyed themselves to the same extent. In fact the two stories did not differ in their 'plots' or in the actual sexual activities described; where they did differ was in the amount of affection expressed by the couple. In the first (affectionless) story it was made clear that the lovers had no bond except their interest in sexual gratification, whereas the second (affectionate) version described how affection as well as lust was present in the relationship. The people who came to the experiment got one only of the two versions to read, and their reactions during the reading measured. They were also given questionnaires on which to describe their sexual activity in the 24 hours before they read the story and the 24 hours after. The first main finding of the study was that men and women did not differ from each other in their preferences for the affectionless or affectionate story, although one might have expected the women to dislike the affectionless story. Also after reading either story both men and women were emotionally aroused and reported feelings of tension. Roughly 90% of the men registered partial erections during reading the stories, and a quarter of them had a full erection. One-sixth had what Masters and Johnson called a 'pre-ejaculatory emission' — the first stage of emission in males thought to serve to lubricate the vagina and appearing some time before the full ejaculation. Among the women, one-quarter experienced vaginal lubrication and a tenth experienced sensations in the breasts. One of the 120 women masturbated herself to orgasm during the reading. Both women and men were equally likely to be sexually excited by either version of the story.

The questionnaire about feelings and behaviour in the 24 hours after the experiment were compared with those for the 24 hours before and showed that both sexes felt more sexual tension and were generally restless. Women especially reported also more sexual activity, more orgasms, more sexual fantasizing, talked more about sex, and were more interested in films, pictures, or books with sexual themes, and seemed to have been more affected than men by the stories — not less as Kinsey had found

What of Kinsey's third hypothesis given that the first two have not stood up very well? For fairly obvious reasons it is more difficult to do an experiment to determine whether women would be more sexually aroused by touch than men, and no such study has been reported yet.

However, it has been established that right from birth girls receive more physical affection than boys, in our society at least, and it is possible that this piece of sex-role learning — teaching boys not to be cissies or mothers' pets — could affect adult sexual behaviour.

To conclude, the idea that men and women differ substantially in what turns them on is almost certainly a myth. Yet like most other myths about human behaviour it can be self-fulfilling; if enough people believe it to be a well-established fact with a firm biological basis, men and women will be forced to behave as if it were true. But why should people subscribe to this particular fallacy? Probably because a universal belief that men are more quickly aroused retains for men the expectation that they can take the initiative in sexual encounters. It also excuses men's occasional sexual misdemeanours, while making less excusable those of women. This creates the kind of sexual world that, on balance, most men prefer. In it men are encouraged to enjoy frequent sexual arousal because that is proof of their sexuality, while women are discouraged because a more gradual arousal is proof of theirs. The passive-active dimension of human behaviour which is commonly equated with the expected roles of both sexes is being exploited in a particularly subtle way. A stable society built on monogamy and the family can be more easily maintained if women at least demand greater minimal requirements for intercourse (like affection and love) than men do.

Thus in almost every respect our sexual behaviour — including arousal and attraction — is heavily influenced by social rather than biological considerations. Sexual attraction may be linked to reproduction and the survival of the species but is essentially a cultural phenomenon with greater scope for individual differences in preferences. Our physiological systems of sexual arousal which underlie attraction are more complex than those of animals, including apes and monkeys, and are much more under the control of the higher brain-centres. Again this permits freedom for the section of cultural and individual influences. Finally, our well-established beliefs about sex differences and about monogamy do not have much biological foundation either. Both sexes have potentially the use of the same senses and mechanisms to make them attractive to others and others attractive to them, but we have chosen by social means to suppress the full sexual potential of one for what is believed to be the greater good of both.

REFERENCES

1. A. Katcher (1955) The discrimination of sex differences by young children. *J. genet. Psychol.* **87**, 131–43.
2. S. M. Levin *et al.* (1972) The development of sexual discrimination in children. *J. Child Psychol. Psychiat.* **13**, 47–53.
3. J. H. Conn (1940) Sexual curiosity of children. *Am. J. Dis. Child.* **60**, 1110–19.
4. A. Kinsey *et al.* (1948) *Sexual behaviour in the human male.* W. B. Saunders Philadelphia.
5. R. J. McGuire *et al.* (1965) Sexual deviations as conditioned behaviour: a hypothesis. *Behav. Res. Ther.* **2**, 185–90.
6. C. B. Blakemore *et al.* (1963) The application of faradic aversion conditioning in a case of transvestism. *Behav. Res. Ther.* **1**, 29–34.
7. J. S. Wiggins *et al.* (1968) Correlates of heterosexual somatic preference. *J. Pers. Soc. Psychol.* **10**, 32–90.
8. P. J. Lavrakas (1975) Female preferences for male physiques. *J. Res. Pers.* **9**, 324–34.
9. S. B. Beck, C. I. Ward-Hull and P. M. McLear (1976) Variables related to women's somatic preferences of the male and female body. *J. Pers. Soc. Psychol.* **34**, 1200–11.
10. H. J. Eysenck (1972) *Psychology is about people*, p.96. Allen Lane, Penguin Press, London.
11. A. M. Mathews *et al.* (1972) The principal components of sexual preference. *Br. J. soc. clin. Psychol.* **11**, 35–43.
12. K. Gibbins (1969) Communication aspects of women's clothes and their relationship to fashionability. *Br. J. soc. clin. Psychol.* **8**, 301–12.
13. N. Worral *et al.* (1974) Personal hygiene cues in impression formation. *Percept. Mot. Skills.* **38**, 1269–70.
14. C. S. Ford and F. A. Beach (1952) *Patterns of sexual behaviour.* Methuen, London.
15. A. Comfort (1971) The likelihood of human pheromones. *Nature* **230**, 432–3, 479.
16. M. Zuckerman (1971) Physiological measures of sexual arousal in the human. *Psych. Bull.* **75**, 297–329.
17. W. Masters and V. Johnson (1971) *Human sexual response*, Little, Brown & Co., Boston.
18. D. Morris (1971) *Intimate behaviour*, Cape, London.
19. A. Sobrero *et al.* (1965) Technic for the induction of ejaculation in humans. *Fertil. Steril.* **16**, 765–7.
20. R. A. Baron (1974) Sexual arousal and physical aggressiveness: the inhibiting influence of 'cheesecake' and nudes. *Bull. Psychon. Soc.* **3**, 337–9.
21. M. E. Luschen and D. M. Pierce (1972) Effect of the menstrual cycle on mood and sexual arousability. *J. Sex. Res.* **8**, 41–47.
22. J. R. Udry and N. M. Morris (1968) Distribution of coitus in the menstrual cycle. *Nature*, **220**, 593–6.
23. K. Freund (1963) A laboratory method for diagnosing pre-dominance of homo- and hetero-erotic interest in the male. *Behav. Res. Ther.* **1**, 85–93.

24. P. W. Hoon, J. P. Wincze and E. F. Hoon (1976) Physiological assessment of sexual arousal in women. *Psychophysiology*, 13, 196—205.
25. T. G. Logan (1975) The vaginal clasp: a method of comparing contractions across subjects. *J. Sex Res.* 11, 353—8.
26. D. Byrne *et al.* (1970) Continuity between the experimental study of attraction and real-life computer dating. *J. Pers. Soc. Psychol.* 16, 157—65.
27. A. Kinsey *et al.* (1953) *Sexual behaviour in the human female.* A. C. Saunders, Philadelphia.
28. V. Sigusch *et al.* (1970) Psychosexual stimulation: sex differences. *J. Sex. Res.* 6, 10—24.
29. L. A. Jacobovits (1965) Evaluation reactions to erotic literature. *Psych. Rep.* 16, 985—94.
30. G. Schmidt *et al.* (1973) Responses to reading erotic stories: male-female differences. *Archiv. Sex. Behav.* 2, 181—99.
31. G. Schmidt (1975) Male-female differences in sexual arousal and behaviour during and after exposure to sexually explicit stimuli. *Archiv. Sex. Behav.* 4, 353—65.

Chapter 2

YOUR FACE IS YOUR FORTUNE

Here the process whereby we come to see others as beautiful and (sometimes) sexually desirable is examined. In the past there have been few international and universal standards of beauty — although most cultures could define an ideal. However, this has all been altered by the spread of American/European films and television shows throughout the world. There is now evidence of increasing standardization of ideals of physical attractiveness of men and women. As these ideals of physical attractiveness come to be shared more widely, they also seem to be desired more and more by those who do not possess them. Thanks to advertising practices which have exploited this envy, there is an increasing tendency for people to forget that beauty is only skin deep. Beautiful people are seen as good people to know; they are an aristocracy who can enjoy many privileges which are denied to others. Several examples are given to support this. The argument goes on to examine how even very young children come to value looks, and evidence is cited to show that young children can be said to select their friends according to adult standards of physical attractiveness. In a final section it is demonstrated that the so-called beautiful face is rarely regular nor does it conform to any recognized aesthetic principle. This underlines the idea that our society's choice of whom to call beautiful owes a fair bit to chance. Even great artists like Leonardo da Vinci have failed to define adequately a 'beautiful' face.

Charles Darwin [1] quotes Hearne ('an excellent observer') who has said:

'Ask a Northern Indian what is beauty, and he will answer, a broad flat face, small eyes, high cheek bones, three or four broad black lines across each cheek, a low forehead, a large broad chin, a clumsy hook nose, a tawny hide and breasts hanging down to the belt' [p.289].

Darwin, of course, is underlining the fact that there are few, if any, universal standards of physical attractiveness. What is sauce for the Western European goose is not, it seems, sauce for ganders in many other parts of the world. This opinion has been echoed so frequently that any statement about disagreement over standards of human beauty has become uninteresting. What is, therefore, the more surprising and fascinating is the fact that any two cultures or sub-cultures agree at all about human attraction.

One of the more convincing demonstrations [2] of this point began in 1960 with the publication, in England, of 12 black-and-white photographs of young women in the now defunct national newspaper, the *News Chronicle Dispatch*. The 12 photographs appeared in two sets of 6 in successive issues of the paper and readers were asked to record their preference for the faces in rank order on a special form and to indicate their age group, occupation, and address. The photographs themselves had been selected to provide as great a range of facial shapes, colouring, eye shapes, etc., as possible. All the girls in the photographs were aged between 20 and 25 and none was a professional actress or model. To ensure that the photographs were comparable, all showed a three-quarter profile of the head and shoulders in which no clothing or jewellery was visible. In addition, all photographs were taken by the same photographer using identical lighting.

When the preferences of newspaper readers for the girls were examined* one rather surprising fact emerged. There was a marked agreement among the average orders of preference of men and women of different age groups from many different walks of life. The only real deviations from this consensus occurred in the age group 55 years and older and among members of unskilled occupations. Even these deviations were not dramatic, and evidence seems to point towards there being some standard idea of female facial beauty in the United Kingdom.

Five years after this British study had been published, another emerged to enlarge and strengthen its conclusions [3]. This time a

*A total number of 4355 readers sent preferences.

national Sunday supplement published in the United States was chosen to display identical photographs of the same girls used in the British work. Again, readers were asked to rank the girls in order of prettiness and to give some background information about themselves. The surprising fact is that readers in the two countries agreed so much in their standards of beauty. The first three ranks in each national sample were occupied by the same three girls in the same rank positions. Only three photographs showed some deviation, the greatest of which was that the girl who was placed last by British newspaper readers was placed exactly in the middle by Americans.* It may be clearly seen just how close the cultural contact between these two countries has become. Two additional facts are of interest to members of both cultural groups. First of all, there was no marked difference between preferences of the unskilled group of workers and the others in the United States as there was in Britain. This is consistent with the idea that class is of greater relevance as a social variable in the latter country. Secondly, although those over 55 years of age in the United States tended to differ from the rest of the population† in their preferences just as in Britain, within every age range the American preferences are more uniform than in Britain and thus seems to emphasize the greater uniformity of American tastes.

Of course, these two studies have limitations. In particular, black-and-white photographs emphasize static features and lack the colour balance as well as the expressiveness of living faces. Perhaps, too, physical attraction has as little to do with choosing a face as speculating on the Miss World contest has to do with choosing a wife. Nevertheless, consensus over a concept of 'prettiness' has been demonstrated in a sample representative of 250 million people in two countries of the Western world and it is worth speculating on how even this result could have come about and what its implications are.

When a large number of people can reach agreement about any measurement, it suggests that some standard exists against which they are making their judgements. In the case of physical measurements of heaviness or distance, standards are readily available in the form of

*Although 101,000 readers sent preferences in the American study, only 6162 responses were actually analysed.
†No indication of racial differences within the American sample is given.

weights or rulers. In the case of facial measurements, it is probably the appearances of models in magazines or the physiognomy of the film star which provides the universal comparison. But even if we agree that it is the film-makers and the advertising men who remind us about what is attractive, such an explanation will not take us very far. Why should a certain face or body form become a universal standard? Why should physical attraction be so important that we should want to measure it? Why should physical attraction help sell goods or contribute a reason for going to the cinema?

The third question will be taken first because it is the easiest to answer. Physical attraction helps sell goods because so many other socially desirable human attributes are associated with it. Indeed, it was Schiller's (1882) statement of that fact, 'Physical beauty is the sign of an interior beauty, a spiritual and moral beauty', that led to a study of whether such an assumption is true today [4]. Sixty male and female undergraduates at the University of Minnesota were each given three envelopes — each envelope containing a photograph of someone their own age. One of the photographs was of a physically attractive person; another was of a person of middling attractiveness; and the third was of a relatively unattractive person. These ratings of attraction were taken from the judgements of 100 Minnesota undergraduates who had participated in an earlier study. Half of the undergraduates in this present study were asked to look at photographs of girls and the others to look at boys.

The task of the undergraduates in this study was to rate the person portrayed in the first envelope he or she opened (and the study was so arranged that only a third of those taking part saw the physically attractive person first, or the unattractive person first, etc.) and then to open the other envelopes one at a time and to do the same. They were asked to rate altruism, sensitivity, outgoingness, warmth, and a large number of similar traits. Other estimates were also required in the areas of marital happiness, parental happiness, social and professional happiness, and occupational success. As the experimenters expected, the physically attractive people portrayed in the photographs were assigned more socially desirable personality attributes than the middling attractive group who, in turn, were assigned more than the unattractive group. In addition, it was expected that undergraduates in the study would assume attractive people to be more likely to hold prestigious jobs, experience happier marriage, be better parents, and enjoy more fulfilling social and occupational lives. All these expectations were met except in the case of parenthood, where the middling, followed by the least attractive, were estimated to be likely to make better parents. Beautiful girls are not seen as good all the way through, however; they may be rated as warm, intelligent, outgoing, and all the rest, but they are also seen as vain, egocentric, bourgeois, and unsympathetic to the poor [5]. Perhaps the last word on the beauty stereotype should be left to a rather tasteless recent experiment. [6] Asked to select the people most likely to be epileptic, from ten photos, subjects picked unattractive girls 69% of the time, and unattractive boys 83% of the time.

One problem that is always present is to say just how much people's behaviour outside the psychological laboratory reflects the assumptions they seem to make within it. In this case there is evidence to support a link between physical attractiveness and social desirability. It is known, [7] for example, that high school girls in the United States will choose a physically attractive male counsellor to advise them rather than a counsellor who is said by his peers to be warm, friendly, enthusiastic, capable, caring, and responsible. It is also known that women in the street are more likely to give other women explicit directions to a destination if those other women are attractively dressed as opposed to having ungroomed hair, army jackets, and jeans [8]. There is evidence, too, to suggest that a woman made up to look physically attractive will influence the opinion of a male audience more greatly than if she appears before them looking unattractive [9].

In 1972 William Raspberry, a *Washington Post* columnist, voiced a widely held suspicion — that physically unattractive women are discriminated against when applying for jobs, and demanded 'equality for uglies'. In an experimental test [10] of Raspberry's accusation, professional interviewers, as well as student volunteers, put 12 applications in order of merit for a specified job. The applications were systematically varied according to academic qualifications, sex of applicant, and — by an attached photograph — for attractiveness. It turned out that an attractive face was worth on average just over two rank positions to its possessor, and the effect was as great for handsome men as for pretty women. Women incidentally were discriminated against as a sex, being placed nearly a full rank position lower than the males.

Of course one could argue that there is logic of a sort in choosing an attractive employee if one is going to spend a lot of time with him or her, but there is evidence that people will favour the good-looking, just for the sake of it, even when they know they will never meet. The 'lost letter' technique has been popular with American psychologists over the last decade: a letter is 'accidentally' left in a public place, and the readiness of passers-by to put themselves out to the minimal extent of posting it in a nearby postbox forms the psychologists' data. If the letter takes the form of an application for a college course, complete with photo, it is possible to study the effects of race and attractiveness [11]. As had been found before, white Americans discriminate against black Americans even at the trivial level of being disinclined to post on their lost letters. They discriminate just as strongly against unattractive Americans, whose letters were sent on by only one in three finders, while letters with attractive photos were rescued half the time.

It seems that we like and trust the physically attractive more on first acquaintance than the physically unattractive. That we do so is undoubtedly due to a straightforward piece of psycho-logic which we employ and which is discussed more fully in Chapter 3. It is sufficient to say here that it can be thought of in terms of two concepts: one is of the beautiful body and the other is of the beautiful soul. We try to force these together because it helps simplify our view of the world and the judgements we make of the people in it. Even though knowledge of a person's qualities may be our goal they are not easily visible from appearance and so we link them with the most likely physical attributes. Physical attraction is visible, personal and admired in itself and therefore becomes an obvious candidate for the kind of association referred to above.

One of the most convincing demonstrations of this lies in the association of a highly visible and admired physical attribute like male height with other desirable human characteristics. As male height increases, so does an expectation of socially desirable personal qualities. In one study [12] students, asked to estimate the heights of the assistant director of their school, their instructor, and two fellow-students, overestimated the heights of the staff members and judged their fellow students to be shorter than they actually were. In another, [13] five different student groups had to estimate the height of a Mr. England who was introduced to them as either a student or a demonstrator or a lecturer or a senior lecturer or a professor from the University of Cambridge. Height estimates were shown to be significantly different between status levels one level apart. So, as authority level increases so does the tendency to see the individual as taller than a person of lesser status. It seems, too, that this height phenomenon extends to the area of politics. 'It is not by chance', one sociologist, Feldman, said in 1971, 'that every American president elected since at least 1900 has been the taller of the two major political candidates' [14]. Indeed, shortly before the American presidential election in 1960, 3018 Californian voters were asked which of the two candidates, Kennedy or Nixon, they personally favoured. They were also asked which of the two they thought was taller. A positive relationship between voting preference and judgement of height was found among respondents of both sexes [15]. Similarly, in another study [16] Lyndon Johnson's height was estimated as greater by those men who liked him than by those who did not. The result was only partially confirmed for women estimators, but in the case of the popularity and height of Lady Bird Johnson it was confirmed in the case of members of both sexes who guessed. Finally, in one survey [17] of recent University of Pittsburgh graduates' reported in the *Wall Street Journal*, it was stated that the taller students (6 ft. 2 in. and over) received an average starting salary 12.4% higher than those who were under 6 feet tall.

Returning to Nixon and Kennedy again and the 1960 election, several experts thought that Nixon may have lost partly because of his appearance, described as 'weak', 'pale', 'flabby', 'drawn', and 'tired', which compared unfavourably with Kennedy's 'healthy tan'. The story about the combination of Nixon's heavy beard and the slight X-ray effect of TV cameras making Nixon look unshaven is also often told. A recent analysis [18] of the 1972 Canadian federal elections showed that a politician's appearance and the votes he gets are, indeed, linked but in a more complicated way. A sample of 79 candidates, standing in 21 seats, had obligingly contributed photos of themselves to a local paper, so it was easy to get 70 students, male and female, to rate them for attractiveness — some time after the election when they were no longer recognized as candidates — and compare these ratings with their success at the polls. At first sight the effect of being good-looking was staggering; the 15 most attractive candidates received an average of 32% of the vote and seven of them won their seats, whereas the 15 least-attractive candidates received an average of only 11% and only one got in. It would be premature, however, to condemn elections as mere beauty contests, because it turned out that the unattractive candidates were mostly standing for fringe parties who had little hope of winning, so it is impossible to say whether voters were voting for the three major parties or for attractive candidates or a bit of both. This leads naturally to the question why candidates for fringe parties should be less attractive; the authors of the study offer four reasons: (a) unattractive people become malcontents and naturally gravitate towards extremist fringe groups, (b) major parties are conventional in outlook and choose conventionally acceptable, i.e. physically attractive, candidates, (c) attractiveness helps one advance in any large organization including the major parties, and, finally, (d) the major parties deliberately choose attractive candidates because they think they stand a better chance. All four suggestions are controversial but none so much as the first which says that unattractive people become 'alienated' from society and want to change it, in other words that radicals and revolutionaries are projecting their personal problems in their desire to change things. It would be reasonably easy to test this theory, at least superficially, and any competent psychologist could design a suitable experiment, collecting a proper sample of radicals, left and right, and a sample of moderates, equated for age, social class, and so on, and photographing them under standard conditions — no clothes visible or all wearing smocks, no make-up, uniform hair and beard lengths — to avoid clues to outlook and consequent bias. The need to get volunteers to have hair and beards trimmed might prove quite an obstacle, but the real reason no such study has appeared yet is almost certainly the fear of what it might prove.

One small piece of evidence has already been published, however, on attractiveness and women's liberation. When the movement first started attracting attention, many people were quick to dismiss its members as misfits, and one form this attack took was saying they were ugly. In fact this idea is still alive, as an experiment [19] published in 1975 shows;

both men and women tended to pick out photos of less-attractive women as supporters of women's liberation, and surprisingly this was true even for supporters of the movement. The experiment also showed that the mis-fit accusation was false, at least so far as appearance went, because the supporters of women's liberation were just as attractive or unattractive as girls who were opposed or indifferent.

It would not be surprising to find that just as we associate physical attractiveness and desirable qualities in the contexts discussed above, we also associate them in a context which has important personal relevance. This is the situation in which we date and, ultimately, marry an opposite sex partner. In order to get some idea of the importance of physical attraction to dating couples, some psychologists in the United States went to the trouble of arranging a 'computer dance' for over 750 freshmen students at the University of Minnesota [20]. They advertised the event with the statement: 'Here's your chance to meet someone who has the same expressed interests as yourself', and gave prospective participants to understand that if they gave the computer some information about their personalities, it would match them with a like-minded date. When students turned up to buy tickets for the dance (a few days before the event) and complete their personal assessment profiles, their physical attractiveness was independently estimated by four confederates of the experimenters. At this point the investigators had measures of the social skill, personality, and intelligence as well as the attractiveness of each student, but they chose not to use any of this information in the subsequent matching. Instead, they paired all the couples on a random basis with the only proviso that the man should be taller than the woman. Their assumption was a simple one. They reasoned that the couples who liked each other best would be those who had similar levels on an index of socially desirable attributes taken from measures of popularity, intelligence, sociability, physical attractiveness, and the like.

Questionnaires were given out at the intermission of the dance and partners completed these individually and in private saying how much they liked their dates. Then, 4–6 months after the dance, all participants were contacted again and asked whether or not they had dated after the dance. When all this information was examined, only one item out of all the original data gained about the participants proved to be consistently relevant to the prediction about whether either partner liked his or her date, or how much he or she wanted to see the other again, or how often the man asked his partner for dates afterwards. That item was the partner's physical attractiveness, and even high intelligence and exceptional social skill could not match it for predictive power in this situation. When this investigation was repeated using smaller numbers of couples by two psychologists working at another university, very much the same result was obtained [21]. This time only 29 couples were allowed to attend the dance and they were randomly assigned with the qualification, as before, that the boy be taller than the girl (in order to conform to a very well-established social norm). Two hours after the dance had started participants were asked privately about how good looking they thought their partner was, about his or her interests, intelligence, attitudes, etc., and about whether or not there was anyone else at the party they would like to date. Answers about the partner's attractiveness were almost completely predictive of answers to the question Would you like to go out with your date in the future? The results were the same for both men and women. In addition, the inquiry about who else might be dated produced a total of 14 names — 13 of these were of people spoken of as very attractive by their assigned dates and by two observers placed at the dance by the investigators.

Of course, computer dances are a special case (in more senses than one, being largely unknown in Britain). Physical appearance might well be the key to attraction in first encounters, but what of subsequent meetings? The computer dance technique was extended in a subsequent study [22] to a series of five meetings and, as in the computer dance experiment, measures of personality — characteristic anxiety level — were taken. Contrary to expectation, anxiety did not take over from appearance as a predictor of (progressively decreasing) attraction; appearance remained as all important on the fifth date as on the first.

Further relevant data comes from two surveys on the link between frequency of dating and appearance. Both showed that more attractive girls get more dates but reported conflicting results for men. One survey [23] found that appearance and dating frequency were not related in men, whereas the other [24] found modest correlations between male appearance, dating experience, sexual experience, and absence of dating anxiety. The difference between the two surveys seems to be that the first asked about dates on three specific, special occasions, New Year's Eve, school dance, etc., for which, it might be argued, every man eventually finds a partner because he keeps asking until someone says yes (unlike the girl who has to wait to be asked), whereas the second asked about dating experience in general. The really telling comparison would involve the ratio between offers made and offers accepted — likely to be low for attractive girls and high for attractive boys.

Of course, those taking part in the computer dance studies were college students, or even high school students, and one could argue that as people get older physical attractiveness in a partner becomes less important; even if it does, the realization may come too late for many people who married or become engaged at college. Several surveys [25] have shown that the attractiveness of husband and wife, rated independently, are similar, even in the middle age [26]. This, of course, follows from the facts that most people go out with partners of comparable attractiveness, marry young, and keep their relative place on the hierarchy of attractiveness. It would be interesting to discover whether marriages concluded after long courtships, or after several engagements, or later in life, show less matching for appearance. If they did show less matching, this would be the ultimate proof of the theory, explicit or implicit in much of the research, that marrying someone for their looks is somehow wrong or immature.

Why do teenagers want to go out with someone good-looking? At one level this is a silly question because it is circular; a good-looking person is virtually by definition someone other people want to go out with. At another level it is asking about the aesthetics of good looks, which is discussed later in the chapter. At a third level it is not a silly question, as studies on 'radiated beauty' demonstrate. A man was seen with either an attractive girl or an unattractive girl and his personality was rated. There is logically no close link between a man's personality and the appearance of the girl he is with, but it emerged [27] that a man associated with a good-looking woman was seen as more self-confident, likeable, and friendly than when he was associated with an unattractive one. It was shown, too, that men who were being rated could predict accurately the impressions they were likely to give in the different paired situations, and it is difficult to believe that in everyday life people's behaviour is not affected by this kind of knowledge. Good-looking people probably make their partners feel good and apparently even change people's views of themselves (see Chapter 3).

The rewards which a person gets from having a physically attractive partner seem exactly like those he or she might get from owning a new car. Indeed, this idea was the topic of a paper written about American college dating in 1937 [28]. The sociologist who put forward the notion believed that selection of a partner was made with 'competitive-materialistic' considerations uppermost in many partners' minds and that such considerations were irrelevant to harmonious marriage. The conclusion may be unsound but the premise probably is not. Good looks confer prestige on those who possess them and on those who are linked with those who possess them: good-looking people know this and their partners or potential partners know this. What repercussions does this fact have? For one thing it grants to physically attractive people the power to determine other people's sexual worth. This has been demonstrated in a number of experiments on dating [29]. In one, men and women whose physical attraction has been assessed by independent judges, had to choose a date from a range of partners varying in sexual attractiveness who were offered to them. Physically attractive dates were chosen by everyone, but there was little doubt that the less-attractive men and women chose less-attractive dates than did the more attractive. People seemed to know their own level of looks and to make their own estimates about who would make a match for their level of good-lookingness. In a related study [30] involving men as choosers and women as choices it was shown that men would choose a more physically attractive woman as a date when her acceptance was promised to them than when it was not. Equally, they estimated that a highly attractive woman would be less likely to accept them than one who was not. Both these results are unremarkable. Most important for the present argument was the demonstration, in the same study, that the attractive men estimated their chances of acceptance as much higher than those who considered themselves to be low in physical attractiveness.

There is evidence, too, that the social power and prestige held by the physically attractive leads to their being more upwardly mobile. A sample of women born in the early 1920s were studied during adolescence and adulthood in the United States and those who became upwardly mobile through marriage were compared with the others who remained 'in their own class' [31]. Upwardly mobile women were characterized by high physical attractiveness, a desire to impress and control others, and an avoidance of steady dating. The effect of physical attractiveness was most marked among members of the working class where it was more predictive of marriage to a man of higher class than educational attainment was. Good grooming and sexual restraint were also related to a rise from this class. In a separate study [32] conducted in Michigan, 50 girls who had been rated for physical attractiveness were asked about the preferred occupations of their future dates. Those low in physical attractiveness said they would prefer dates within the occupations of intermediate status (like electricians, bookkeepers, plumbers) or within the higher status occupations or professions. Highly physically attractive girls, however, rejected even the intermediate occupations and opted (on paper) only for the professions. It is evidence such as these studies provide that has frequently given rise to a mild panic among theorists who suppose that the upper strata in our society will eventually possess the overwhelming share of its good looks as well as its wealth and brains. This idea is discussed in Chapter 3.

Although it may be seen that people tend to make their initial choices of others in terms of physical attractiveness, and that the physically attractive are often upwardly mobile members of society, if you ask people what they seek in a partner they will relegate good looks to a low place in their priority. In an early study of this, physical attractiveness was said to be sought for only after 'pleasing behaviour', 'affectionate disposition', 'individuality', and 'sincerity' [33]. A more recent piece of research compared the evaluations Canadian and American students gave of the characteristics they sought for in a mate in 1967 with answers given by similar groups in 1956 and 1959 [34]. Women at all three times rated good looks as last or next to last: men showed an increase in evaluation of the characteristic over the years but even in 1969 they gave it eleventh place. In another investigation 'looks' was said to take third place in importance behind 'personality' and 'character' [35]. In yet another, physical attractiveness was judged by both men and women to play only a 'moderate' part in eight varied situations of heterosexual attraction which were presented to them [36]. One conclusion which might be drawn from all this is that people participating in these inquiries are not being truthful about the influence of physical attraction on their heterosexual choices. It is far more likely, however, that a gradual process of socialization has made people unaware of such influence.

Evidence of such socialization has only recently come to light and it makes fascinating reading because it seems to show quite clearly that even very young children are able to assimilate adult values concerned with physical attractiveness. One investigator [37] at first estimated that it would take children around 10 years to learn the simple cultural associations connected with body-build. Accordingly, he asked boys aged 10–20 years to look at photographs portraying fat, medium, and thin adult males and to give an indication of the character traits held by the different types. The results showed clearly that a common body-build stereotype exists in this age range. The medium, muscular build is associated with positively valued traits and behaviours, whereas the other two builds are assigned descriptions which are relatively unflattering. The same investigator then carried out two more researches, [38] this time with five-year-old children, and found to his surprise that even kindergarten children have a preference for physiques consistent with their society's favourable opinion of average body-builds.

Of course, to show children pictures of adults and ask them to make judgements may be different from getting their opinions about their peers of whom they have more direct experience. Underlying this is the idea that stereotypes derive from fleeting acquaintance with people or from ignorance associated with the social distance between them. At least one investigation [39] — primarily intended as an inquiry into reactions to skin colour — has explored this idea in relation to children. Here, 504 children aged 10 and 11 who all attended schools in south-east London with a coloured population took part; 195 of these children were classified as 'coloured' and the rest as 'white'. The technique used for the study was to show children six specially drawn pictures of children the same age and sex as themselves and to ask them to rank them in order of preference. ('Tell me which boy (girl) you like best.' 'Which boy (girl) do you like next best?') The following six pictures were used:

A child with dark skin colour and no visible physical handicap.
A child with white skin colour and no visible physical handicap.

A child with white skin colour with crutches and a left leg brace.
A child with white skin colour and a left forearm amputation.
A child with white skin colour and a slight facial disfigurement.
A child with white skin colour who is obese.

The point of presenting so many variations of the picture of the white child was to allow some measurement of the 'preference gap' between the white and black pictures portraying a child without handicap. Is this gap so big that even blemished white skin or exaggerated body-build is preferred to average black? The results show that it is not. On average, the picture of the white child who is not handicapped is the most liked and that of the coloured child without handicap comes second. This finding holds for all four sets of children used in the study (white, non-white, boys, and girls) except for the white boys who rated the coloured child as third most liked. The preference order for all four groups is shown in Table 2.1. Two features of this table are immediately striking. First of all, even coloured children prefer white children to black and, secondly, obesity is considered by almost all groups to provide the greatest barrier to liking. The former finding has been frequently attained in the United States and it clearly demonstrated how strong the transmission of cultural values is. Minorities

TABLE 2.1. PREFERENCE RANK ORDER FOR COLOURED AND WHITE 10–11-YEAR-OLD BOYS AND GIRLS FROM SOUTH-EAST LONDON, ALL SCHOOLS COMBINED

Picture	Boys Coloured Rank order	Boys White Rank order	Girls Coloured Rank order	Girls White Rank order
Non-handicapped white child	1	1	1	1
Non-handicapped coloured child	2	3	2	2
Facial disfigurement child	3	2	3	3
Crutches and leg brace child	5	6	4	4
Amputation left forearm child	4	4	5	5
Obese child	6	5	6	6

can be persuaded to denigrate themselves on no better grounds than those of skin colour. The second finding demonstrates the same point about cultural transmission but suggests in this case a reason for the judgement made of the obese relative to the handicapped at least. Handicapped children probably elicit some sympathy from other children because their injuries are assumed to be no fault of their own. The obese, on the other hand, are judged harshly to have let themselves go, to have overeaten or taken little exercise, and therefore to have character traits which will make them unpopular. Thus it seems that cultural values enter into children's judgements of the attractiveness of their peers just as they do into their judgements of adults.

However, this result, interesting as it is, leaves important areas still to be investigated. Body-build associations may be easy to learn but an important source of physical attraction which we called 'facial beauty' may not be discriminated quite so readily by children. Even if it is, it may not be associated by children with the qualities that make one person.more popular than another. Both these considerations were central to an investigation [40] carried out in a summer camp which provides 3-week vacations for children who live in low-income areas of New York City. Children at this camp were aged 9–14, and on arrival at the camp they were assigned to 'bunk' groups of about six age peers each; two bunk groups were housed in each of six cabins. Camp activities were not entirely organized around the bunk or cabin groups, but a large amount of the child's social interaction was confined to them. During the last week in camp the authors of the study set about finding boys who could be assigned either to a group high in their social acceptability or to a group low in acceptability according to three different measures. Firstly, a boy had to be known by name by more or fewer campers outside the bunk group than was the average individual in his cabin. Secondly, he must receive more 'like' or 'dislike' choices from boys outside his group than did the average boy in his cabin. Thirdly, he must be ranked either first or last in the order of friendship choices for boys within his living group. By these criteria a number of children could be placed as high or low in serial acceptability, and eventually five were selected to represent each group. Selection was performed on the grounds that each representing group was to have a similar racial composition (in fact, three blacks, one Puerto Rican, and one Caucasian) and that a head-and-shoulder photograph of every boy in the groups showed no evidence of a physical disability.

Seventy-three boys at a later camp session who had never met any of the ten selected boys were shown their photographs. For this part of the study the photographs were paired at random with the exception that each pair had to comprise a boy high and a boy low in social acceptance. There were three such sets of pairings made and every boy who later judged the photographs saw one of these three sets. Every one of the five times that he saw a pair of photographs he was asked: 'Which of these boys would you like to have as a friend?' From their answers an overall order of preference was calculated and this was compared with the original popularity ratings of the boys. The results show that across all pairings of photographs the boy earlier determined as highly socially acceptable was preferred to his counterpart an average of 63.9% of the time. In other words, a fairly good prediction of popularity after 3 weeks' interaction could have been made in this case from a sight of facial photographs alone. What was it about the faces in the photographs which made this possible? To answer this the investigators selected 15 boys to be representative of the group high in acceptability and 15 to be representative of the low, and showed photographs of these boys to both boy and girl campers who did not know them, a year after the camp sessions had ended. Again all 30 photographs were randomly paired and individual children who looked at the photographs were either asked to select the child in each pair they thought they 'would most like as a friend' or asked to select the child they thought was the 'better looking'. Thirty-one girls and 47 boys were given the first task and an independent group of 33 boys were given the second. Results showed that 12 out of 15 boys chosen as a friend were members of the group known to be high in acceptability and there was no overall difference between girls and boys in the choices. Boys who were known to be more socially acceptable were also judged to be more physically attractive in 11 out of 15 cases. Overall, 14 out of 15 boys chosen as a 'friend' by one group were independently chosen as the more physically attractive by the other. The overall conclusion seems to be that attractive physical appearance is an important determinant for young boys, even after a few weeks' interaction, of a playmate's likeability.

The children involved in the above study were all over 9 years old, but recent evidence [41] suggests that the same effect can be detected among the friendship choices of nursery school children. The procedure used was to pin photographs of a child's classmates on to a large board and to ask individual children privately to point to photographs of those they liked and those they disliked. Children were also asked to indicate those children who behaved in certain ways like 'fighting a lot'. Each photograph was rated for physical attractiveness by a group of adults. A comparison of the different sets of data indicated, as will now be expected, that unattractive (judged by adults) boys were liked reliably less by other children in their class than were attractive boys. This was true of preferences made by the younger group of children 4.4—5.4 years) just as it was true of preferences made by the older (5.5—6.10 years). The findings for little girls were slightly different. The very young unattractive girl was significantly more popular than her attractive peer. However, this trend reversed and older attractive girls were significantly more popular than the older unattractive girls. This may show a growing awareness by children of the cultural value placed on attractiveness, but such an idea does not explain the complete switch from one value to an opposite one in the case of girls or the earlier awareness of the correct cultural value in the case of boys. Other data in the study is consistent with the adult stereotypes discussed earlier in the chapter. The children believed that aggressive, anti-social behaviour like yelling, hitting and fighting was more characteristic of attractive boys than of unattractive. Attractive children of both sexes seemed to their peers not to be frightened of anything, to be likely to enjoy doing things alone, and not to need help from anyone. It would seem that even at this age attractive nursery school children are seen by their peers to be self-sufficient and capable of accomplishing whatever they wish.

In adults — in the person of first-year university students — the relationship between popularity and attractiveness becomes more complicated. The more popular groups were more attractive, but paradoxically the most attractive students are the least popular. The investigators [42] divided their sample into four groups: the positively popular, the positively unpopular, the averagely popular, and the 'isolates' who were not mentioned as friends or enemies by anyone. The popular group were more attractive than the average group but not as attractive as the unpopular men and women, who got the highest attractiveness ratings. Fortunately the investigators collected some personality data from the sample, which go some way to explaining their results; attractive girls were ambitious, independently minded, and not very affiliative — rather 'abrasive' personalities. Furthermore the measures were of popularity with one's own sex, so jealousy and fear of competition probably played a part. The least attractive group of students were the 'isolates' who simply failed to make any impression at all on their fellows.

Being attractive makes a big difference to a person's social and sexual life, right from early childhood. Does it also have, therefore, an effect on his or her personality? A lifetime — or at least half a lifetime allowing for looks fading — of getting one's own way relatively easily is surely bound to leave its mark. Rather little research has been reported until relatively recently, perhaps because people were afraid of what they might find, a few findings have now emerged [43]. Attractive girls are happier, less neurotic, and have a higher opinion of themselves. Attractive men, on the other hand, do not differ from their unattractive fellows. Attractive girls are also more assertive and are far quicker to correct a piece of rudeness contrived by the experimenter; perhaps the attractive girls have higher standards or perhaps the unattractive girls have found by bitter experience that other people do not appreciate their efforts to assert themselves. Ultimately, however, it is likely that attractive and unattractive women will be re-united in the democracy of old age and fading beauty. No systematic survey has been published on the reversal of the effects of being attractive and desirable, so it is impossible to say at what age it happens, how quickly, or whether there are any sex differences. Clare Luce Booth does provide a poignant description of how this fate overtook one particularly beautiful woman.

> 'Somewhere along the grapevine I heard that, disillusioned with love and life, she had become a recluse. And then a few years ago in Paris, on a chance walk in the gardens of the Tuileries, I encountered her. . . . . . I recognized her at once despite what the year had done to her. . . . . A ruin, yes, but a lovely ruin . . . . We talked for a bit, and I invited her to a dinner I was giving. She shivered and shook her head. "I never go anywhere anymore," she said. "I can't bear to show this battered old face in public. I can't even bear to look at it anymore in my own mirror." ' [44]

The argument so far in this chapter will be clear. It is a feature of our thinking about other people that we select certain faces and bodies and call them beautiful. We often go further than this and attribute additional personal qualities to those who have 'beauty'. This may mean that we prefer their company, are more likely to employ or date them, and it certainly means that we teach our children to recognize them and treat them according to our standards. But how do we ourselves learn to recognize beauty in the first place? Well, the answer is not simple, for beauty — especially facial beauty — as we shall see, cannot be defined

Those who do try to define beauty usually talk in terms of 'harmony' or 'proportion'. For the Greeks a well-proportioned face could be divided into sections of one-third each. If you draw an imaginary line from the hairline to the chin, then the brow should be one-third of the way along this line and the mouth two-thirds. Also, the width of the face ought to be two-thirds of its height. Others have had the same notion of proportion but based it on the number 7. Imagine you are looking at a face from the side. The hair should occupy the top seventh, the forehead the next two-sevenths, the nose the following two-sevenths, and the shape between nose and mouth and chin the last two-sevenths respectively. The artist Leonardo da Vinci was one of those who expected the perfect face to be the well-proportioned one, and he wrote out his thoughts in much detail, thus:

'The ear is precisely as long as the nose. The length of the ear should equal the distance from the bottom of the nose to the top of the eyelid. The space from the chin to the beginning of the bottom of the nose is the third part of the face and equal to the nose and to the forehead.'

Da Vinci was especially preoccupied with facial proportions (indeed, the face of the Mona Lisa conforms closely to the latter part of this description). But those who look at some of the faces in Leonardo's sketch books are not particularly struck by their beauty. The problem seems to be that there is more to a beautiful face than perfect proportion. Indeed, some faces which are agreed to be beautiful may not have perfect proportion at all. You can see this if you take a full-facial magazine photograph of some well-known beauty like Raquel Welch or Jacqueline Kennedy Onassis. Get a vanity mirror and put the edge of it as close as you can to an imaginary line drawn down the middle of the face from hairline to chin. Now, hold the mirror at right angles to the page so that you see half of the face on the page and the same half reflected in the mirror. You will now be looking at a face which may not have perfect proportion according to the thirds or sevenths principle but at least one-half will have the same proportion as the other because it is a mirror image of the other. The great majority of the faces to which you apply this test will look very different (and you may even believe that some are improved!). Some will look so different that they are almost unacceptable. The point is that often the most beautiful faces can be poorly proportioned and even asymmetrical (i.e. they have two differently shaped sides, right and left). The secrets of beauty cannot be understood in this case by applying some idea of regularity of form.

Other attempts to understand facial beauty have concentrated on the size and shape of its individual features. Based on these is the notion of a 'beauty score' which largely depends on points given to various features of the face one by one. One such system is reproduced here [45]. You can see that the ideal face according to the (Table 2.2) is oval in shape with a clear complexion, has large blue eyes, a straight nose which looks 'diamond-shaped' from the front, and a moderate mouth (neither wide nor narrow). The ears ought not to protrude nor have small lobes, the eyelashes ought to be long, and in men the eyebrows need to be bushy while in women they need to be fine. You can lose some of your score if your face is badly proportioned. The mouth-to-chin distance ought to be less than the height of the forehead, and the width of each cheek ought not to be greater than the width of the mouth. The only drawback about this way of calculating beauty is that even if you get a top score it is not guaranteed that everyone will consider you another Helen of Troy or Apollo. Beauty seems to involve more than just good facial features, and indeed some people may be considered beautiful but still be less than perfect in this way. Symmetry, regularity, and fineness of features are not necessary, and they are certainly not sufficient for a face to be considered beautiful. Every face seems to have its own harmony, and plastic surgeons are among those who realize this, for they depend on few of the foregoing theoretical considerations about beauty for their work. Instead, their working manuals emphasize the individuality of a face, thus:

> 'Great care must be taken to keep all incisions curved. As we know, the general rule is to have the curve of the incision follow or harmonize with

existing lines or the outlines of the facial features nearest it. Second, certain lines and curves of a face, particularly in an adult, are essential for expression and, therefore, communication. It is essential that we distinguish not only between these expression lines and mere lines of ageing, but also between good and bad expression lines.' [46]

TABLE 2.2. BEAUTY SCORING METHOD BASED ON A SURVEY MADE IN AMERICA IN 1962

		Male	Both	Female	Score Male	Score Female
Hair	straight		4		___	___
	wavy		3		___	___
	wiry		2		___	___
	crinkly		1		___	___
Eyebrows	bushy	2		1	___	___
	fine	1		2	___	___
Eyes	small		2		___	___
	large		3		___	___
	protruding		1		___	___
	blue		2		___	___
	other colours		1		___	___
Eyelashes	notably long		2		___	___
	not long		1		___	___
Nose	straight *in profile*		4		___	___
	upturned		3		___	___
	droopy	1		2	___	___
	roman	2		1	___	___
	straight *front view*		2		___	___
	blobby *large tip*		1		___	___
	diamond-shaped		3		___	___
Complexion	clear		4		.....	.....
	freckled	1		2	___	___
	marked		1		___	___
Shape of face	oval		3		___	___
	round	1		2	___	___
	squarish	2		1	___	___
Ears	protruding		1		___	___
	small lobes		2		___	___
	neither		5		___	___
Mouth	notably wide or narrow		0		___	___
	fine lips		1		___	___
	neither		3		___	___
	Add total from *Overall proportions*[a]				___	___

(a) Additional score for overall proportions: *start with 20 points. deduct 5 points if brow-height is not greater than chin-height. Deduct 5 points if twice cheek-width (viewed from front) is greater than mouth-width. Add to 'features' score. Maximum possible beauty score = 55 points.*

As well as near regularity of features, there must be additional reasons why many of our favourite film stars, the models we see in cosmetic advertisements, and even the girl or boy we see regularly on the way to work, attract us physically.

There are a whole variety of these additional reasons to choose from and one or all of them may be appropriate to explain a particular judgement. Take the simplest idea of all which suggests that the more we see something the more we are attracted to it. This can certainly explain our fondness for certain pieces of popular and classical music, and it may explain individual and collective liking for certain faces too. Someone once cut several photographs of faces from the yearbook of a North American university and showed each one to the same audience a different number of times [47]. When everyone was asked afterwards to say how much they liked the face in each individual photograph it was shown that the frequency of a photograph's exposure was linked directly to its popularity. The more often a face was seen the better it was liked, and the effect showed no signs of diminishing even though some of the photographs had been shown a great number of times. In the second investigation, the same procedure was adopted [48]. Certain photographs were shown to a panel of judges up to 11 times, whereas others were shown only once. This time an effect of frequency of exposure was demonstrated but not for all photographs. Only those which had been shown in photographic positive (i.e. 'normal' photographs) were affected by the number of times they were seen, whereas those shown in photographic negative were not any more liked even though they were also seen up to 11 times. In addition, there were individual faces which did not gain in popularity as much as others. All this suggests that familiarity alone will not account for liking, but the interesting thing is that it can help (and rarely hinders) our preference for particular faces.

Another thing which may help explain our attraction towards certain faces is termed the 'Bambi effect'. Walt Disney's drawings of Bambi in common with teddy bears and other soft toys hold an appeal for nearly everyone because of the shape of their bodies, particularly their heads. Some psychologists [49] have suggested that they remind us of babies and very young children and when we feel drawn to these forms we are answering an innate call to love and protect the young of our species in much the same way as a bitch takes care of her puppies. If this is true, we would expect that the more a head resembled the domed head of a baby the more we would like it. Also, we might expect women to be more prone to this effect than men. In essence, this is what has been found. When 330 men, women, and children of various ages were shown profile drawings of children and animals, they liked those with domed foreheads best; they also showed an additional preference for foreheads which were much more domed than normal relative to the rest of the face. The effect could indeed be 'instinct', and it seems to depend on the onset of adolescence. Girls do not show the marked preference for the exaggerated form until they are in the sixth grade (i.e. aged 11–12 on average) when it develops suddenly. Males develop a less marked preference much more gradually [5]. Some facial beauty may stem largely from the possession of baby-like features and in particular the shape of the upper part of the head. This instinctual preference for a particular shape is probably unique; most of our preferences in this area are surely learned.

The idea that we *learn* to recognize beauty does not mean that there are no ideas about it that are common to all cultures. There are, but these are few and have mainly to do with physical repulsion. It is claimed, for example, that no culture finds extreme fatness attractive, nor is a poor complexion liked anywhere [51]. Equally, relative youthfulness in girls is usually sought after and most cultures consider old or masculine-like women to be the least attractive. Those ideals of beauty which are not shared between cultures have sometimes to do with the association between beauty and the values of a particular society. In the West, certain faces, while not perfectly proportioned, are nevertheless revered because they have physical properties which happen to be those associated with mental properties our societies admire. People will say some men are handsome because they have a *firm* jaw (determination), a *strong* nose (dependability), or *clear* eyes (honesty). They might also describe a woman as pretty because she has large, wide apart eyes (innocence), smooth skin (sensitivity), full mouth and soft lips. (sensuality), small chin, nose and ears (vulnerability). The preference is sexist to the same extent that our culture is sexist. Generally, women with big faces and men with small are not idealized in the West.

Another reason why we find certain faces beautiful and others not so beautiful is that we are told to think of them as so. Initially it is our parents who give us this information, but as we grow older we let advertisers and film producers do the selection for us. When this happens, concepts of beauty and ugliness are often established according to the principle of non-conformity. Attractive and unattractive faces have been known to share the distinction of being unusual. In a study [52] conducted in Scotland, two psychologists had several photographs rated for 'high', 'medium', and 'low' attractiveness. Following this up with a facial recognition test 5 weeks later, they found that people best remembered the attractive and unattractive faces and had much more difficulty in saying whether they had seen the 'average' ones before. This is probably because attractive and unattractive faces have distinctive features that make them more easy to remember. By persistently using faces that are unusual in the same ways an advertiser can get our attention, glamorize the face by putting it on a page with desirable material goods like furs and fast cars, and soon convince us that such a face is beautiful. Eventually we want to have our hair done according to that style, or to use the lipstick the owner of that face uses, or to apply the same razor blades to our face as the man in the picture does. This is how our taste can be shaped and how we can learn to like the faces made standard in the magazines.

The chapter is coming full circle, for it began with the assertion that there are few, if any, universal standards of physical attractiveness. A person's physical beauty cannot be estimated fully from knowledge about the regularity of the facial features or the shape of the body. It depends also on the qualities admired by a particular culture and very importantly for those in wealthy, materialist societies; it depends on how our admiration of these qualities is exploited by those like advertisers and film-makers who can shape our taste. Beauty is bestowed by a culture or society and it is universal to the extent that one society's values are shared with or foisted upon another's. It is easy to see the effects of this in the United States. When blacks and whites were asked to rate photographs showing representatives of both races for their physical attractiveness, both black and white men showed a clear preference for white girls (women did not show such a clear preference between races) [53]. This would seem to indicate how successfully the cultural ideal of the beautiful white girl had got across to both races. The same trend may be seen among recent entries for international beauty competitions like Miss World or Miss Universe. Oriental and African countries no longer seem to send girls who are the most representative of internal standards of beauty. They seem instead to send those girls who look most like European girls, and undoubtedly their internal standards must be changing in accordance with this principle. Once the standard has been accepted it is taught to children. Indirect evidence of this was quoted earlier, but there is also more direct proof available. If 5-year-olds are asked to rank for attractiveness photographs of teenage boys and girls, they will not do so very systematically and their opinions will agree little with the consensus of adult judges. By 6 years, however, they come more into line with adult opinion, and by 7 years of age there will be little to choose between the preferences of children of this age and others of 12, 17, as well as adults of up to 50 years old. [54] By 7, therefore, the great social process which standardizes facial taste is more or less complete.

REFERENCES

1. C. Darwin (1971) *The origin of species by means of natural selection: the descent of man in relation to sex*, Limited Editions Club, Adelaide.
2. A. H. Iliffe (1960) A study of preferences in feminine beauty. *Br. J. Psychol.* 51, 267—73.
3. J. R. Udry (1965) Structural correlates of feminine beauty preferences in Britain and the United States: a comparison. *Sociol. soc. Res.* 49, 330—42.
4. K. Dion *et al.* (1972) What is beautiful is good. *J. Pers. Soc. Psychol.* 24, 285—90.
5. M. Dermer and D. L. Thiel (1975) When beauty may fail. *J. Pers. Soc. Psychol.* 31, 168—76.
6. R. O. Hansson and B. J. Duffield (1976) Physical attractiveness and the attribution of epilepsy. *J. Soc. Psychol.* 99, 233—40.
7. G. B. Browning (1968) The effect of perceived physical attractiveness of male counselors on ninth grade girls' choices of a counselor. *Diss. Ab.* 30, 198—A.
8. R. S. Schiavo *et al.* (1974) Effect of attire on obtaining directions. *Psychol. Rep.* 34, 245—6.
9. J. Mills and E. Aronson (1965) Opinion change as a function of the communicator's attractiveness and desire to influence. *J. Pers. Soc. Psychol.* 1, 173—7.
10. R. L. Dipboye *et al.* (1975) Relative importance of applicant sex, attractiveness and scholastic standing in evaluation of job applicant résumés. *J. appl. Psychol.* 60, 39—43.
11. P. L. Benson, S. A. Karabenick and R. M. Lerner (1976) Pretty pleases: the

effect of physical attractiveness, sex and race on receiving help. *J. exp. Soc. Psychol.* 12, 409—14.

12. W. D. Dannenmaier and F. J. Thumin (1964) Authority status as a factor in perceptual distortion of size. *J. Soc. Psychol.* 63, 361—5.

13. P. R. Wilson (1968) Perceptual distortion of height as a function of ascribed academic status. *J. Soc. Psychol.* 74, 97—102.

14. S. D. Feldman (1971) The presentation of shortness in everyday life — height and heightism in American society: towards a sociology of stature. Paper read to the Am. Sociol. Assoc.

15. H. H. Kassarjian (1963) Voting intentions and political perceptions. *J. Psychol.* 56, 85—8.

16. C. D. Ward (1967) Own height, sex, and liking in the judgements of the height of others. *J. Personality.* 35, 381—401.

17. Feldman, *op. cit.*

18. M. G. Efran and E. W. J. Patterson (1974) Voters vote beautiful: the effect of physical appearance on a national election. *Can. J. Behav. Sci.* 6, 352—6.

19. P. A. Goldberg *et al.* (1975) Another put-down of women? Perceived attractiveness as a function of support for the feminist movement. *J. Pers. Soc. Psychol.* 32, 113—5.

20. E. Walster *et al.* (1966) Importance of physical attractiveness and dating behaviour. *J. Pers. Soc. Psychol.* 4, 508—16.

21. R. W. Brislin and S. A. Lewis (1968) Dating and physical attractiveness: a replication. *Psychol. Rep.* 22, 976.

22. E. W. Mathes (1975) The effects of physical attractiveness and anxiety on heterosexual attraction over a series of five encounters. *J. Marr. Fam.* 37, 769—74.

23. D. Krebs and A. A. Adiniofi (1975) Physical attractiveness, social relations and personality stereotype. *J. Pers. Soc. Psychol.* 31, 245—53.

24. G. R. Kaats and K. E. Davis (1970) The dynamics of sexual behaviour of college students. *J. Marr. Fam.* 32, 390—9.

25. B. I. Murstein (1972) Physical attractiveness and marital choice. *J. Pers. Soc. Psychol.* 22, 8—12.

26. B. I. Murstein (1976) Physical attractiveness and marriage adjustment in middle-aged couples. *J. Pers. Soc. Psychol.* 34, 537—42.

27. H. Sigall and D. Landy (1973) Radiating beauty: effects of having a physically attractive partner on person perception. *J. Pers. Soc. Psychol.* 28, 218—24.

28. W. Waller (1937) The rating and dating complex. *Am. Soc. Rev.* 2, 727—37.

29. E. Berscheid *et al.* (1971) Physical attractiveness and dating choice: tests of the matching hypothesis. *J. exp. Soc. Psychol.* 7, 173—81.

30. T. L. Huston (1973) Ambiguity of acceptance, social desirability, and dating choice. *J. exp. Soc. Psychol.* 9, 32—42.

31. G. H. Elder, Jr. (1968) Appearance and education in marriage mobility. *Am. Soc. Rev.* 34, 519—33.

32. G. van Gorp *et al.* (1969) Dating attitudes, expectations and physical attractiveness, unpublished, Univ. of Michigan.

33. F. A. C. Perrin (1921) Physical attractiveness and repulsiveness. *J. exp. Psychol.* 4, 203—17.

34. J. W. Hudson and L. F. Henze (1969) Campus values in mate selection: a replication. *J. Marr. Fam.* 31, 772—5.

35. A. Tesser and M. Brodie (1971) A note on the evaluation of a computer date. *Psychon. Sci.* **23**, 300.
36. H. L. Miller and W. H. Riverbark (1970) Sex differences in physical attractiveness as a determinant of heterosexual liking. *Psychol. Rep.* 701—2.
37. R. M. Lerner (1969) The development of stereotyped expectancies of body — behaviour relations. *Child Dev.* **40**, 137—41.
38. R. M. Lerner and C. Schroder (1971) Physique identification, preference and aversion in kindergarden children. *Dev. Psychol.* **5**, 538; and R. M. Lerner and C. Schroder (1971) Kindergarten children's active vocabulary about body build. *Dev. Psychol.* **5**, 179.
39. S. A. Richardson and A. Green (1971) When is black beautiful? Coloured and white children's reactions to skin colour. *Br. J. ed. Psychol.* **41**, 62—9.
40. R. E. Kleck *et al.* (1974) Physical appearance cues and interpersonal attraction in children. *Child. Dev.* **45**, 305—10.
41. K. K. Dion and E. Berscheid (1972) Physical attraction and peer perception among children. *Sociometry.* **37**, 1—12.
42. Krebs and Adiniofi, *op. cit.*
43. E. W. Mathes and A. Kahn (1975) Physical attractiveness, happiness, neuroticism and self esteem. *J. Psychol.* **90**, 27—30; and J. J. Jackson and T. L. Huston (1975) Physical attractiveness and assertiveness. *J. Soc. Psychol.* **96**, 79—84.
44. C. B. Luce (1971) The beautiful girl syndrome. *Cosmopolitan*, Sept. 1971, see E. Berscheid and E. Walster, Physical attractiveness, in L. Berkowitz (ed.), *Advances in Experimental Social Psychology*, vol. 7, p.204.
45. M. Brislin, unpublished, undated report.
46. J. F. Crosby Jr. (1973) Aesthetics: the ideas and ideals of beauty in F. W. Masters and J. R. Lewis (eds.), *Symposium on Aesthetic Surgery of the Nose, Ears and Chin*, vol. 6, C. V. Mosby, St. Louis.
47. R. B. Zajonc (1968) Attitudinal effects of mere exposure. *J. Pers. Soc. Psychol.* monog. suppl., part 2, pp.1—27.
48. D. Perlman and S. Oskamp (1971) The effects of picture content and exposure frequency on evaluations of negroes and whites. *J. exp. Soc. Psychol.* **7**, 503—14.
49. B. Huchstedt (1965) Experimentelle Untersuchungen zum 'Kindenschema'. *Z. exp. angew. Psychol.* **12**, 421—50.
50. W. Fullard and A. M. Reiling (1976) An investigation of Lorenz's babyness. *Child Dev.* **47**, 119—23.
51. C. S. Ford and F. A. Beach (1952) *Patterns of sexual behaviour* p.94, Methuen, London.
52. J. W. Shepherd and H. D. Ellis (1973) The effect of attractiveness on recognition memory for faces. *Am. J. Psychol.* **86**, 627—34.
53. G. L. Parrott and G. Coleman (1971) Sexual appeal: in black and white. *Proc. Ann. Conf. Am. Psychol. Assoc.* **6**, 321—2.
54. N. Cavior and D. A. Lombardi (1973) Developmental aspects of judgement of physical attractiveness in children. *Dev. Psychol.* **8**, 67—71; and J. F. Cross and J. Cross (1971) Age, sex, race, and the perception of facial beauty. *Dev. Psychol.* **5**, 433—9.

Chapter 3

LOVE AT FIRST SIGHT?

There is a very romantic idea that the most durable sexual relationship begins with a glance between two strangers who immediately fall in love with each other. Not only is this likely to be a rare occurrence, but it is a poor description of the psychological process whereby we come to know and trust other people. This chapter suggests that most of us are likely to be very inaccurate if we try to sum up other people early in a relationship. If we do so, we take enormous chances with our judgements. A side-effect of our general ineptness when making judgements of others has become widely known as the 'self-fulfilling prophesy'. Such prophesies occur when we act towards others in ways calculated to make true the first impression we had of them. For the reason given in the previous chapter — that we tend to associate physical attractiveness with personal warmth — the working of the self-fulfilling prophesy gives physically attractive people a clear edge over others. This is not just true in sexual matters, but generalizes to wider aspects of everyday social life. Examples of the privileges that the physically attractive are likely to enjoy in the classroom and the courtroom are given and these are supported by empirical evidence. The chapter ends by analysing a fictional first encounter between two strangers who are attracted to each other.

We can make up our minds about people from very little information. If people are shown photographs of physically attractive and unattractive individuals they will assess the personalities of those pictured with little hesitation. In one published report [1] they said that the attractive* were more curious, complex, perceptive, amiable, confident, pleasure-seeking, assertive, outspoken, and active than the unattractive individuals. The ability to make such quick assessments of others on the basis of such little information is the subject of this chapter. How do strangers form impressions of each other? How do they build on this initial impression and decide whom to go out with and whom to marry?

There are six principal techniques for forming an impression of a stranger and all of us use them frequently. The best known of these techniques is *stereotyping*. This is the process whereby we pick up pieces of information about somebody else — e.g. their age, sex, religion, or nationality — and use them to make a statement about their character. Stereotyping is the action of assigning attributes to a person solely on the basis of the class or category to which he or she belongs. There should also be marked agreement among people about the correctness of the characteristic for the judgement to be termed a stereotype. Thus most Englishmen believe that French girls are passionate. From this piece of information any Englishman meeting a French girl begins a simple chain of reasoning. It says:

(1) All French girls are passionate.
(2) She is French.
(3) Therefore, she is passionate.

This is a straightforward example of a stereotyped judgement and everyone makes judgements of this type every day. If you accuse people of doing so they will protest strenuously, for they use stereotypes without awareness.

A good illustration of this point was made over 20 years ago when an investigation of American college men's attitude to girls who wore lipstick was reported [2]. Every man taking part in this study talked to six girls for 10 minutes each; three of the girls he talked to wore lipstick and three did not. This was not pointed out to him. The girls themselves took part in several such interviews and for half the interviews they wore lipstick but for the other half they did not. When the men were asked to describe each girl afterwards they spoke of those who wore lipstick as more frivolous, silent, unconscientious about work, and more overtly interested in the opposite sex. When asked to say what had influenced their judgements it was clear that none of the men was aware that it was probably the use of lipstick that had done so. Indeed, none of them seemed to have noticed the lipstick at all.

There are lots of similar physical cues that give rise to judgements such as these, and again we are probably not aware of using them. University students attribute favourable personal attributes to men with beards — even those at the most conventional universities [3]. Men with long hair are similarly regarded by students [4]. There are stereotypes associated with hair colour too [5]. Despite the adage 'gentlemen prefer blondes', dark men seem to prefer the personalities of brunette women, but the preference of blond men is equally divided between blondes and brunettes. Most women prefer dark men with the exception of artificial blondes who, according to one survey, do not seem to care what colour of hair a man has.

Stereotypes associated with occupations are reported too. Most men suppose that nurses and air hostesses are promiscuous, and in Britain at least there is a widespread belief that single girls who go to holiday camps are sexually available [6].

A second way we have of judging people is to use what are termed *implicit personality theories*. We often assume that certain personality traits go together. Thus we might believe that those who are sociable and able to get on well with others must also be intelligent. This starts us on another chain of reasoning. Thus:

(1)   All sociable people are intelligent.
(2)   He is sociable.
(3)   Therefore he is intelligent.

It is particularly common for admired personal attributes to be linked with one another in this way. Just as in the example the two admired characteristics 'intelligence' and 'sociability' are put together, so links with looking attractive and looking unattractive are often formed. In the example reported at the beginning of this chapter, physical attraction — a desirable attribute — suggested that the underlying personality was complex, amiable, confident, perceptive, and assertive. As with stereotyping, these implicit personality theories about which dimensions of personality belong with which others are widely shared by members of a cultural group.

Ideas about people which are not shared are termed *personal personality theories*, and this is the third means we use of judging others. We develop such theories because some isolated incident involving another person sticks in our mind. These pet ideas are really like superstitions. A man may distrust any girl with red hair because he was once jilted or snubbed by a girl like that. A girl may think she will get on better with boys with blue eyes just because she did so once. Most people can produce examples like these: they are judgements which others laugh at but which we are personally convinced are quite sound.

The fourth means we use to assess others quickly often involves personal observations too. This is where we form an opinion on the basis of a *single incident or piece of behaviour.* Sometimes we think of someone as friendly because they happen to be smiling on one occasion, or suppose that they are always miserable because they happen on one occasion to be scowling. Girls who are once heard to swear can be thought of as promiscuous; so are girls who tell a dirty joke or even listen to one. Misconceptions of this sort are encouraged by popular writing on sex. Take the example of 'the first kiss'. The anonymous author of *The Sensuous Woman* [7] advises her readers that a man's kiss is a sure sign of his later sexual performance; a dry peck or a slobbery kiss are invariable signs that a man will be 'equally dull in bed'. There is no reason why the connection should be invariable but, convinced it is, 'J' can hardly be said to move from kiss to later events with a completely open mind. All of us are just as likely to be misled into thinking that an early incident will tell us something general about people we meet.

A very personal basis for judging someone is the fifth means we use — *projection*. This is a concept originated by Sigmund Freud and there is much controversy among psychologists about when and how it occurs, if it occurs at all. According to Freud, the person who 'projects' reduces a secret fear, usually about sexuality, by projecting it on to others. A man who is anxious that he might be a latent homosexual suspects other men — unjustifiably — of being homosexual. The sexually repressed or frustrated spinster imagines that men are following her or plotting to rape her. It has become a cliché that the person who complains about pornography is 'projecting' his or her secret desire to read or see it. It might also be claimed that the anti-pornographer, by projecting his or her own unacceptable impulses to sex or violence, is able to enjoy some direct expression of those impulses by describing what others see and do. Like many Freudian theories, this is difficult to prove and there is no positive demonstration of it beyond its appearance of plausibility.

The sixth basis of our impression of others is the frequent assumption that they are similar to ourselves or to someone we already know. This is termed the *assumption of similarity*. A small fact or feature that someone shares with us or someone else can lead to a chain of reasoning like:

(1)   He went to Harvard.
(2)   My husband went to Harvard.
(3)   He is like my husband in one way.
(4)   Therefore he must be like my husband in other ways.

The same reasoning is often applied to people who look alike. Of course, an assumption of similarity can also lead to liking, as was noted in an earlier chapter. Some studies have shown that certain men assess women according to how similar they are to their own mothers. It is also common to assume that others — particularly our friends and our sex partners — are like ourselves. When we reason like this we often let our vanity run away with us and suppose that others are much more like us than they really are. One study [8] found that each member of several pairs of married couples thought their political attitudes similar to the other's to the point of being almost identical. In fact, the political attitudes of each couple were only slightly related. Similar distortion occurs when married couples describe their own marriage ideals and what they take to be their partner's ideals. There is some similarity but that expected by the couples themselves is a great overestimation. In the same way, it is possible to assume a stranger has a lot in common with us and be quite wrong in this assessment.

Most people would prefer not to believe they form impressions of others in any of the six ways set out above. Certain people speak with pride of their 'intuition' which gets to work when they meet a stranger. There is no such thing as intuition if that means we assess others often without thinking about what we are doing. Judging people is a skill and for a lot of our lives we learn what to look for when we meet someone and what it means when we see it. It is not wholly surprising that the term 'intuition' is often given to this process, for we work quickly and without awareness of what is going on in our heads. A greater number of people will object to the listing of techniques for a different reason. Nearly all of us like to believe that we treat others as individuals and so the idea that we stereotype and all the rest is not a popular one. Unfortunately it is just as much nonsense to believe in our capability to individualize people as it is to believe in intuition. The reason is not obvious and it will be necessary to give a lengthy explanation.

To understand why we rarely individualize, it is necessary to understand exactly what is meant by the terms 'forming an impression' or 'making a judgement'. The point of forming impressions about other people is to help us *anticipate* or *predict* the behaviour of someone else. When we say that someone is kind, we mean that their behaviour in the future is likely to be kind. We make predictions like this for good reasons. For one thing, they help us formulate a plan or strategy about how we should behave next towards somebody or what we should say. For another, our ability to make anticipations can protect us against people who might harm us in some way. Just as prevention is better than cure, anticipation is better than being taken by surprise. Thus, we constantly go around making statements to ourselves about what people are going to say and do next.

It is very difficult always to say what individuals will do next because each one of us has such a wide range of possible behaviours. Many 'experts' offer to provide the key to understanding and predicting our own and other people's behaviour. These include physiognomists who read faces, phrenologists who study the shape of the skull, fairground gypsies who read palms, and graphologists who interpret handwriting. All these claim to provide insights into 'character' and although the claim is attractive it is bound to fail. At the same time, psychologists working on the science of 'personality' have met with little more success. Where does the difficulty lie? The real barrier to predicting our own and other people's behaviour is its apparent irregularity and inconsistency. When it is said that someone is an extrovert that can hardly mean their behaviour is *always* extroverted. Sometimes they will do what an extrovert is expected to do — slapping others on the back, telling dirty jokes, making a lot of noise. At other times they will be quiet, well behaved, and even quite reserved. The reason is the degree of extroversion they show depends largely on how they see the situation they are in or the person they are with. If you try to predict precisely how someone will behave by using the vague and general characterizations of gypsies and graphologists or even by noting his or her score on a personality test, you will not do very well.

We are all of us put under some pressure by the fact that there are no easy ways to predict another's behaviour. It is particularly important for everyone to be able to anticipate the behaviour of certain people like their wife, husband, boss, mistress, and close friends who occupy key positions in their lives. How do we get to know the preferences and likely behaviour of such people? We seem to do so by applying a simple rule. We say, 'a person's behaviour in the future is likely to be the same as his behaviour in a similar situation or towards a similar person in the past'. Thus possessive individuals learn the occasions on which their otherwise virtuous partners flirt with other people and attempt to control their spouses or the situations to prevent a recurrence. Anxious courting couples learn which of their friends or relations the other does not like and keep them apart to prevent unpleasantness. If we want to use the past/future rule, it poses problems for our memory. Just think of the number of small facts that can be recalled about the behaviour of the people nearest to us. 'He only likes drinking at weekends'; 'she is always bad-tempered on Sunday evenings'; 'he prefers not to go to discos by himself'. We remember all these things because it stops us putting our foot in it and possibly disturbing a close relationship. Husbands and wives, lovers, friends, near relations, bosses, and employees all maintain daily harmony by filling their heads with each other's idiosyncrasies.

It is all very well to try and keep this kind of information in our heads, but we are likely to run into difficulties if we try to remember too much. The greatest problem for our memory is not finding somewhere to store facts, it is being able to place them in such a way that they can be got at quickly and efficiently. Technically, the operation of finding information that has been stored in memory is called 'retrieval'. If we are to retrieve quickly specific information about the behaviour of the most important people in our lives, then other information about people less important must take second place. How this works is that we devote the greater part of our retrieval capability to recalling the ways in which those nearest to us are individuals, that we have very little left over for the recall of the behaviour of people who are not so important. As a consequence, these others are all aggregated together in our minds and are formed into groups in which all 'individuals' are assumed to be alike for the sake of convenience. These groupings are what are commonly described as 'stereotypes'.

There is evidence that our minds work in the way described above and we do tend to remember best the information about those important to us in some way. If you ask people to recall eight living acquaintances who have a common christian name (e.g. John) and then ask them to rank the people recalled in order of liking, you will find the order of recall is almost exactly the same as the order of liking [9]. A different kind of study [10] has also been made of social recall. Forty-eight dating couples (dating length ranged from 1 week to 3 years) were asked to take part in an experiment. They were then divided into groups of 12 (i.e. 6 dating couples) and seated in a square. In every case one of each couple was seated halfway round the square from the other. Then every person taking part was asked to turn up a word card in front of him or her and read a single word out loud. When a number of successive words had been read in this manner, everyone was tested for their recall of all the words read out. It was found that people had by far the best memory of the words they themselves had read out, and usually the words read out by their partners came a close second. The best recall of a partner's performance was made by couples who touched each other most and who reported the strongest liking for each other. These results suggest that memory is affected by the amount one person cares for another.

This memory model of how we form impressions of others has some interesting implications. It suggests that each one of us has the capability to remember as individuals only a handful of the people we know. The limitations of our ability to retrieve information from memory *forces* us to lump together the great majority of our acquaintances and does not allow us to treat them as individuals at all. It has to be emphasized that this happens no matter how much we might want to treat people as individuals; we simply do not have the capacity to store and retrieve information about their individual patterns of behaviour. This situation has its compensations, however. The groupings of people that we make in this way help us to get to 'know' strangers very quickly. Roughly speaking, all we have to do is to decide in which category a stranger belongs and we can say something about his or her likely behaviour. The truth is that we really do not form impressions of people at all; we simply slot them into pre-existing impressions.

When we face most people in everyday life we have only an approximate idea of how they are going to behave. This is because we have either forgotten what they did in a similar situation in the past or they are strangers to us and we have never had a chance to learn about their behaviour. As a result we are forced to make an informed guess about most people and we are very often likely to be quite wrong. It is at this point in any interaction between people that certain interesting things happen. Both parties usually try to force each other into the impression they have formed by treating each other in an appropriate way. When one or the other succeeds, his or her judgement is termed a *self-fulfilling prophesy*. Anyone who has been at the receiving end of such a prophesy will understand how it gets its name. Should someone you meet have a fixed idea that you are 'stupid', 'bad tempered', 'good fun', or have any one of a host of other characteristics, they work on you in such a way as to make it difficult for you to show you are not any one of these things. If several people share the same fixed impression of you, it soon becomes difficult not to believe them. As a result many people end up acting in ways that others expect rather than in ways they would prefer. One survey found that medical students almost all had the firm impression that nurses were sexually permissive. The idea originated partly from first and second-hand experience and partly from the notion that nurses, because they had detailed knowledge of bodily functions and had often to attend to them in male patients, must somehow regard sex differently. Nurses who went out with medical students found it difficult not to live up to the behaviour expected of them because if they did not, they were not asked out again [10].

The initial stage in the process of the self-fulfilling prophesy is known as *labelling* — the business of applying an impression to somebody. One of the most commonly applied labels has to do with physical attractiveness, and psychologists have recently uncovered many examples of just how advantageous it is to be labelled in this way. The simplest illustrations concern smart appearance and, of course, being well dressed is usually an easy way of increasing one's attractiveness. As might be expected, people are rated differently by others when they are wearing smart clothes (e.g. evening dress) as opposed to casual [11]. This demonstrates the superficiality of our impressions when we meet people for the first time. What is surprising is that people who are *fairly well acquainted* with a person will often rate him or her as different in personality if that person wears different clothes. This was shown when girls in a class were assessed on two occasions 3 weeks apart by their fellow students [12]. Those dressed similarly on both occasions got the same rating each time, but those wearing different clothes on the second occasion were seen as having changed in personality. As everyone who goes to a white-collar job interview knows, smart appearance carries with it an air of desirability and earns the individual who has it additional social status. It has been shown [12], for example, that more people will jay-walk at a 'don't walk' traffic sign if a smartly dressed person leads the way than if a poorly dressed person does so. Similarly, better dressed people will be able to get more market research opinions from people they stop, collect more signatures on petitions, and obtained rides more quickly when they hitch-hike. Only sometimes does good appearance work against an individual. It has been found that being casually dressed is much the best if you want 'to scrounge money' on a university campus to make a telephone call, or if you want to hitch a ride in the higher class areas of American cities [12].

It is not necessary to look far for a reason why many people prefer to be smartly dressed. The clothes that a person wears are a compromise between how a person sees himself or herself and how he or she would prefer to be. The wearer is making a statement such as 'I am sophisticated' and he or she hopes that acquaintances are also likely to say 'You are sophisticated'. If they do, it makes it much easier for that person to 'act sophisticated'. This sequence of 'Look good' — 'feel good' — 'act good' is an illustration of how the self-fulfilling prophesy can work. People who meet a smartly dressed person label that person in a desirable way and treat him (or her) as if he had those qualities. The well-dressed person (who usually enjoys being seen this way) acts as if he possesses them. Although the examples given have referred only to smart clothes, the same considerations probably apply even more when clothes worn are both smart and very fashionable. Indeed, it is interesting to notice in the latter case that for women at least, fashionable clothes increase not only social status but also sexual status. Even women who see other women so dressed imagine them to be passionate, free, romantic, wild, thrilling, approachable, adventurous, flirtatious, and sexy as well as having a lot of other desirable characteristics which unfashionably dressed women are assumed not to have. A separate study confirms this [13]. There wearers of fashionable clothes were universally judged to have different dating patterns, sexual morals, and smoking and drinking patterns from other girls. Presumably, very fashionably dressed people are helped and encouraged to act out the kind of role dictated by such characterization because of the label they are given by the people they meet.

Of course, just as having a label put on them can help people act out roles they enjoy or find desirable, so it works in the opposite way also. Unfashionably dressed women will find it more difficult to behave wildly, adventurously, and flirtatiously because others do not expect such behaviour of them. It is probably similar for unfashionably dressed men in most company. Everyone prefers to have their prophesies fulfilled and as most of us do not really expect the badly and unfashionably dressed to be flirtatious we never encourage them to be so. But if the effects of labelling the sexually attractive and unattractive were limited to men not making passes at girls who wear glasses, it might not be terribly important. However, there is ample evidence to show that physical appearance has a strong effect on people's behaviour in other situations besides those already mentioned here. Some of the available examples, as will now be seen, reveal a more disturbing side to the process of labelling.

The judgements we make of other people's behaviour usually assume that a person causes his own behaviour. Children explain natural events by this principle: the sun rises because it wants to, and goes down because it is tired. Primitive societies think the same way about such events. In Western society adults usually do not attribute intentions to inanimate objects, but they tend to suppose that *people* do things intentionally and with the deliberate aim of producing those effects their behaviour may have. Psychologists have frequently seized on this general rule that we attribute intentions to others and have attempted to show that when exceptions are made to it, these exceptions have a certain consistency. Thus it has been shown that if people like someone and that person behaves in a certain way, then providing that behaviour is approved by those who like him, it will be assumed to have been done deliberately. On the other hand, if a piece of a liked person's behaviour is not approved of, it will be assumed to have been caused by something outside that person's control. The opposite applies to people who are disliked. The bad things they do are done deliberately and the good things happen by accident. Actions which are inconsistent with how we feel about somebody are attributed to events outside that person's control, while those which are consistent are not.

It has been claimed many times in this book that we are disposed to liking those who are physically and sexually attractive and to disliking those who are unattractive. It is not surprising, therefore, that a strong effect has been found linking physical attraction with attribution of causality along the lines suggested above [14]. In one study, people were shown a photograph of a woman and given details of her job. The photographs were deliberately varied and so were the job details so that some people saw a physically attractive woman and heard that there was a possibility of the company she worked for going bankrupt and her losing her position. Others saw a physically unattractive woman and heard that her company was successful and that there was a good chance of her being promoted. Reversals were also made so that certain people had the good-looking woman linked with the good job prospects and others the unattractive with the bad prospects. In every case those taking part in the study were asked to say how responsible the woman was for her impending fate. Judgements reached were most unfair; unattractive women received the blame for being in the jobs with poor prospects but not the credit for being in the promotable positions, while attractive women were given credit for being in the favourable positions but not the blame for being in the poor ones.

Many people will be wondering if this result has wider implications. For example, do juries allow themselves to be more swayed by physical attractiveness than they will admit? Are they more likely to be lenient towards attractive offenders than others on the grounds that the offence was 'not their fault'? Anecdotal evidence is available which suggests that beautiful women are convicted less often of crimes they are accused of but no direct evidence is obtainable on this point because experiments cannot be conducted in courts. Simulated courtroom procedures have been used however, and these do show a link between physical appearance and recommended punishment of a criminal offender [15]. In one such study a number of all-male or all-female juries were set up from a pool of university undergraduates. When the juries met they were asked to suppose they were members of a university court which consisted of both students and staff members. This particular court was said to be hearing the case of a student accused of cheating in an examination. They were given a 650-word fact summary to read and this revealed that the defendant's professor and a junior assistant had repeatedly seen the defendant talking to another examinee and looking at the other student's paper. Some details were also given which seemed to support the defendant's case. All jurors were reminded that each one of them was duty bound to base their decision on the *facts as stated.*

Some of the jurors had a photograph of an attractive* undergraduate attached to the papers, some an unattractive undergraduate, and others were given no photograph at all. All the male juries 'heard the case' of female defendants and the female juries the cases of males. After they had read the facts, individual members of the juries stated whether or

*The photographs used had been selected from a series of 341 photographs of male and female undergraduates by a group of male and female undergraduate judges who had rated them for their attractiveness.

not they felt the defendant was guilty and indicated the severity of the punishment they would recommend. The results of this study showed that being attractive was a great advantage if you were a defendant in this kind of situation. Attractive undergraduates were felt to be less likely to be guilty and less deserving of severe punishment at equivalent levels of presumed guilt than unattractive undergraduates. Cases in which the facts only were presented without an accompanying photograph received recommendations for punishment which, with a single exception, fell between those given to the attractive and unattractive. It was also found in this study that male jurors were much more susceptible than females to the defendant's physical attractiveness.

At first sight the attitude of the male and female jurors towards attractive and unattractive offenders appears most irrational. There seems to be no good reason why those who differ in physical appearance should be considered more and less blameworthy for a crime. On the other hand, it is possible to see a certain kind of logic in the jurors' behaviour. Inasmuch as attractive people are seen as having desirable personal characteristics, it makes sense to treat them leniently. Presumably they are less likely than those who do not seem to possess such qualities (i.e. the physically unattractive) to repeat their crime in the future, and this must enter into the deliberations that go into a juror's verdict. To test whether this kind of thinking does underlie the decisions made by mock juries, another study was carried out [16]. This time jurors were asked to consider defendant's guilt on two kinds of crime. One was a burglary and the other a swindle. It was reasoned that if jurors really were aware of taking a defendant's physical attractiveness into account, this would affect the verdicts reached in the two cases in different ways. Attractive defendants would be punished more leniently for the burglary but less leniently for the swindle. This is because physically attractive people who swindle are much more likely than unattractive to do so again because they can more easily take advantage of their God-given physical gifts. The study carried out to test this reasoning actually divided into two parts. Jurors (male and female undergraduates) were given details of the burglary; one-third of them were also given photographs of an attractive female defendant, another third given photographs of an unattractive female defendant, and the remaining third no photograph at all (although they were informed that the defendant was a woman). The second part of the study involved exactly the same procedure but this time the case concerned a female defendant who was alleged to have swindled a middle-aged bachelor by making friends with him. In both cases, burglary and swindle, the value of the money lost was $2200. The results supported the idea behind doing the study. Attractive burglars were treated more leniently than unattractive, but attractive swindlers less leniently than unattractive. At least this seems to indicate that jurors are thinking about the relationship between attractiveness, the crime, and the sentences they recommend. It is also interesting to note that the sentences given both to the unattractive and to those whose photographs were not seen by jurors were almost identical. There is a crumb of comfort here for it would suggest that most people are treated similarly and only the very attractive receive special (favourable or unfavourable) treatment in court. These laboratory treatments are quite different from the actual court-room. People make decisions that they know are not going to have any consequences for the defendant and they make them by themselves rather than in discussion with other jurors towards a common verdict. Nevertheless, it is known that people do take such role-playing situations fairly seriously (after all, their qualities as fair-minded citizens are being tested), and it would not be unreasonable to suggest that the effects noted here do not operate in real trial proceedings. After all they do in other areas in public life (see Chapter 2), and real juries are made up of lay members of the general public who are all influenced by the conventions of our society to form judgements in the ways outlined in the present chapter.

These studies of juries not only have immediate practical implications, they are also related to a growing body of knowledge about how the physically attractive and unattractive can be judged and treated for a good part of their lives. If the physically unattractive really are treated less leniently by the courts, it would seem to be yet another example of the differential treatment they are likely to have received since childhood. In a demonstration [17] of this point, one psychologist reasoned that adults are likely to blame and punish attractive and unattractive children differently for the same misdemeanour in precisely the same way as the jurors did other adults in the instances cited above. The method chosen was to ask female college students to read an account of a mild or severe misdemeanour ostensibly committed by a 7-year-old child. Given with the description of the misconduct was background information consisting of the child's name and age as well as a photograph of the child. It was this photograph that was changed on the accounts read by different people. Photographs of attractive and unattractive boys and girls were used and one photograph selected from these four categories was pinned to each account. The expectation was that women who read about misdeeds that they thought were done by attractive children would be more likely to excuse them and would recommend less severe punishment than when the misdeeds were thought to be committed by unattractive children. However, no such difference was found when the misdeed that had ostensibly been committed was mild. But when the transgression was severe, the women felt that the behaviour of the attractive was much more excusable. For example, when the severe transgression was attributed to an attractive child, one of the women said:

'She appears to be a perfectly charming little girl, well-mannered, basically unselfish. It seems that she can adapt well among children her age and make a good impression . . . she plays well with everyone, but like anyone else a bad day can occur. Her cruelty . . . need not be taken seriously'.

When the same act was committed by a physical unattractive child, another woman inferred:

'I think the child would be quite bratty and would be a problem to teachers . . . she would probably try to pick a fight with other children her own age . . . she would be a brat at home . . . all in all, she would be a real problem'.

When the misdemeanour was serious, women also felt that it was the unattractive child rather than the attractive who was most likely to repeat it. So at least a part of the experimenter's original expectation is supported. Another part of it was not supported, however. No difference in punishment was recommended for attractive and unattractive children guilty of the same act. Regardless of the crime, the women felt that it should be discussed with the child, and alternatives such as physical punishment and withdrawal of love were eschewed. Such a point of view is not consistent with the idea that the unattractive children are much more likely to behave this way again, and it is possible that the women in the experiment were simply reiterating modern ideas about child rearing; it is not clear that they would really behave this way if they did have to punish the children concerned. Of course, such a criticism can be levelled at the whole study. It is not known how the women would have behaved had it been a more real situation and the children involved had been their own. It could well be that mothers are more lenient towards their unattractive children in order to compensate for the unfairness they expect to be shown by the world outside.

The study just quoted probably gives some clues to how strangers or acquaintances will treat children who misbehave. There are a number of such people such as teachers, child minders, youth leaders, and the like who do have a significant influence on the child's life. So, too, do other children, and if it is true that other children prefer attractive children as friends (see Chapter 2) and unattractive children really are less popular, then plain children are almost certainly penalized by their looks. It is known that children are more likely to sneak on unpopular children [18] and it is known also, from the studies quoted here, that adults are much more likely to believe the worst of unattractive (unpopular) children. Further information on this question comes from work done in schools [19]. Teachers, who each represented one of 400 schools in the State of Missouri, were all given a report card on a student and asked to evaluate him or her. The evaluation was required to contain the student's IQ, his parents' attitude towards school, the pupil's social status with his peers, and an estimate of his educational potential. The report the teachers saw contained a good deal of information about each student. There was a note of his absences throughout the year as well as his grades in eight subjects. There were also ratings of his 'personal development', 'work habits', and attitudes towards 'healthful living'. Finally, a picture of the student, either one of six attractive 11-year-old boys and girls or one of six unattractive 11-year-old boys and girls, was fixed to one corner of the report. The point of the study was to show that even when the information given to each teacher was identical, their expectations would be different according to whether the photograph in the corner of the report showed an attractive or an unattractive child. In fact, this is just what happened. The more attractive the child, whether male or female, the higher the educational potential the teacher assumed the child to have. This came about when the evaluations were made by either male or female teachers. The attractive boy or girl was assumed to have the higher IQ, was expected to attain more education, and was assumed to have parents who were more interested in his or her education than the unattractive child. It was also assumed that attractive children enjoyed better social relations with their peers than unattractive children.

Teachers are not being deliberately selected here as a group who are especially misled by looks, for all of us are guilty of that. Staff in psychiatric hospitals, for example, direct their comments, especially the approving ones, to the better-looking patients, a form of discrimination not practised by the patients themselves [20]. However, what can happen when the teacher assesses a pupil may be used as a perfect illustration of a grander social conspiracy. Earlier in this chapter the notion of a self-fulfilling prophesy was put forward. The initial stage in that process whereby we apply our expectations about somebody, called labelling, has just been reviewed in relation to physical attractiveness. The second and final stage can now be explained using the classroom example. Many people have suggested that there is a positive relationship between a teacher's attitude towards a student and that student's subsequent school performance. Indeed, it has even been suggested – but on rather poor evidence – that a child's measured IQ is likely to rise if his teacher imagines him to be cleverer than he really is. Certainly, it is known that children get on well at school subjects if they like the person who teaches them. Relatedly, particular teachers can do a lot to encourage or discourage a child's belief in himself and his school ability. Supposing, then, a teacher believes a child is clever because he *looks* clever. Then, if the teacher encourages that child he is more likely to do well, i.e. appear clever. Similarly, if a teacher imagines a child to be stupid, he can discourage him by spending less time explaining things or by saying what he thinks of him in front of the rest of the class. By these methods, a teacher is likely by his own behaviour to affect performance in a direction consistent with his initial expectation. This is how the self-fulfilling prophesy works. The teacher, like all of us, can act in such a way as to make his first impression come right. Fortunately there seems to be limits to the self-fulfilling prophecy of ability. Teachers and parents may expect the more attractive child to do better at school, they may even help him or her by giving better grades and ratings [21]; but their influence stops short of ability as measured objectively by the Thorndike Lorge intelligence test or by written tests of reading, spelling, and mathematics [22]. A more elaborate study might, however, discover more complex interactions – perhaps the attractive pupils do not have to try so hard, or perhaps the unattractive children find themselves cast in the role of swot or grind.

The technique of the self-fulfilling prophesy amply illustrates the deficiencies of our ability to form impressions of other people. Because we are unable to think of most others as individuals and yet we like to see ourselves as good judges, we try to make people turn out as we always thought they would. Often we do this so well that we never see fit to question our ability to make judgements. The most successful self-fulfilling prophesies are perpetrated collectively. There are social conspiracies (usually unacknowledged) for us all to see and to treat groups of people in agreed ways — 'physically attractive people are nice to be with', 'Italians are romantic'. We apply these judgements regardless of their truth and work together through individual applications of the same prophesies to make people act in the ways that are collectively expected It is this agreement among others about the characteristics of old and young, men and women, fat and thin, that creates pressure for individuals who belong to these groups, to conform. If they do, social illusion becomes reality and people's behaviour is kept within the bounds of our common understanding. Of course, there is an opposite point of view. Individually and collectively, we may be correct in our judgements. For example, it could well be the case that all people born with good looks are also born as more intelligent, outgoing, complex, happy, and trustworthy than other people. However, such an idea is not very plausible. What is more likely is that people tend to take on the characteristics with which they are labelled. Unfortunately, there is not much direct evidence on this point; what little there is will be discussed in Chapter 4.

So far this discussion has dealt mainly with the initial impression one person makes on another. Such first impressions are important, if only because a lot of the contacts we make in everyday life do not get beyond this level of superficiality. The canvassing political candidate, the job applicant at interview, the defendant in court are all examples of cases where appearance can easily sway an important decision. However, it is quite possible that looks are important only over such a short duration of contact between two people, and there are some who maintain that looks steadily decrease in importance thereafter. Such a supposition is probably optimistic. For one thing, an individual's initial impression of the person he is talking to greatly affects the way he plans the rest of the encounter. We are often put out when the other person does not confirm the early judgement we make and we work especially hard on such people to make them fit into our first impression. For another thing, these people who value good looks in another may not encourage further encounters with a physically unattractive person if they have the choice. When people do not have such a choice, as, for example, when they are at school or work together, interesting effects are noticed when they rate each other's physical attractiveness. In one study [23] of this, some 11- and 16-year-old boys and girls were asked to make ratings of the attractiveness of their classmates when they were shown to them in photographs. Identical photographs were also rated for good looks by children of the same age who went to a different school and who did not know the individuals they rated. The first group of judges was termed 'knowers' and the other was called 'non-knowers'. Knowers had attended school together and had generally been in the same class since the first grade. When ratings of knowers and non-knowers were compared, it was found that there was much greater agreement about the attractiveness of those in the photographs among non-knowers than among knowers. Girls and boys who knew each other made many flattering judgements about each other's looks than the strangers did. It seems that the more a person is known to somebody the more attractive they are judged to be. In fact, this effect is at its greatest when the person being judged would be considered by most other people to be of average attractiveness. In these cases we seem to make very flattering judgements of people if we know them well. The latter is certainly not a general rule, and independent evidence suggests that our favour towards the appearance of acquaintances may easily be lost. A study has shown that if it is pointed out to us that a person's opinions differ greatly from our own, we frequently begin to see them as much less attractive than other people do. All this confirms a recurrent idea of this chapter. Because people do not have their worth tattoo on their foreheads we use their most visible attributes, such as their physical attractiveness, to make some estimate of the characteristics they possess. It follows that initially we should use a person's attractiveness as a guide to their value, but when clear independent evidence of their value is brought to our attention we revise our estimate of their looks. As noted above, this rule applies most when the attractiveness of the person we are judging is near average.

When two people do begin to talk, they are able to form impressions of each other on the basis of a whole variety of guidance. Consider two strangers — a man and a woman — who have just met on a train or at a bus stop, and let us assume that both are mildly attracted to each other. The conversation will almost certainly open with some banal remark or a question like 'Do you know what time this train gets to Washington?', or 'Do you mind if I smoke?' Questions are more commonly used because they are the more likely to draw another into conversation. The next step is very important. The two people will communicate their interest in each other, one by the way they make the reply and the other by the way they receive it. There is little doubt that the questioner would wish there were more than just an abrupt answer. If the reply is encouraging — for example, if it ends in turn with a question back to the first person — then both parties will begin a sequence of conversation which has two aims. The first is to appear attractive and the second is to appear attracted.

All conversations of this kind are fairly tightly controlled by social rules. We are all taught from a very early age how to treat strangers and we all know how to be polite and listen with interest to other people. Social rules play a very important part in the whole business of forming impressions of other people. They help, in the same way as self-fulfilling prophesies do, to overcome our deficiencies as judges of other people. Rules help take the unpredictability out of an individual's behaviour and therefore make him or her easier to assess. When we meet a stranger at a party we know roughly how they will behave because there are conventions about what to do at such gatherings. Similarly, there are rules about how to buy goods in shops or how to behave at a job interview. In many encounters a knowledge of what ought to be said and done according to convention allows people to interact easily without either one having to think of the other as an individual at all. Again, just as there is an unwritten social agreement to punish those who will not conform to common stereotyped expectations of themselves, there is also a social agreement to punish those who break social conventions. Punishment can take any form from physical assault on those who jump queues to name-calling of individuals who are rude or boorish.

It would be wrong simply to think of these rules as etiquette or good manners. There are a good many social rules that are not strictly of that kind. For example, in some social groups it is frowned upon for women to be outspoken or to contradict men in public. Of course, in such cases the rule that women should be subordinate is not one of etiquette — nor is it made as explicit as rules of etiquette usually are. It is only when women behave in ways which contravene the rule that we notice it existed at all. This and many other rules are only acknowledged when we show or feel annoyance towards those who behave in direct contravention of them. There are rules, too, which prevent men from behaving in certain ways. It would not be bad manners for a man to discuss his emotional life with a group of other men. However, this very rarely happens because it is considered unbecoming for a man to behave in this way in male company. Many men and women are, through men's and women's liberation groups, intent on changing such rules.

In the case of an ongoing conversation, the rules governing the situation often dictate the roles that people have to take towards one another. Returning to the example of two strangers talking to each other, both are probably trying to establish from the beginning the kind of partner the other prefers. Their behaviour will be, in part, determined by the estimate they make. The woman might think, 'He's fairly dumb but quite good looking so I'll pretend to be more stupid than I am'. Her self-presentation here is following the prescription that men in Western society prefer women who are not as clever as they are. Similarly, the man in this conversation will probably say to himself: 'Most women prefer men who are intelligent, physically powerful, wealthy and fairly dominant. Therefore, I must try and act out this particular role, if I am to get any further with this woman'. In fact, a study [24] has been carried out to examine the effects of the man's playing a dominant role on his attraction for women. A number of unacquainted men and women were put together and asked to work on a puzzle set by a psychologist. In cases where the man showed himself to be competent at the problem, girls were more attracted to him than they were to incompetent partners. If the man tried to overcome his incompetence by being dominant in this situation, he lost further ground and became even more unattractive. On the other hand, competent men who were also dominant increased their appeal. The conclusion seems to be that dominance on its own is not enough to make a girl's heart flutter, and in certain cases it can even have an effect opposite to that intended.

The man and woman in our example will find many clues to the kind of person the other is in their appearance alone. By using these clues skilfully they can each present themselves to the other in desired ways. Suppose the man in this first encounter notices that the woman is well dressed and well spoken. He then has a choice between two possibilities. Firstly, that the woman is financially well-off because she is a successful career woman and therefore well educated and intelligent. Secondly, he may think that the woman is financially well-off because she comes from a well-to-do family and so is not necessarily very bright. Either way, he will probably believe that he should present himself as well-off and, until the second is demonstrated, he probably should present himself as rather clever as well. Social rules dictate that if we want to say, 'I have lots of money and am very intelligent' we must do so in a very roundabout way. In such circumstances we usually proceed to make 'casual' and 'chance' references to recent events in our life which are important to the role we wish to adopt. 'I noticed in *The Times* today . . . ', 'One frequently finds that when one is abroad . . . ', 'I have a friend who works at the White House who was telling me . . . ' are all examples of gambits which a man might use to make himself more acceptable to a woman. People from different walks of life have their own indirect ways of referring to things which will increase their sexual status (e.g. claiming an acquaintance with footballers, pop stars, or even criminals). The literal meaning of the phrases they use is not important. 'I have a friend who works in the White House' also means 'I am of sufficient social and intellectual status to have friends who work in the White House'. Messages about personal, social, and intellectual status are wrapped up in this way because it is as unbecoming to state them directly as it is for the wealthy woman to wear every item of her jewellery at the same time.

At the same moment as they are searching for clues about the other person's character, our two people will also be looking for some hints that the other person likes them. Signs such as smiles, nods, eye contact, and the like are all indicators of liking, and they are discussed in Chapter 5. Some people are very good at recognizing and at using these clues, but others are not so skilled. Alternatively, their perception of the clues may be greatly affected by their strong attraction towards the other person. In such cases people usually over-interpret any action on the part of the other — if she smiles it must mean love or if she frowns it can only be disdain. Many people, if they are strongly sexually attracted to another, engage in a kind of wishful thinking and see the other as more sexually receptive than they might do at other times. One very interesting study [25] has shown how this works. Some college men were divided initially into two groups. One group read a very arousing passage about human sexual activity while the other read a rather straight passage about the sexual behaviour of the herring gull. In a second part of the study some men from both groups were ,asked to evaluate a very attractive girl whom they were led to expect they could have a date with. Others were asked to evaluate the same girl but they were not led to expect they could have a date with her (the dates had supposedly been arranged by the experimenters as part of an investigation into impressions formed on first dates. The dates never actually came off; the experiment was finished and the college men told the real purpose after they had given their impression of the girl.) Thus, in the study there were four groups of men: sexually aroused men describing a girl they expected to date, unaroused men doing the same, aroused men describing a girl they would not meet, and unaroused doing the same. The first aroused group are, in psychological jargon, evaluating an emotionally relevant object. The unaroused groups are less motivated. The second sexually aroused group (describing a girl they are not likely to date) are, if anything, slightly frustrated. As expected, it is the aroused groups who see the girl as likely to be sexually receptive and interestingly the aroused but frustrated group see her more in this way than those who expect to be seeing her on a date.

All these observations underline the fact that physically attractive people have a great advantage in man/women conversations. For one thing, they are more likely than others to arouse in their listeners a feeling of sexual arousal, and, of course, we all enjoy this feeling even when it is quite mild. In addition, being with somebody who is attractive gives status to the person to whom they are talking; we prefer to be seen with physically attractive people. Finally, if we are getting on well with attractive people it is possible for us to feel attractive ourselves and because we feel this way we can act out the role of an attractive person. This gives us some additional enjoyment. Returning to a point made near the beginning of this chapter, if we are to extend a relationship with someone then they must make themselves important enough for us to remember their behaviour as individuals. For reasons already explained, we are reluctant to individualize others. Such a step means that we must reorganize a part of our memory to cope with the demands their individual preferences, attitudes, and behaviours make on us. Also, we usually prefer the world the way 'it is' rather than the new way another individual might want us to see it. The only way in which we can be shocked out of our natural conservatism is to be challenged or aroused. Many life-long friendships and affairs begin on the former basis: a disagreement between two people can force both of them to get to know the other as an individual. Anecdotally, many successful marriages are founded in initial dislike. However, many potential relationships are killed in the early stages by the very same means. The much more certain way to have others see one as an individual is to arouse them sexually and this is where physically attractive people have an edge. Their behaviour is more likely to be remembered because society has given them value, whereas the behaviour of the less attractive will be grouped and categorised under most circumstances. Getting to know someone is like a steeplechase, and the good-looking have the advantage of being among those who start beyond the first hurdle.

REFERENCES

1. A. G. Miller (1970) Role of physical attractiveness in impression formation. *Psychon. Sci.* **19**, 241—3.
2. W. J. McKeachie (1952) Lipstick as a determiner of first impressions of personality. *J. soc. Psychol.* **36**, 241—4.
3. C. T. Kenny and D. Fletcher (1973) Effects of beardedness on person perception. *Perc. Mot. Skills.* **37**, 413—14.
4. S. Roll and J. S. Verinis (1971) Stereotypes of scalp and facial hair as measured by the semantic differential. *Psychol. Rep.* **28**, 975—80.
5. E. D. Lawson (1971) Hair colour, personality and the observer. *Psychol. Rep.* **28**, 311—22.
6. J. K. Skipper and G. Nass (1966) Dating behaviour: a framework for analysis and an illustration. *J. Marr. Fam.* **28**, 412—20.
7. J. (1971) *The sensuous woman*, W. H. Allen, London.
8. D. Byrne and B. Blaylock (1963) Similarity and assumed similarity of attitudes between husbands and wives. *J. abnorm. soc. Psychol.* **67**, 636—40.
9. R. J. Cromwell (1956) Factors in the serial recall of names and acquaintances. *J. abnorm. soc. Psychol.* **53**, 63—67.
10. M. Brenner (1971) Caring, love and selective memory. *Proc. 79th Ann. Conf. Am. Psychol. Assoc.* **6**, 275—6.
11. P. N. Hamid (1969) Changes in person perception as a function of dress. *Perc. Mot. Skills.* **29**, 191—4.
12. R. Bull (1974) The importance of being beautiful. *New Society.* **30**, 412—14.
13. K. Gibbins (1969) Communication aspects of women's clothes and their relation to fashionability. *Br. J. soc. clin. Psychol.* **8**, 301—12.

14. C. Seligman *et al.* (1973) Attribution of responsibility for a chance event as a function of physical attractiveness, a target problem: outcome and likelihood of event. *Proc. 81st. Ann. Conf. Am. Psych. Assoc.* **8**, 1428.
15. M. G. Efran (1974) The effect of physical appearance on the judgement of guilt, interpersonal attraction, and severity of recommended punishment in a simulated jury task. *J. Res. Pers.* **8**, 45—54.
16. H. Sigall and N. Ostrove (1975) Beautiful but dangerous: effects of offender attractiveness and nature of the crime and juridic judgement. *J. Pers. soc. Psychol.* **31**, 410—14.
17. K. K. Dion (1972) Physical attractiveness and evaluation of children's transgressions. *J. Pers. soc. Psychol.*, **24**, 207—13.
18. H. Harari and J. McDavid (1969) Situational influence on moral justice: a study of 'finking'. *J. Pers. soc. Psychol.* **11**, 240—4.
19. M. M. Clifford and E. Walster (1973) The effect of physical attractiveness on teacher expectations. *Sociol. Educ.* **46**, 248—58.
20. M. S. McGarry and S. G. West (1975) Stigma among the stigmatised: resident mobility, communicative ability and physical appearance as predictors of staff-resident interaction. *J. Abnorm. Psychol.* **85**, 399—405.
21. G. R. Adams and J. C. LaVoie (1975) Parental expectations of educational and personal-social performance and childrearing patterns as a function of attractiveness, sex and conduct of the child. *Child Study J.* **5**, 125—142.
22. M. M. Clifford (1975) Physical attractiveness and academic performance. *Child Study J.* **5**, 201—9.
23. E. Berscheid and E. Walster (1974) Physical attractiveness, in L. Berkowitz (ed.) *Advances in Experimental Social Psychology*, vol. 7, Academic, (see p.184) New York.
24. J. C. Touhey (1974) Effects of dominance and competence on heterosexual attraction. *Br. J. soc. clin. Psychol.* **13**, 22—26.
25. W. Stephan *et al.* (1971) Sexual arousal and heterosexual perception. *J. Pers. soc. Psychol.* **20**, 93—101.

Chapter 4

YOU CAN TELL AT A GLANCE

The idea (raised in Chapter 3) that we may not always make very accurate judgements about each other is examined in relation to sexual behaviour. This chapter contrasts popular misconceptions about personality and sexual behaviour with other ideas that are much more likely to be valid. The results of research show that there are universal and largely unsupported ideas about the promiscuity (or lack of it) of various groups in our society. There are also mistaken ideas about the behaviour of sexually deviant groups such as homosexuals. It is nevertheless possible to make valid generalizations about sexual behaviour and examples of such generalizations involving social class, age, occupation, and appearance are given. The chapter ends with a discussion of love and how it distorts the judgements we make of our sexual partners.

> 'He wished, as often in the past, that he was a really mature man who 'knew' things like that 'by instinct'. He tried to draw a mental picture of someone who looked like Emilia and who 'was just waiting for you to try it on so she could slap your face' and then of someone who looked like Emilia and who 'was bloody sitting up and begging for it'. Both pictures were highly plausible and resembled each other even more closely than they resembled Emilia.' [Kingsley Amis, *I Like it Here*]

This quotation from an early novel by Kingsley Amis illustrates a problem familiar to very nearly everyone — how to tell what someone is thinking about them, how to tell what the other expects them to do, and how to predict what the other will do if they commit themselves by making a pass. The problem has also attracted the attention of psychologists. Thus in a recent experiment [1] a number of college students were asked what they expected should happen on a first date, and what they thought the other person would expect to happen. This was to see whether the boy's idea of what to do and the girl's idea coincide, or whether they misunderstand each other and go out on their date with inconsistent ideas about how to behave. College men were asked if they expected a girl to let them kiss her after a first date, and college women if they expected a man to want to; slightly more than half said yes to these questions. Next the subjects were asked to predict what the other sex thought was expected, to see if the girls think the boy expects a kiss, and if the boys think girls expect them to try. The results showed conclusively that the two sexes systematically misunderstood each other. In Amis's problem situation one could rely on people to guess wrongly quite often. These misunderstandings taken an interesting form that have highly significant consequences. Whereas only half the men and women actually expected or wanted to kiss after a first date, rather nearer three-quarters thought it expected of them. This inaccuracy of students' perceptions of what the opposite sex thinks will tend to cause an increase in permissiveness, for if everyone thinks the people around them are more permissive or sexually active than they really are, and if they live up to this wrong impression, it will be made true — an example of a self-fulfilling prophecy. In fact another study [2] found that college women generally overestimated rather than underestimated the proportion of their peers who were not virgins; on average they thought less than half of other college women were virgins, whereas in fact more than half — 57% to be exact — were virgins.

In any relationships beyond the most transient, much depends on the similarity of outlook of the men and women, and something on their personality and 'role expectations' These tend to match in actual couples, so that people tend to be drawn to someone whose personality or outlook matches their own — 'birds of a feather' — or, to be precise, whose personality and outlook *seems* to match their own. The research showing how people pair off according to personality, intelligence, and outlook used questionnaires, tests, and opinion polls, but the couples who meet outside the laboratory have to sum each other up without the benefit of scientific measurements of personality — unless they use a computer dating service. Instead they must rely on their ability to observe and interpret how the other behaves, on their judgement of human character in fact.

Most research on the way people interpret each other's character — and there has been a lot — has painted a depressing picture of partial or total misunderstanding, [3] yet there are some grounds for expecting courting and married couples to do better. Most psychological research has studied opinions formed by people who have no pressing need to form them, about people they have little contact with and will never meet outside the laboratory. A courting couple are in a much better position to get to know each other, besides having much stronger reasons for needing to, if only they can avoid wishful thinking. A number of studies of how clearly couples see each other have appeared, over the last 20 years, and have yielded mixed results. It is true that some evidence that couples see each other correctly is generally found, like the evidence for similarity of personality in couples, it is very limited. For example, in one piece of research [4] married couples were asked to say how much upset was caused in the marriage by various typical problems, such as sexual demands, or one partner 'not listening' to the other. The researcher found that husbands and wives were not just guessing what the other thought, but were a very long way from perfect agreement. Many other studies have obtained the same sort of result. Another typical study [5] tried to estimate how accurate engaged peoples' judgements of their fiancé(e)s' personalities were, using a personality test. When men were describing their fiancées' personality, accurate judgement of what the girl was really like was small; most of what the man said was pure guesswork. Girls did slightly better but were still very inaccurate.

Perhaps the samples studied in these experiments included a lot of unhappy marriages or engagements that were fated to break up. This line of argument has been pursued, again with limited success. For example, the study on problem areas in marriage failed to find any difference between happily married couples and a group who were getting divorced. Other studies have found differences but they are not very large. For example, suppose you asked married couples to predict each other's answers to a number of questions — a form of test often adapted these days into a TV panel game. One researcher [6] who did an experiment like this asked happy and unhappy couples to say how each other would answer 55 questions. Since the questions were answered 'yes' or 'no', anyone could score about 27 or 28 just by guessing, but how did the married couples fare? Not a lot better than guesswork in fact; the happy couples got an average of 38 right, 10 or 11 better than guesswork, and the unhappy couples an average of 33, only 5 or 6 better than guesswork. Even the happy couples are much nearer the bottom of the scale than the top. This experiment is also interesting because it took a simple precaution, not taken in earlier work, nor in all later work, nor for that matter in the TV quiz show or newspaper versions of the task. Of the 100 original questions 45 were dropped because more than two-thirds of the people gave the same answer; if everyone answers the question in the same way the person making the prediction does not have to consider what his or her partner would say, just what people in general would say, or else he or she can assume the other says the same as himself or herself, with some chance of being correct. In general, research shows engaged couples, who see each other's personality or marriage expectations clearly, are more likely to marry and are less likely to break off the engagement, but again the effects seem to be modest. Certainly it is far from true that all couples who knew each other well are destined to get on well; perhaps some of them do not like what they see. By the same token not all couples who misunderstand each other drift apart; many get married in haste and repent at leisure, but some never realize they are by conventional wisdom incompatible.

Shared opinions and personality merely make a person more eligible, but of the large number of possible partners we must choose just one, or at least just a few. Even if one person perceives another's opinions and personality, and even if they match, attraction does not automatically follow of course. Similarity of personality, outlook and appearance may be a necessary condition for attraction, but certainly are not sufficient. Other factors play a significant role, not the least being chance or luck. Deciding that someone is similar is just the first and perhaps the least important step. Indeed, for many people it is relatively minor, because a high proportion of the people they meet are similar enough to be 'eligible'. For example, when a college student narrows his or her choice — not necessarily consciously of course — to someone who is outgoing, reasonably intelligent, about his or her own age, reasonably attractive, and liberal but not radical in outlook, he or she has not narrowed it all that much, probably not to below a three-figure number, or even below four figures on a large campus. So how does the college man or woman, or others in the same sort of situation, settle on a partner? The answer is — in all sorts of ways, many of which defy rational explanation, but they might get on a lot better by choosing someone who likes them, in preference to someone — equally similar in outlook, etc. — who happens not to.* A fair amount of research has been done on how good people are at seeing who likes them or dislikes them, and who is merely indifferent.

Most of the research on the perception of liking covers friendship only, and generally same sex choices at that. Everyone in a particular group — often school or college classes — is asked to nominate perhaps three people they like and three they dislike. This is called 'sociometry', [7] and yields a 'sociogram' — a diagram showing who likes who, who is popular, who is rejected, and who is isolated (neither popular nor unpopular). The next stage is to ask everyone in the group to predict others' choices, to say who likes who, who likes them, etc. The experimenter can also go on to find out why unpopular people are unpopular by asking other people in the group to describe those they dislike and why they dislike them. When the experimenter asks his group to predict others' social preferences, he finds that people do not just guess but can see who likes who, but nevertheless are far from being perfectly accurate, and that predictions depend as much on what the perceiver expects or wants to see as on what is actually there. People expect liking to be reciprocated, and while they are often correct — so that the people they like like them too — people exaggerate this reciprocity. We are apparently worse at seeing dislike than like. Most people have had the experience of finding that someone does not really like them, so are a little wary of committing themselves, and will have less blind faith in the correctness of their judgement. The early stages of love affairs particularly are not characterized by perfect mutual trust, for boy and girl are constantly seeking reassurance from each other. When affairs come to an end it is often a relief to both and the result of

*Of course people choose dates who do not, initially at any rate, like them for lots of reasons, ranging from physical infatuation to what one might call 'the thrill of the chase'.

developing indifference, but in about 30% of cases, according to one survey, it is 'unilateral' and often gives the rejected partner a nasty shock.

People seeking a fiancé(e) or companion obviously pay more attention to personality, outlook, or social background than people just looking for a sexual partner. The latter will focus on sexual attitudes and behaviour. People differ markedly in their attitudes to sexual behaviour and practices, especially for the unmarried. The psychologist sets about measuring these differences with questionnaires. Such questionnaires can be used to type people into those who believe in absolute freedom, those who believe in premarital intercourse only if the couples are involved emotionally, those who disapprove of sex before marriage for anyone, and those who subscribe to the 'double standard' — the idea that men should be free to have sex before marriage or outside marriage, or, indeed, positively ought to have some experience, whereas women definitely should not.* It would come as no surprise to anyone to learn that permissiveness diminishes with age, but one survey found more complex and interesting relationships, for that permissiveness increased slightly up to age 20, reaching a peak there, and then decreased particularly in those who have children, reaching a peak in parents of girls in their late teens. Women at all ages are less permissive — on average that is — whereas American Negroes are more permissive. Not surprisingly, people who are deeply religious are less permissive too. [8] However, it would be a mistake to rely on someone's expressed attitude towards sex, when trying to decide what they actually do or are willing to do; for example, a study [9] that found that more attractive girls were twice as likely to have had premarital intercourse than average also found no difference at all in their attitude to sexual intercourse. What people do and what they think they ought to do are far from being the same thing. Another survey [10] found that young Danes were very permissive in outlook, had had more sexual experience, but wanted more still, whereas young Americans in Utah did not have a permissive outlook, had had less sexual experience, and tended to regret even what they had done.

*The 'double standard' still has a strong grip on Western society, but is gradually losing its influence. It creates two classes of girls 'good' and 'bad', and leads ultimately of course, to prostitution.

Actual sexual behaviour, as opposed to attitudes about it, has been exhaustively studied; the Kinsey reports [11] and their numerous successors went into this in great detail, asking men and women if they were a virgin or not, and, if virgin, how much of a virgin — how much sexual experience they had had. Kinsey and his followers use a simple-scale, based on the largely correct assumption that one thing leads to another, that, for example, couples who do not kiss are most unlikely to engage in heavy petting.* A British version [12] of Western sexual progression runs as follows:

(1)   Little or no contact with opposite sex.
(2)   Limited experience of sexual activities, e.g. stroking clothed breast.
(3)   Sexual intimacies falling short of intercourse, e.g. genital stimulation.
(4)   Sexual intercourse with one partner.
(5)   Sexual intercourse with more than one partner.

The boy or girl — and this is more of a teenage preoccupation — who wants to decide how far his or her partner has gone and hence how far he or she is likely to go, has essentially two sources of information — gossip and inference. People make love in private in all human societies (whereas animals are generally indifferent to an audience), so it follows that people can only know another's sexual status if they tell someone about it (assuming that 'peeping toms' keep their discoveries to themselves). If the couple tell a social scientist, they provide information for making inferences; if they tell their friends and relations they provide information by way of gossip. But who tells others about their sexual experiences and why? A recent survey [13] of college students answered the first question and produced quite remarkable results. The students certainly do not keep their experiences to themselves; only 1 in 5 of men *did not* tell anyone about their first experience of intercourse, and only 1 in 4 of girls did not. Men tended

*There is no logical reason of course why they should not. Some societies regard kissing as a very intimate act, and some do not do it at all.

to broadcast the information — over half told 5 or more of their friends about it, whereas only 1 in 5 of the girls did. These friends were, as one might expect, of the same sex; in particular virtually no men told female friends about their exploits. (They do tell their parents however — about 60% of the men and 40% of the girls said their parents knew.) As the author of the survey remarks, these figures imply that 'a woman's decision to enter coitus also implies that she is creating for herself a sexual status which will have a relative pervasive distribution' — in other words there is good chance that a lot of men will get to know about it. The same is true for lower class American society. Information about the 'sexual status' of local girls is spread freely through the group. The same seems true to the authors for British college students. Information about more exotic societies is limited, but of 200 societies examined in one report [14], there were about 60 in which sex outside marriage was forbidden and severely punished, implying that people would not talk about it.

Younger men and women talk about sex more; the urge to tell someone else lessens with age, especially in men. Only 16% of males still at school did not tell anyone, as opposed to exactly half of the men in the third and fourth year at college. The depth of the relationship also matters. Not surprisingly men are keen to tell their friends about sex with 'casual dates or pickups', but what is more surprising is that 60% do tell their friends sooner or later even when 'planning to marry'. The same holds for girls; 4 out of 5 tell their friends, even about intercourse with casual dates, while slightly fewer — 70% — tell their friends about sex with their fiancés. Lester Kirkendall's [15] interviews with a number of boys about their premarital experiences show that they tell their friends partly to boast and prove their manliness, but also to pass on useful information, exchanging notes about who is an 'easy lay', and describing the best way of seducing different girls. According to the author of the survey, girls seem to have different reasons for discussing their sexual experiences. They talk about it not so much to let each other know which men are willing (although some may tell their friends which men are willing *and able*) as to relieve feelings of guilt or to reassure themselves they have done the right thing.

Evidently gossip is a very good way for young unmarried boys to size up girls, it probably plays a less important role elsewhere. More mature people are less likely to be curious about others' sexual behaviour, and would tend to assume – more or less correctly – that anyone over the age of 25 or so, married or not, would be sexually experienced. Adults do express an interest in what sociologists call 'deviant' behaviour, notably homosexuality. There is no systematic information about disclosure of homosexuality, but with the removal first of legal sanctions, and currently of moral stigma, many homosexuals feel no obligation to pretend to be heterosexual. As one might expect, homosexuals in professional and managerial jobs prefer to remain under cover more than those in traditional homosexual occupations like hairdressing or acting.

There is a substantial body of research on various correlates of sexual experience, and also on correlates of homosexuality. The logic of the exercise is not unlike that behind car insurance. Given statistical information on how many people at various ages, in different social classes, with different personal histories have had intercourse, it is possible to guess at the behaviour of a particular person by adding up all the information arriving at an estimate of their status. Like car insurance, this yields probabilistic judgements and does not pretend to predict whether a person will or will not be a virgin, any more than car insurers try to predict particular accidents. Both processes concentrate on identifying *the sort of person likely* to be more experienced or have more accidents. Both are therefore in a sense unfair to the individual. The process is largely additive; one piece of information does not change its significance in the light of another. To that extent it may seem to many 'mindless' and again somewhat of an affront to human dignity.

The Kinsey reports – on male and female sexual behaviour – give some illustrative data on demographic correlates on sexual status. Starting with the most obvious sign, the older a man or woman is the more likely he or she is to have had intercourse. For women the curve rises steadily from age 15 where only 3% were experienced, to age 30, where 44% had. (These data refer to unmarried girls only of course.) Decade of birth also makes a difference, for regardless of age, the longer ago a girl was born, the less likely she was to have had premarital intercourse. By now Kinsey's data on women born before 1900 have only academic interest, but the tendency has continued and perhaps even accelerated since the fifties. One recent survey [16] found a marked increase in sexual experience among college women between 1958 and 1968, particularly in more casual liaisons. For example, the number of girls who had intercourse with casual dates increased from 10% to 23%, with steady dates from 15% to 28%, and with fiancés from 31% to 39%. It is quite possible that these two trends have cancelled each other out — the increase in experience with age being equalled by the increase due to being born later, in a more permissive age.

The most recent survey available [17] shows that pre-marital intercourse is getting steadily more general in American college youth. By 1972 three-quarters of students, male and female, had had intercourse, and the overall sex difference had at last vanished, although slightly more women — 45% against 32% — still confined their experience to a single partner.

In the United States, race is a reliable indicator; Negroes have more sexual experience and sooner. Kinsey found that women who live in urban areas are more sexually experienced. Of late, national differences have been studied extensively. One study [18] found quite large differences between American and Danish students, while another study [19] looked at student samples in the United States, Canada, Germany, Norway, and England, producing some surprising results. About 60% of American men, aged 20—22, had had PMI, a similar proportion of Canadian men, slightly fewer German men, rather more Norwegian men — 67% — and three-quarters of Englishmen. The picture for women was similar but not identical, around 40% American and Canadian women had had premarital intercourse, just over half of the Norwegian women, and around 60% of German and English women. The most striking results were the answer to a question about premarital intercourse with 'one night stands'. Here the English sample were far more experienced than any other, especially the women, where a third said they had had such an experience, opposed to 12% in Norway and rates under 1 in 10 for the other nationalities. This data comes as a surprise to many English people who do not usually regard themselves as especially sexually adventurous, particuarly compared with the Scandinavians. British people who feel worried or affronted by this apparently greater promiscuity can find some consolation in another survey comparing British and American sexual behaviour. This study was done in 1970 and compared over 2000 American men and the same number of women, with a large British sample; they found British boys and girls much *less* experienced at ages up to 17 — in apparent flat contradiction to the first. However, subjects in the second survey were younger and a representative cross-section of the population, whereas in the first survey they were all college students. There is no survey data for France or southern European countries, but the latter are likely to have far lower premarital intercourse rates given that the sexes are not allowed to meet or to be alone before marriage. The same goes for Indians and Pakistanis including, to judge from press reports, those who have settled in Britain. It has been reported [20] that East German youth have less sexual experience than their West German compatriots. It should be emphasized that these are all probabilistic data; saying that 58.2% of American men and 74.8% of English men, aged 20—22, have had sex before marriage tells one nothing about *a particular* American or Englishman. Even *a particular* Danish man may be one of the 5.3% who is sexually inexperienced.

People often wonder how reliable survey data of this type are and suspect the informants lie, either because they are ashamed to tell the truth even in anonymous interviews, or perhaps because they resent the whole proceeding and lie to spite the investigator. Malcolm Muggeridge declared publicly that he 'never under any circumstances tell(s) the truth about sexual experiences' and concludes that 'the data collected by Dr. Kinsey and other toilers in that vineyard is, to put it mildly, suspect'. One study [21] has been reported that provided an independent physical check on the truth of men's reports of intercourse; analysis of urine samples, for presence of sperm cells, served to confirm the men's reports of their activities. Another check which can be made is to ask husband and wife separately; their reports usually agree fairly well.

A person's social class can be a guide to his sexual behaviour, although the results of the four or five surveys on this subject in America and Britain have produced somewhat ambiguous results. Thus the Kinsey Report, on *Sexual Behaviour in the Human Male*, mentioned that more lower-class men had had premarital sex and that they had it younger than middle-class men. Kinsey's conclusion has been questioned on the ground that his lower-class sample included a lot of convicts and was not representative. The same objection cannot be made about a later survey [22] of American women, which also found very large class differences and in the same direction as Kinsey; 30% of upper-class women had had premarital intercourse as opposed to 80% of lower-class women. Similar data were obtained in a 1970 survey [19] also in America, showing that working-class girls were more likely to have had sex before marriage. However, two other surveys, one in Britain and one in the United States, have found that middle-class girls were *slightly more* sexually experienced, not *far less* experienced. In the United States, the Kinsey Report, *Sexual Behaviour in the Human Female*, published several years after the report on male behaviour, found a smallish tendency for women whose fathers had better jobs and who themselves had had a better education to be more likely to be sexually experienced. In Britain [12] only one social class difference has been reported; more − 53% to be precise − middle-class teenage girls had had extensive 'petting' experience compared with working-class girls, only 35% of whom had 'petted' a lot. The most recent American survey [23] done in 1971, found no class difference in white youth, but large differences for black youth, in the direction of the poorer boys and girls having intercourse earlier than the better off. If we regard the better off blacks as upwardly mobile within white society, then this finding is an example of what Kinsey called 'anticipatory socialization' − adopting the values and behaviour of the class you hope to join, in preference to those of the class you currently belong to.

Psychologists prefer to explain the way people behave at a more individual level and are less interested in class, race, or national differences. Their approach to explaining why some people have had a varied sex life before the age of 16 while others do not have intercourse until after marriage (and not even then sometimes) relies more on personality, on the one hand, and on concepts like learning, on the other. An early study [24] of the sexual behaviour of dominant and submissive women is typical of their approach. Dominance was assessed by interview and questionnaire, and proved to have a strikingly large relation with sexual behaviour. What emerged was that all the submissive women − with hardly a single exception − were virgins, whereas only about a third of the dominant women were. The researcher also found that the dominant women were more promiscuous, and that they masturbated much more. The results of this survey are interesting because they are not quite what 'commonsense' psychology would expect. Surely, one might argue, 'submissive' women ought to give in to male demands more readily — remember women's liberation was a long way off in 1942 — but the data suggest rather that it was the women who were getting their own way.

More recent research used standard personality tests such as the Eysenck Personality Inventory (EPI), which assesses two aspects of personality — 'extroversion', or the extent to which a person is outgoing, sociable and impulsive, and 'neuroticism', or the extent to which the person worries about things. A large survey of university students in West Germany [20] used the EPI and found very large differences in the sexual behaviour of extroverted and introverted students of both sexes. The extrovert group were more likely to have had sexual intercourse, had done so at an earlier age, had had intercourse with more people, had experimented with a greater variety of coital positions; and were also more likely to have tried oral sex. The differences between the groups were quite substantial. For example, 45% of the extroverted men had had intercourse by the age of 19 as opposed to only 15% of the introverted men, and of those that had had intercourse at the time of the study, the extroverted men had it on average 5 or 6 times a month, as opposed to the introvert's average of 3 times. The difference for women was even more striking: the introverted women had intercourse 3 times a month, whereas the extroverted women achieved an average of 7½.

Similar research has been reported in Britain by Professor H. J. Eysenck on the sexual attitudes of people with different personalities [25]. People with psychotic* tendencies presented 'an interesting combination of promiscuity, pre-marital sex, and curiosity, with hostility and lack of satisfaction'. The extrovert is also more promiscuous, but has no anxieties and is satisfied with his sex life, whereas people with neurotic tendencies suffered from guilt feelings and did not enjoy their sex lives. Higher neuroticism scores were associated with male impotence, female frigidity, male premature ejaculation and female failure to have an orgasm, although these tendencies were all very modest — one or two scale points. An earlier survey [12] found that

*A psychotic is someone out of touch with reality, liable to disorders of language and thought, or social withdrawal.

the teenage boys who were rated more talkative during the survey interview were also more experienced. Given that extroverts had intercourse more often and with more partners, it is not surprising to learn that they catch VD more often [26]. Several other studies [27] in America have found that guilt feelings — measured on the Mosher Sex Guilt Inventory — are associated with less sexual experience.

In a further analysis [28] of his data, Eysenck looked at the actual sexual behaviour of 100 of the students who had 'hysterical personalities', people who are both highly extrovert and highly anxious or neurotic. An extrovert wants stimulation and variety in his or her sex life and, as we have noted, tends to get it, while an anxious person tends naturally enough to worry about sex. The combination of a keen interest in sex and strong anxiety about it will create conflict; the person with a 'hysterical personality' will be sexually experienced but guilt-ridden, which is precisely what Eysenck found. When they were compared with 100 'stable introverts' the hysterics emerged as more sexually experienced but also as very worried. More of the hysterical men (86%) had experienced intercourse compared with 62% of stable men. The differences between hysterical women and 'stable introvert' women were larger and more extensive; twice as many — 50% — of hysterical women had experienced intercourse. Furthermore they had had more extensive experience of prolonged kissing, being kissed on the nipple of the breast, and handling of the male genitals. Despite — or perhaps because of this — neither they nor the men were contented, and a high proportion said 'yes' to questions like 'sometimes sexual feelings overpower me' and 'I have felt guilty about sex experiences', compared with the stable introverts. Psychiatric reports about men and women with actual hysterical neuroses confirmed the picture painted by Eysenck of maladjustment; women hysterics were 'coquettish and frigid' and hysterics of both sexes tended to 'sexualize non-sexual relations', while, however, becoming frightened and tending to draw back if actual sexual relations were proposed.

The problem with information about personality differences is, as was remarked earlier, that one has first to assess personality. This presents difficulties outside the laboratory, for obviously questionnaires cannot be used, but the only alternative — subjective estimates — is very unreliable. Can research offer any other clues to sexual behaviour that are more directly visible? One or two interesting pieces of data have emerged incidentally. Signs of sexual status can be more specific; for example, smoking and drinking are quite good cues to teenagers' sexual experience. Inexperienced teenagers rarely get drunk, whereas 56% of experienced boys and 45% of experienced girls had been drunk three or more times according to a British survey [12]. The obvious explanations — that girls get drunk and are seduced easily, or men are more aggressive when drunk — may be dismissed for the author of the survey said that alcohol played little part in the couples' actual decision to have intercourse. It seems rather that drinking is symptomatic of a particular type of teenager. The same survey found that sexually experienced teenagers smoked more; in particular teenage girls who smoked more than twenty cigarettes a day were hardly ever virgins. A recent American study [29] found that 62% of female drug users — college students — were sexually experienced, opposed to 49% of those who did not use drugs. Furthermore, girls who smoked marijuana tended to have or have had several partners, whereas most of the non-smokers restricted their activity to a steady boyfriend. A psychological explanation of these effects would be in terms of personality and attitudes, arguing, for example, that more liberal-minded people are more likely both to have sexual intercourse readily and to take drugs. Sociologists would probably prefer an explanation in terms of 'sub-cultures', and would argue that patterns of behaviour, involving drinking and premarital intercourse, become customary in particular teenage or student circles. The sociologists seem nearer the mark, for two interesting recent studies [30] have shown that people's friends, and their sexual behaviour and attitudes, exert a powerful influence on the person's own behaviour. One showed that three times as many students whose friends were sexually experienced were experienced themselves, compared with students whose friends had little experience. The other found that sexually experienced males and females had at least one experienced friend, and that most inexperienced females had no experienced friends (there were too few inexperienced males to make any comparison).

Where the girl lives and what sort of family she comes from both play a significant role in sexual experience for American teenagers. Girls, black or white, who live away from home are far more likely to be sexually experienced than ones still living with parents or other family, while girls living by themselves are the least likely to be virgins. Black teenage girls living alone are hardly ever virgins, nor are the great majority — 70% — of white girls in the same circumstance. Girls living in flats or the like with other young people tie for second place with a rather different group of girls — those living in a household headed by a man or woman who is not a parent. Girls living in more conventional families are far more restrained but the biggest difference results from having their own fathers at home. The lowest teenage rate of activity — 20% — is found in white teenage girls living at home with both natural parents. This data [23] was collected in 1971 and throws an interesting light on the true scope of the 'sexual revolution'.

Another clue to behaviour that is even easier to observe than smoking or drinking is physical appearance. When people think about the relation between appearance and sexual behaviour they tend to argue on the following lines. Obviously the more attractive the male, the more conquests he will make and the sooner he will make them, but for attractive girls the situation is rather different. Assuming — rightly or wrongly — that girls are often reluctant to have sexual relations before marriage, one might predict that the prettier the girl the easier she will find it to attract partners, and the easier, too, she will find it to avoid pressure to give sexual favours to keep her partners. Is this reasoning correct? Two surveys, one in Britain and one in the USA [31] found a strong tendency for more attractive boys to be more experienced, but only a slight tendency in girls (in the same direction). However, more detailed American data [9] found a large effect of attractiveness in girls, and suggests further that the relationship may be a more complicated one. Sixty-two per cent of attractive girls were not virgins, 31% of average girls, and 39% of unattractive girls. There is evidently a strong tendency for better-looking girls to be more sexually active, contrary to our layman's reasoning but also a smaller tendency for unattractive girls to be more active, this time consistent with the layman's ideas. The same survey showed that the attractive girls had a fuller social life, having twice as many male friends (but no more female friends), having more dates, and having been in love more often — which perhaps accounts for their greater sexual experience. It could also be a 'reference group effect' as the attractive girls said that more of their friends had had intercourse — but then perhaps their friends are more attractive too. One commentator [32] has pointed out that the assumption behind most sex manuals is that practice makes perfect, and if this very reasonable assumption is true, it would appear to follow that more attractive girls would also be better in bed than their less-attractive friends. Needless to say, no research has been published on the erotic capabilities of attractive girls or of any group of men or women.

Rather a lot of the research described so far in this part of the chapter could be described as a mere exercise in bookkeeping, or 'virgin counting', with not enough attempt to explain why boys and girls decide to remain a virgin or not. No information is available about how or why boys make up their minds, and the assumption tends to be that lack of opportunity is the only reason in most cases, forgetting how important religious and moral principles are to some men. Some account of how girls make up their minds has been offered recently [33] and it takes the form of six categories of girl, identified by an interview probing the girl's 'sexual philosophy'. There are three types of virgin — 'inexperienced', 'adamant', and 'potential non-virgins' — and three types of non-virgin — 'engaged', liberated', and 'confused'. The inexperienced virgin is the girl for whom the whole question has not arisen yet because she has not had any serious relationships and has not progressed beyond kissing and light petting. The 'potential non-virgin' is similar, having had more experience and involvement, but she has not met the right man, at least not in the right place; when she does, she thinks she would probably be willing to have intercourse. The adamant virgin believes very firmly in waiting until after marriage, for religious reasons, or because that is what her parents taught her. She tends generally to a 'law and order' mentality. The engaged non-virgin is a familiar type; the large pre-war surveys of engagement and marriage found that very many engaged girls would have intercourse with their future husbands before marriage but not with any other man. The liberated non-virgin enjoys her sex, as sex, and does not insist on an established relationship necessarily, while the confused non-virgin does not really know why she has intercourse, but vaguely thinks it will help her get or keep a boyfriend.

So far all the discussion and all the data have centred round 'normal' male-female relations, but some word ought to be said about other sexual preferences, especially about homosexuality. For a long time people worked on the assumption that homosexuality was such a significant deviation that it must have large and far-reaching correlates; viewing from a different, perhaps more sensible perspective, people are now not surprised to learn that it is rather difficult to establish any 'cause' of homosexual behaviour, although the old idea that all homosexuals are effeminate is still quite widespread. (Some of course are; it would be interesting to know how many effeminate men are not homosexuals.) The 'biographical' approach to homosexuality runs the risk of triviality; it is not impressive to be told that homosexual men can be identified by their attraction to their own sex or because they date girls less often. One study [34] traced child-guidance clinic records of men who were identified as homosexual by the army, and found they had had poor relations with other children long before they were identified or labelled as homosexual. The Freudian approach looks at relations with parents, or at whether one parent was absent, but no reliable effects have been found. Several studies [35] have reported that female homosexuals having psychiatric treatment have had poor relations with their parents compared with normal women, but a recent report found this was not specific to homosexuality, for women going to a psychiatrist for other problems reported exactly the same frequency of bad relations with parents. Early research has also largely disproved the notion that homosexuals have hormone disorders or feminine physiques, although one more recent study [36] did find some physical differences but too small to be of any use in identifying homosexuals.* However, there is the strong suggestion from studies of identical and non-identical twins that there is an inherited component in homosexuality. A recent Czech study found that homosexuals had considerably higher intelligence than the heterosexual men who came to the same clinic, and suggested that increased intelligence and homosexual tendencies both result from a hormone disorder; one would need to rule out some simpler explanations before accepting this.

Despite the change in the moral and legal climate, homosexuality is often dangerous for those who practise it, so they are often at pains to conceal their sexual preferences. Not all succeed in remaining 'covert' homosexuals — especially in the US Army where homosexuality is

*Why should we want to *identify* homosexuals? Often no doubt out of nosiness or malice, but also to avoid wasting time courting people who are not likely to be interested.

commonly grounds for a dishonourable discharge. Of those who suffer this fate, the great majority are informed on, through malice, or by someone who has been caught and names names, or by someone who gives names of partners after confessing his own behaviour to secure dishonourable discharge [37]. Less than 1 in 5 are actually caught in the act.

Once a couple have assessed each other's personality and have formed opinions about each other's sexual standards and behaviour, they are ready to begin courting in earnest. This is the time when many begin to look for clues about whether the other will be receptive to a deeper relationship. From now on, they will be constantly observing and evaluating each other, partly to check up on their initial impressions of personality and outlook, sexual status, and so forth, but also to pick up the other's reactions to them, to see what mood the other is in, and to try to guess what their current state of sexual willingness might be. They have to watch for things that change as well as for enduring personality traits. Some of the most important of these changes involve emotions — happiness, anger, sadness, and the like.

Judging emotional expressions has long been a favourite topic of psychological research, and a large number of experiments going back 100 years to Charles Darwin have shown that people can judge with moderate accuracy what other people's facial expressions and tones of voice mean. A lot depends, however, on the context; in a standard laboratory demonstration of this, people are shown a photograph of someone apparently in great agony, who is in fact winning a 100-metre race. All these experiments have looked at emotions like anger, happiness, sorrow, but is there a specifically sexual emotion? And if so does it have any visible and *specific* signs? Some physical changes, such as reddening or blushing have been suggested, that these also may occur when someone is angry or embarrassed, so they convey little information *out of context.* Many if not most animals have distinctive mating calls, but humans seem not to have, although one should be wary of dismissing the idea out of hand, bearing in mind that it has recently been suggested that there are distinctive human sexual odours (see Chapter 1 for more details). At present there is no positive evidence for a characteristic 'sexual emotion' in humans, so claims like those of Desmond Morris in his book *Intimate Behaviour* [38] that blushing and sweating are sure signs of sexual arousal, are, as Chapter 1 noted, very misleading.

When a couple meet and start getting to know each other, each has an idea, of course, of what they want from the relationship, but must also make some sort of assessment of what the other wants too. There is ample scope for misunderstandings for couples often go out on dates with potentially quite serious misunderstandings of each other's intentions. Where the sexes stick to their traditional roles in courtship — which they mostly still do — a more or less complementary situation exists in which the girl is trying to decide what the man's intentions are — honourable or dishonourable, short term or long term — while the man is trying to decide whether the girl is willing to fall in with his plans or not. As Lester Kirkendall's [15] interviews testify, the girl is often misled and exploited, and is led to believe the man is entering a long-term relationship, leading to marriage, or that he is in love. Sometimes, of course, women mislead and exploit men, but usually for money rather than sex.

A recent survey [39] has looked at what makes men or women unwilling to have intercourse and at whether each sex understands why the other is willing or not. The actual reasons men give for sexual restraint are fear of pregnancy and their inability to persuade the girl to agree, whereas girls refrain because they do not love the man, would feel guilty afterwards, or because it is against their principles. Significantly, in the light of the data on sexual gossip reviewed earlier in the chapter, they are not afraid of losing their good reputations, which perhaps they should be. Neither sex avoids relations because they are afraid of 'being caught'. There is a lot of misunderstanding between sexes. Women think men refrain for fear of pregnancy more than they do, but do not realise that men often refrain because no *mutual* decision is reached. Instead women see men as more sexually aggressive than they are, and think they refrain only because the girl will not let them. (This is often true, but not as often as the girls think.) Men, on the other hand, think women refrain because they are afraid of pregnancy and afraid of losing their reputation, rather than through shame or because they are not in love. Inasmuch as men often do 'spoil a girl's reputation' by boasting of their 'conquest' to other men, it makes sense that they attribute this fear to her.

When people of different cultures meet, misunderstandings are particularly likely to result. For example, men in Mediterranean cultures — where boy and girl are not generally allowed to get together unsupervised — are often confused or misled by girls from further north, sometimes regarding a girl travelling on her own as some sort of travelling prostitute. Many Greeks, Italians, Turkish, and Yugoslav men go to Switzerland and Germany, as 'guest workers', where they encounter girls who are neither 'good' — i.e. strictly virginal — nor prostitutes. Some of them have difficulty understanding this combination, and a few are so upset by it that they develop delusions of witchcraft. [40] A similar situation has arisen in parts of Israel or Israeli-occupied territory, where there is a large Arab population. Arab courtship customs are rather Mediterranean in character, with no sexual freedom for girls and strong emphasis of male virility, leading to a double standard and reliance on prostitution, whereas Israeli courtship and marriage customs are definitely Western in character. The Arabs observe the freedom enjoyed by Jewish youth and are envious, especially as their traditional outlet, via 'red-light quarters', is not available. An observer [41] remarks: 'Arabs feel that Jewish girls are sexually uninhibited and that they have sexual relations with Jewish boys as a matter of course. They believe that their own approaches, however, would be rejected by the same girls, because they are Arabs.' The Jewish boys are suspicious and hostile towards the Arabs, and are afraid they will 'steal their women'. They are also worried because they tend to 'impute extraordinary sexual prowess to Arabs'. The Arab boys solve their problems occasionally by pretending to be Oriental Jews, and courting Jewish girls, but mostly are drawn to foreign tourist girls, especially from Scandinavia. They watch these girls, discuss them, classify them as likely prospects or unlikely, and over-interpret what they see. 'They are . . . enormously pre-occupied with sex. . . . They eagerly interpret any clue from a girl as an invitation, often on rather flimsy grounds.'

Many readers will at this stage of the book be wondering if any mention will ever be made of 'love', or whether the authors are too cynical or coldly scientific to consider it; it is, indeed, important, and the time has come to say something about it. The most obvious thing about someone in love is that they idealize the loved person. The person in love is often blind to the faults of the loved one, even though these may be obvious to others and forcibly drawn by them to his or her attention. In extreme cases it is clear to everyone but the person in love that he or she is being cynically exploited for sex or material gain by the other person, but it still is hard to get the victim to realize that he or she is being used. Very often all that happens to him or her is systematically re-interpreted to fit the existing view of things – to accord in fact with his or her 'implicit personality theory' about the other person. When the realization does come, it may be very shattering, or it may not, for many love affairs die a gradual death through progressive mutual loss of interest.

The effect of love on perception may be dramatically distorting, but not always. Very often it simply prevents any accurate perceptions being made. The man or woman never learns anything about the other person at all, or at least leaves large gaps in his or her knowledge. In place of accurate perception, an idealized stereotype is attributed to the other; the loved one is seen as good, kind, considerate and, of course, beautiful, and his or her real qualities and behaviour remain a mystery. One may at this point question how the relationship can be maintained. Of course, it often does not always last. In adolescence, especially, episodes of romantic love are typically brief and numerous. (Perhaps more numerous than adults think. A survey [42] of American college students, aged between 19 and 24, found that men reported having experienced an average of 5 or 6 romantic episodes, and women an average of 7.) Because courtship is (still) largely governed by social customs, the people involved can often 'get by' if they merely follow the roles and react appropriately in the 'stereotyped' manner. They do not need to form very definite opinions about each other as individuals. For couples in Western society who are going to marry, something in the way of romantic feeling is certainly expected, by friends, parents, and relatives, and couples in love are frequently portrayed in the mass media, so everyone will have some idea what is appropriate behaviour. Perhaps many relationships involving romantic love can exist for at least a while, simply because both parties are successfully playing interlocking roles. No perception of each other is needed, merely perception of what is appropriate behaviour. Such play-acting cannot go on for ever, but the sorts of locations and activities customary in courtship perhaps delay the day when the couple really find out about each other.

(Of course, romantic love is more than just a distorting or obscuring influence on perception; it is very pleasant for the people involved and loyalty and affection are involved.)

The first comment one finds about love in any sociology book is that it is peculiar to our culture and our time. In other societies, and in former times in the West, people courted, seduced, and married each other without the benefit of romantic love. Many sociologists seem to think that this was a good thing and regard love as a typical piece of modern degeneration; their reasoning is similar to that in the preceding discussion. They hold that it was not a good idea for people to blind themselves to others' real characters, and a particularly bad idea is to marry someone while still in such a state. However, what matters are the reasons for this cultural difference rather than its consequences — why the phenomenon of love is found in Western society and rarely elsewhere, except as a form of Western cultural invasion. At one level this question has been partly answered already — romantic love is customary in Western society, so people fall in love because they are expected to. Certainly attempts to show that boys and girls in American society who fall in love readily are personally unstable or insecure have not been successful. Slight relationships have been reported; for example, men who fall in love with two girls at once, or girls who fall in love with boys younger than themselves show a very slight tendency to instability. Obviously the explanation must be primarily a cultural one, but why have this custom? An explanation in terms of social custom only puts the real explanation one stage back.

In many societies, such as India (or pre-revolutionary China), marriages are arranged by the parents and contact between the sexes before marriage severely curtailed so that young people have little chance of forming romantic attachments. In tribal societies and in small villages, the number of eligible partners is severely limited, whereas in Western urban society young people have much greater freedom and opportunities to meet potential mates. In other words, in most other societies people have their minds largely made up for them about marriage. The survey of why people choose marriage or bed partners, in Chapter 6, indicates that there was a large element of chance involved. The man or woman usually knows a fairly large number of likely mates, and his or her final choice will be arbitrary — not in the sense that he or she will make it without a lot of heart searching, but in the sense that the outside observer can point to several apparently quite similar people he or she might have chosen instead. This surfeit of available mates is most marked in places like universities and college, where there are great numbers of essentially similar people congregated together, and correspondingly less marked in small villages and rural areas.

There is a well-known psychological theory [43] about what happens when people have to choose between a number of equally attractive alternatives. When they have committed themselves by choosing A, rather than B, C, D, or E, they seek to justify their choice of A by emphasizing its virtues and to justify their rejection of the other possibilities by emphasizing their faults. This has been demonstrated in an ingenious study which showed that people who had recently bought a new car spent a lot of time reading advertisements for it, *after* they had bought it (and avoided reading advertisements for cars they might have bought instead). Perhaps the same sort of thing happens in courtship; when someone has made a partly arbitrary choice of a particular mate, the mate is idealized and his or her faults ignored, in order to justify the choice. In small communities, or where the choice is made by someone else for people, there is no need to distort the perception of the partner, because no desirable might-have-beens exist to cast doubt on their choice. There is some evidence for this suggestion in the finding that romantic love was less characteristic of people from small towns — even though, being American, they were exposed to the same norms. There is further evidence [44] in a report that leaving college sub-culture, with its attendant oversupply of possible mates, causes a decline in romanticism. Recently, an American anthropologist [45] has studied the — rather limited — numbers of non-Western societies where romantic attachments are made, and found that they mostly went in for unarranged marriages, on the Western pattern, and also that the couples moved away from home when they married. Because they had chosen each other they had to justify the choice by romantic idealization, and because they moved away from home and parents, romantic feelings were useful in strenthening the bond between them.

'Biologically' oriented psychologists can supply some alternative explanations, however. All schools of thought agree that a child's relationship with its parents is very important, and certainly the first and most intense relationship he or she forms. There is some evidence that children deprived of this relationship, by being in an orphanage or by being neglected, grow up to be 'affectionless'. Rhesus monkeys raised without a mother, or a mother substitute, show fear and hostility to other monkeys, do not mate normally, and, if they reproduce, do not look after their young [46]. Chapter 6 describes work on the similarities between parents and mates and discussed the idea that people often try to marry a substitute for their opposite sex parent. Perhaps people who fall in love are trying to recreate the intense bond between child and parent; just as they sought reassurance from mother they seek reassurance and support from their mate. Again, the finding that girls that did not love their fathers had ambivalent attitudes to their husbands or lovers, supports the theory.

Falling in love may be learned on an individual basis as distinct from being learned as part of our culture. More attractive girls had been in love more often than less attractive ones, perhaps because, being more attractive, they met more attractive men, and so found romance (and sex) more rewarding. It has also been shown [44] that girls with a stronger sex drive tend to form more frequent and intense attachments. The same reasoning applies; a more highly sexed girl will find relationships with men more satisfying — or at least will be more frustrated by not forming any — and so will find the experience more rewarding. (These findings may, with the benefit of hindsight, seem 'obvious' — consider, therefore, an alternative 'obvious' hypothesis, *inconsistent* with the results. 'Love' is a reaction against the earthiness of physical sex, and so is more likely to be characteristic of girls with low sex drive who prefer to idealize their mates and their relations with them.)

People who fall in love often claim they cannot help it — particularly when telling other people, not always for the first time, how unhappy it makes them. The more cynical observer often suspects an element of self-pity and of poor self-control, and this suspicion is strengthened by a recent survey, [47] that found a close link between romantic attachment to someone and frequency of thinking about that someone; the point of this apparently unsurprising finding is that people can control their thoughts to some extent. If you do not want to think about something or someone, you can avoid doing so, at least up to a point; conversely, if you want to make yourself love-sick and have been persuaded that it's the thing to do, it's easy to bring on the condition by brooding about the other person.

It would seem to follow from all that has been said in this chapter so far that there must be some men or women who are much better than others at summing up their fellows and in particular their sexual intentions and status. A similar thought often occurs to the man or woman in the street, especially when he or she has been made to feel silly after misperceiving someone's intentions. The image of a smooth, self-confident successful person, who understands others better than they understand themselves, tends to spring to mind. In one sense, of course, some part of this person must exist. Social or sexual encounters could not occur at all, unless those involved were capable of perceiving correctly a lot of things about each other. However, there are still grounds for supposing that the image of the super-perceptive person is partly a product of wishful thinking. For one thing most research [48] has failed signally to find any generality in ability to judge others; the man who can sum up someone's character neatly is not necessarily good at predicting what they are going to do next. The man who is good at perceiving personality is not necessarily good at perceiving attraction between people, and the man who is good at perceiving attraction is not necessarily any good at identifying others' emotional states.

What passes for a remarkable ability to see through or into others is often a mixture of self-confidence, and what is called technically 'stereotype accuracy'. This is the ability to guess what most people are likely to do rather than what a particular person will do. Someone who is reasonably well aware of what behaviour, outlook, etc., is typical in his or her group or social circle can easily impress someone who has not noticed such things. (In effect the discussion of 'inferences' of sexual status earlier in the chapter recommended a conscious use of stereotypes — accurate ones, of course.) It is relatively easy, armed with data from Kinsey or his successors, to say that someone does not indulge in bestiality, as less than 1% of men or women do; it is much harder, however, to say whether an American college girl is a virgin or not, since about half are and half are not. One would need more data — age, year in college, attractiveness, personality, the circles she moves in, degree of involvement, before making an informed guess.

It is also easy to fool many people with impressive sounding descriptions of personality and psychodynamics that are actually quite empty — such, after all, is the stock and trade of the fortune-teller or horoscope writer. Dubbed the 'Barnum effect', this involves essentially choosing a very general stereotype and wrapping it up in such a way that it sounds like a brilliant individual diagnosis. Thus it is surprising how many people can be impressed by being told they worry sometimes about their relationships with others or are not quite sure about their sex lives. Who but a full-blown psychopath does not worry about relations with others occasionally? The data on what actually goes with the ability to sum others up paints a rather different picture. For example, in one experiment men who were good judges of feminine character were 'tactful', 'tolerant', and 'timid', whereas girls who judged men well were 'submissive', 'reasonable', and 'accepting'. The men especially do not fit the picture of the smooth talker and great seducer, being rather something of a milksop. Another found that highly sexed men were rather poor at perceiving their fiancée's personality, perhaps because their judgement was distorted by their interest in sex.

REFERENCES

1. J. O. Balswick and J. A. Anderson (1969) Role definition in the unarranged date. *J. Marr. Fam.* **31**, 776–8.
2. E. D. Jackson and C. R. Potkay (1973) Pre-college influence on sexual experience of college co-eds. *J. Sex Res.* **9**, 143–9.
3. M. Cook (1971) *Interpersonal perception* Penguin, Harmondsworth.
4. W. H. Clements (1967) Marital interaction and marital stability: a point of view and a descriptive comparison of stable and unstable marriages. *J. Marr. Fam.* **28**, 697–702.
5. J. R. Udry (1963) Complementary in mate selection: a perceptual approach. *Marr. Fam. Liv.* **25**, 281–9.
6. R. Dymond (1954) Interpersonal perception and marital happiness. *Can. J. Psychol.* **8**, 164–71.
7. R. Tagiuri (1958) Social preference and its perception, in R. Tagiuri and L. Petrullo (eds.), *Person perception and interpersonal behaviour*, Stanford University Press.
8. I. Reiss (1967) *The social context of premarital sexual permissiveness*, Holt, Rinehart & Winston, New York.
9. G. R. Kaats and K. E. Davis (1970) The dynamics of sexual behavior of college students. *J. Marr. Fam.* **32**, 390–9.
10. H. T. Christensen and G. R. Carpenter (1962) Value-behaviour discrepancies regarding premarital coitus. *Am. Sociol. Rev.* **27**, 66–74.

11. A. C. Kinsey *et al.* (1948) *Sexual behaviour in the human male*, Saunders, Philadephia and A. C. Kinsey *et al.* (1952) *Sexual behaviour in the human female*, Saunders, Philadephia.
12. M. Schofield (1965) *The sexual behaviour of young people*. Longmans, London.
13. D. E. Carns (1973) Talking about sex: notes on first coitus and the double standard. *J. Marr. Fam.* **35**, 677–88.
14. C. S. Ford and F. A. Beach (1952) *Patterns of sexual behaviour*. Methuen, London.
15. L. A. Kirkendall (1961) *Premarital intercourse and interpersonal relations*, Julian Press, New York.
16. R. R. Bell and J. B. Chaskes (1970) Premarital sexual experience among coeds: 1958 and 1968. *J. Marr. Fam.* **32**, 81–4.
17. K. E. Bauman and R. R. Wilson (1974) Sexual behaviour of unmarried students in 1968 and 1972. *J. Sex. Res.* **10**, 327–33.
18. E. B. Luckey and G. D. Nass (1969) A comparison of sexual attitudes and behaviour in an international sample. *J. Marr. Fam.* **31**, 364–79.
19. A. M. Vener *et al.* (1972) The sexual behaviour of adolescents in Middle America: generational and American-British comparisons. *J. Marr. Fam.* **34**, 696–705.
20. H. Giese and G. Schmidt (1968) *Studenten-Sexualitat: Verhalten und Einstellung*, Rowohlt, Reinbek.
21. W. H. James (1971), The reliability of the reporting of coital frequency. *J. Sex Res.* **7**, 312–14.
22. E. J. Kanin (1960) Premarital sex adjustments, social class and associated behaviours. *Marr. Fam. Liv.* **22**, 258–62.
23. J. K. Kanter and M. Zelnik (1972) Sexual experience of young unmarried women in the United States. *Fam. Planning Pers.* **4**, 9–18.
24. A. H. Maslow (1942) Self-esteem (dominance feeling) and sexuality in women. *J. Soc. Psychol.* **16**, 259–64.
25. H. J. Eysenck (1974) Personality, premarital sexual permissiveness and assortative mating. *J. Sex Res.* **10**, 47–51.
26. B. W. P. Wells (1969) Personality characteristics of VD patients. *Br. J. soc. clin. Psychol.* **8**, 246–52.
27. D. L. Mosher and H. J. Cross (1971) Sex guilt and premarital sexual experiences of college students. *J. cons. clin. Psychol.* **36**, 27–32.
28. H. J. Eysenck (1971) Hysterical personality and sexual adjustment, attitudes and personality. *J. Sex Res.* **7**, 274–81.
29. I. Arafat and B. Yorburg (1973) Drug use and the sexual behaviour of college women. *J. Sex Res.* **9**, 21–9.
30. J. J. Teevan (1972) Reference groups and premarital sexual behaviour. *J. Marr. Fam.* **34**, 283–91, and A. M. Mirande (1968) Reference group theory and adolescent sexual behaviour. *J. Marr. Fam.* **30**, 572–7.
31. H. J. Eysenck (1971) Personality and sexual adjustment. *Br. J. Psychiat.***118**, 593–608; and W. Simon *et al.* (1972) Beyond anxiety and fantasy: the coital experiences of youth. *J. Youth Adol.* **1**, 203–22.
32. E. Berscheid and E. Walster (1974) Physical attractiveness. *Adv. exp. soc. Psychol.* **7**, 158–215.
33. J. F. D'Augelli and H. J. Cross (1975) Relationship of sex guilt and moral reasoning to premarital sex in college women and in couples. *J. consult. clin. psychol.*, **43**, 40–47.

34. M. Roff (1966) Some Childhood and adolescent characteristics of adult homosexuals, (unpublished report).
35. D. W. Swanson *et al.* (1972) Clinical features of the female homosexual patient. *J. nerve. ment. Dis.* **155**, 119—24.
36. R. B. Evans (1972) Physical and biochemical characteristics of homosexual men. *J. cons. clin. psychol.* **39**, 140—7.
37. C. J. Williams and M. S. Weinberg (1971) *Homosexuals in the military: a study of less than honourable discharge,* Harper & Row, New York.
38. D. Morris (1971) *Intimate behaviour,* Cape, London.
39. R. H. Driscoll and K. E. Davis (1971) Sexual restraint: a comparison of perceived and self-reported reasons for college students. *J. Sex Res.* **7**, 253—62.
40. M. Risso and W. Boker (1968) Delusions of witchcraft: a cross-cultural study. *Br. J. Psychiat.* **114**, 963—72.
41. E. Cohen (1971) Arab boys and tourist girls in a mixed Jewish—Arab community. *Int. J. comp. Sociol.* **12**, 217—33.
42. W. M. Kephart (1970) The 'dysfunctional' theory of romantic love: a research report. *J. comp. fa, Stud.* **1**, 26—36.
43. L. Festinger (1957) *A theory of cognitive dissonance,* Row, Petersen; Evanston, Ill.
44. A. Ellis (1949) A study of human love relationships. *J. genet. Psychol.* **75**, 61—71.
45. P. C. Rosenblatt (1972) Courtship patterns associated with freedom of choice of spouse. *J. Marr. Fam.* **34**, 689—95.
46. H. F. Harlow and M. K. Harlow (1969) Effects of various mother—infant relationships on rhesus monkeys' behaviour, in B. M. Foss (ed.), *Determinants of infant behaviour,* vol. 4, Methuen, London.
47. A. Tesser and D. L. Paulhus (1976) Toward a causal model of love. *J. pers. soc. Psychol.* **34**, 1095—1105.
48. U. Bronfenbrenner *et al.* (1968) The measurement of skill in social perception, in D. C. McClelland *et al.* (eds.), *Talent and society,* Van Nostrand, Princeton.

Chapter 5

THE THRILL OF THE CHASE

Previous chapters have considered situations in which people are observing others and making judgements about their sexual behaviour. The present chapter looks at how they behave towards each other during longer interaction sequences such as courtship and seduction. These are interesting because the initial judgements made can determine the future behaviour, e.g. whether to approach or not and also what type of approach is made. Moreover, the response to the first more typically determines what the second move is, and so on. Performing these sequences of moves in any encounter can be viewed as a skilled performance and the constituent parts can be identified. It is part of the practice of this skill to be able to recognize cues such as involuntary gestures of acceptance or repulsion. Examples of these are discussed along with their psychological basis. Also considered are ideas about natural male and female smells which are said to be emitted during courtship. Finally, there is discussion of what can go wrong in short-term or long-term relationships to make the whole process break down.

We have seen that similarity of personality, outlook, and background are all important in dating and mating relationships, as are physical appearance, and the realization that the other is attracted too. However, realization is one thing but it is quite another to act on it. Scope for action is limited because although nearly all human behaviour is governed by laws and by social customs, this is especially true of sexual behaviour.

It is also true of all societies although the different, more liberal rules of some societies may give the false impression of complete freedom. For example, in Western society a man who tries serious advances without first going through the preliminaries of kissing and embracing would be thought crude and aggressive, whereas the Crow Indians of North America have radically different customs. The man looks for a mate by crawling up to a tent at night, putting his hand inside and trying to find a woman, whose genitals he then stimulates; if successful he may persuade the woman to have intercourse.

A basic rule in courtship concerns who should take the initiative. In animals, initiative is fairly equally divided; sometimes the male of the species makes the first move, sometimes the female, often both, but in humans the initiative generally lies with the male, although there are a handful of exceptions to the rule. Maori women try to attract a man by pinching or scratching his hand surreptitiously. Among the Kwoma, in New Guinea, the men are afraid of offending the girl's family by unwanted attentions, so they leave it to the girl to take the initiative. A few South Sea Island societies make no distinction; the man or the girl can start courtship. In all other societies the man is expected to make the first move and usually to continue in the dominant role, whereas women are not supposed to give a direct invitation to men, although generally they are allowed to show an interest indirectly. Sometimes not even this is permitted; the Mondu in Africa consider the slightest sign of interest by a girl to be shameful. The custom of male initiative is probably part of the more general pattern of male dominance observed in nearly all societies [1]. It is worth noting that more than 20 years ago an American survey found that most college men would prefer the initiative to be shared, but women, on the hand, mostly would not.

Of course, an analysis of courtship involves more than the notation of certain rules like that concerning 'initiative'. Psychologists have preferred recently to place the notion of rules inside a description which terms courtship as a skill or a game. To 'get off with' someone depends on following a complicated sequence of moves, presenting oneself favourably, reassuring the other, and adapting the performance to their reaction. Courtship is very like a game of snakes and ladders (or chess if one prefers to play down the role of luck and regard it more intellectually). As Kingsley Amis [2] puts it:

'Even before she spoke I could see that, after mounting a series of short but cumulatively valuable ladders, I had just gone sliding down a major snake.'

For some people a better analogy might be to liken courtship to a minefield.

Whether courting with a view to marriage, or merely intent on seduction, it is reckoned by psychologists that the same principles apply, principles which furthermore apply to many other social encounters, and in a slightly simpler form to 'skilled' performances like driving a car, playing tennis, or operating machinery. For one thing all these have goals or purposes; goals in sexual relationships can vary. In a short-term relationship the couple are seeking companionship, social activity, and, of course, what Kinsey called a 'sexual outlet'. In animals the strength of the sex drive is closely related to hormone levels, so that these can be used to measure it; indeed, in some monkeys hormone changes produce clearly visible changes in the animals' genitals. This is not true of humans, where no substantial or consistent relation between hormone levels and sex drive has been discovered. At one time it was thought that sex might work like hunger, building up during deprivation, so that the longer one went without the stronger the drive became. In fact, length of deprivation is only slightly related to strength of drive, measured either by how much sexual tension people report or by how easily aroused they are. Interest in sex, and strength of sex drive, depends in fact largely on previous experience in that the more (pleasant) experience the person has had, including fantasy, the more easily aroused he or she is. A simple questionnaire measure of how much sexual experience people have had has been devised: Larsen's 'Appetitional Index' which includes items of this type — 'I find a variety of different partners makes sex more interesting' — and it has been demonstrated that scores on this questionnaire give a better indication of how easily aroused people are than length of the time they have been without sex [3].

Some men and women doubtless do seek a succession of joyless mechanical seductions because they are uncertain of their own sexuality — and hence motivated by anxiety rather than sex — but surely more men seduce women, and vice versa, because they enjoy sexual intercourse. It is very easy to over-extend psychodynamic explanations about why people 'really' do things. On the other hand, it is likely that quite a few men and women have goals other than sex in mind when they seek each other out. A minority of both sexes do not enjoy sexual intercourse, but need things most conveniently supplied by or through it – like close physical contact or affection.

The goals of longer-term relationships are somewhat vaguer, for in a sense the relationship itself is the goal and the couple simply wish to stay together for the sake of being together rather than for external things they can get out of each other. However, there is more to courtship than this. Firstly, of course, the long-term couple enjoy the benefits of the short-term couple, companionship, going to social occasions, sexual satisfaction, reassurance, material support, etc. In any case, saying that their goal is maintaining the relationship is not quite as vague and circular as it sounds, since 'maintaining the relationship' in Western society involves a series of quite definite sub-goals. Having achieved a first date and then further dates, the next aim of the man or woman (or both) is to exclude rivals by reaching an agreement that they are 'going steady', while also arranging different, more intimate sorts of meetings. Subsequently the two major sub-goals enter into most relationships – engagement and marriage, which many couples see almost as goals in themselves, not just as the formal recognition that the relationship exists and is developing. For some couples an important sub-goal is living together. In America 'pinning' can be a sub-goal to be reached before engagement; this has a parallel in Britain in semi-formal agreements to become engaged on a particular date – being 'engaged to be engaged'.

Behaviour towards an attractive person can be seen as a sequence of self-presentation tactics governed by many unwritten but firm rules, just as to appear to be attracted requires another set of rule-governed behaviours concerning how much to look at the other person, how close to sit, etc. The total performance of which such examples are part may be described as *socially skilled*. There is a psychological model for describing such behaviour and it is set out below. The model shows a sequence of events which are numbered 1 to 5, seen from one person's point of view [4]. The person has a goal (1), e.g. to ask the other person for a date, but in order to achieve this he or she first of all 'translates' this (2) into some form of behaviour (3). As a preliminary to asking for a date a man engages in a friendly chat to 'soften up' the girl.

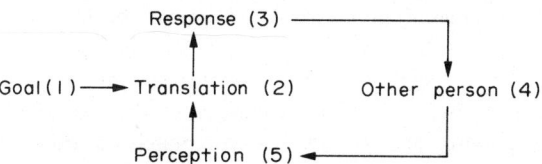

According to how the girl behaves (4) he decides what to do next (2), again) by looking for certain reactions in the other (5). Of all the parts of this sequence, *perception* (5), i.e. 'knowing what to look for in the other's behaviour', and translation (2), 'knowing what to do when you see it', are the most important.

The goal or purpose of a first encounter is usually quite clear — to ask for a date or to engage in some sexual activity. In order to achieve these goals both people have to achieve a series of sub-goals as well, such as making the other laugh, taking his or her hand without causing alarm, etc., goals which are rarely made explicit. Indeed, one or other partner may take great pains to hide his or her intentions from the other, trying to appear very casual towards the other just before negotiating a further meeting. Similarly, an invitation back to the other's room for coffee frequently means music, low lights, and sexual advances, but however plain it is that the second factor follows from the first, both men and women are reluctant to state their intentions fully.

'Translation' is the least obvious part of the model; it means that the person selects a tactic that will have the result he or she wants, the problem being that the same tactic will not be effective on every occasion. To take an obvious example from a non-sexual context, when driving a car turning the steering wheel to the left makes the car turn to the left, whereas turning it to the right makes it turn right. Similarly, in courtship different methods are needed for different people, so that a man courting a worldly, experienced woman will use different tactics from a man courting a nervous, inexperienced girl, and a woman trying to attract a man will act in one way at a party, but in another way at work. One observer has declared herself 'willing to generalize that with the male propositioner the directness of the proposition is positively correlated with his perception of the chances of acceptance' [5].

In social exchange theory terms, set against the higher 'rewards' to be gained from a more desirable partner, is the greater likelihood of rejection, which is 'costly', at least to most people [6]. It follows that people will learn, by their own experience, or by watching others, or by advice from parents and friends, approximately whether they stand in what has been called the 'secret ranking', [7] a concept included in exchange theory, too, but called more prosaically 'comparison level'. When a man or woman weigh up a possible date, they also take into consideration or 'comparison' what else is available; for the attractive girl, or the handsome wealthy man, accepting one invitation means rejecting a lot of others, and starting a particular relationship implies passing up several other opportunities, whereas an unattractive man or woman has to adopt different standards in deciding to accept or not. However, courtship is not quite as cut and dried, or depressing, as the comparison of balance sheets, and there is scope for what one might term enterprise and initiative, or even ambition. Someone with a high opinion of him or herself — a high 'level of aspiration' — will aim higher, and unless he or she aims unrealistically high have some chance of success.

Quite a lot of people — mainly men, given the rule of male initiative — are reluctant to make any approach to the other sex because they are afraid of being rejected. (Women suffer from the male initiative rule in a different way, when either the man they would like to go out with does not ask them, or if they are unlucky, no one asks them.) Male fears can be measured by personality tests, and it has been shown that men who do not date often get high scores on tests of 'social avoidance and distress' and 'fear of negative evaluation'. Alternatively, these fears can be tested directly by asking the man to ring up a girl for a date or talk to a girl for a few minutes; shy men often dry up or cannot get started at all, as well as having a higher pulse rate during the test. Over the last few years university student counsellors in the United States have started trying to help men who are worried by shyness or inability to get on with girls.

Their approach is based largely on behaviour therapy, which is very specific treatment intended to reduce anxiety, or to teach men the right thing to do. There are all sorts of techniques available — 'role-playing' or practice in talking to girls, feedback from impartial observers or from other anxious men, feedback by watching films of how they are doing and how they look to other people, as well as watching films of people doing it properly. One line of behaviour therapy concentrates on reducing anxiety by arranging meetings for shy men with girls who are part of the therapist's team; the particular point of this approach is that the men were assured the girls would not reject them, so the meetings went off fairly well, and the self-confidence this gave the men carried over into relations with girls who were not part of the experiment. The other main approach is to build up the man's social repertoire, so he knows how to approach girls and how to avoid putting them off. This type of treatment generally uses practice and filmed feedback, or sympathetic comment by the therapists and his assistants pointing out what the man is doing wrong — talking about himself too much perhaps — and suggesting what he might do instead — such as asking the girl about herself for a change. Programmes of this sort have produced measurable and significant improvements in shy males' performance, leading them to be less hesitant, less anxious, helping them create a generally better impression with girls and with their friends generally, and in one study producing such a specific change as an increase in the time they looked the girl in the eye while trying to make friends.

In fact an ideal programme of help for shy men should combine the two approaches, as one of behaviour therapy's failures has shown. A technique that works very well in curing anxiety caused by dogs or spiders or the like, failed to help men who were anxious about approaching the opposite sex. Watching films of people getting more and more friendly with dogs, or closer to a series of ever larger and hairier spiders, reduced fear — a convenient fact for the therapist who does not want his office cluttered up by real dogs or live spiders; watching films of men asking for dates with girls, and being accepted, did not reduce shy males' problems at all. The difference probably lies in the fact that people know how to stroke dogs or move closer to spiders once they have overcome their anxiety, but the shy man does not know how to go up to a girl and ask her for a date, and that, as well as anxiety, is his problem [8].

Most investigations of behaviour therapy* include groups of men who get more traditional treatments, usually with rather sobering results. The traditional treatment is the 'talking cure', in the shape of counselling or

*More studies of this type have been reviewed by Curran [9].

psychotherapy, where the therapist discusses the man's anxieties and tries to get him to see things differently, put his fears in perspective, and so on. Men who get this treatment do not benefit much from it; it seems that a very specific approach is needed rather than the broad attack of psychotherapy. One could liken the effect of psychotherapy to trying to improve someone's golf or tennis by giving him a lecture on the sport, when what he needs is practice coupled with expert advice. Of course, a shy male who found his way to a psychoanalytic counsellor or therapist probably would not even get a general lecture but would be likely to be told his fear of girls was symbolic and symptomatic, and was 'really' a fear of castration or the effect of repressed homosexuality, and hence part of a wider, deeper problem.

Following a change of outlook among some psychologists and psychiatrists, a similar type of help has been made available to homosexual students whose problem is plucking up the courage to 'come out', i.e. be overtly homosexual [10]. Twenty-seven students went through a graded series of homosexual assertion tests, starting with carrying a folder bearing the label 'homosexuals demand equality' and progressing through canvassing signatures for a gay liberation poster and finishing with visiting a police station to complain about having been refused service in a restaurant because of homosexuality. The procedure made the people more self-confident but did not affect their behaviour significantly.

The 'perception' box in the model really contains two parts. The 'first impression' helps the person decide what to do initially — how to select their first response. Thus a man might weigh up the evidence and reach the conclusion that he is dealing with a promiscuous girl and so decide that a fairly direct approach is the best. However, 'first impressions' are notoriously unreliable, and are often modified in the light of further experience. The effects of a first move, e.g. putting a hand on the girl's knee, show whether the first impression was right or not. If the girl moves away, the man knows he has misjudged her and that she was not as ready as she seemed. This perception of the results of one's moves towards a person or object is called 'feedback' because the information is 'fed back' from the other person or object, and in courtship feedback, or 'knowledge of results' as it is also called, is vitally important, for first impressions almost always need revising in the light of what happens.

Looking at courtship in this way raises the problem that people are not aware of going through the moves of assessing the other, and then choosing a tactic from a repertoire according to a goal. This is not an important objection because most people are able easily to verbalize what they think of somebody and why they say or do something when another person behaves in a certain way. They rarely think like this during an ongoing encounter because they are concentrating harder on other aspects. The 'social skill' model is merely the minimum necessary model to explain how courtship could proceed, a model that accounts for other familiar activities, like driving a car, typing, playing tennis and other games, or operating machinery where the same sequence of perceiving, selecting a response, making a response, and observing the effects of the response occur.

The last box in the diagram contains, so to speak, the other person, obviously a vital link in the chain. One may object that he or she is being considered as a passive object, but this is not really correct, for the other person is also perceiving, selecting a response according to his or her goal or purpose, making the response. This complicates the model a little, but does not mean that it is unsatisfactory. The other person is aware of what the first is doing and will try to guess *why* he or she is doing it. One consequence of this may be that both are often prevented from following the most obvious course of action, precisely because it is too obvious to the other person. In courtship people often have to try to predict the other person's reaction to the next move and make allowance for it, which can obviously lead to great complications of bluff, double-bluff, or an infinite regress of the 'he thinks I think he thinks I think . . . ' type.

Because people do not make their responses without thinking what the other person will do, couples are often considering a pair of responses when selecting their own response; and thinking about the other person's behaviour may often lead people to act differently. For example, if the man anticipates that the woman will reject his advances, he will tend not to make any because he finds it unpleasant or worrying to be rejected, whereas if we expect his advances to be welcomed he will make them readily. If both parties are afraid of rejection by the other, they will never make a move and the relationship will never get started. It has been suggested that the balance between anticipated rewards and costs will sometimes lead to a hostile encounter, not the starting of a courtship. Being friendly is always a risk because the other person might reject one, whereas being unfriendly and rejecting the other person is not risky, because even if it is less rewarding it is more certain. There will be the slight but certain satisfaction of spurning someone which is preferable to the larger but less certain reward of being friendly and being accepted. (This presupposes, of course, that there is some slight satisfaction derived from rejecting someone, a cynical assumption which is unfortunately sometimes true.)

The skill model emphasizes the motion of sequence and strategy in courtship — just as the snakes and ladders or chess analogies do. These sequences and strategies naturally differ, at least superficially, from culture to culture and from sub-culture to sub-culture.

One of Lester Kirkendall's informants described his method, highly developed over a long series of conquests [11]. He started by locating a partner and creating a good first impression; working in a women's clothes shop took care of the first problem, and possessing a good wardrobe of smart clothes solved the second. On the first date he impresses the girl by his car, his experience of motor racing, and by showing how many friends he has by greeting them at dance or party. At this stage he aims to relax the girl and ensure that she is enjoying his company and his 'smooth, good manners' while forming a private assessment of her willingness for intercourse by asking the girl for favours and by listening for any flattery from her. Generally by the second date he has succeeded in getting the girl in the right frame of mind to steer the conversation to more intimate topics and subsequently to make advances, starting with kissing, not just on the mouth but on the throat, neck, or ears. Her reaction practically always tells him whether he can proceed to intercourse, but often he encounters token resistance that soon caves in.

Kirkendall's information takes from what psychologists rather disparagingly call 'anecdotal' form. We do now have a direct test of what distinguishes a successful man from an unsuccessful one [12]. A dozen or so successful men who had a lot of dates and a dozen or so unsuccessful men who got a lot fewer dates than they would like each did three tests: talking to an attractive girl for 10 minutes with a view to getting to know her well enough to ask for a date, making a phone call to the same girl some time later, as one might do after meeting someone at a party, and, finally, undergoing the 'taped situation test', essentially a test of having a ready answer. The men were told to imagine themselves at a party and that they had asked a girl for a dance, at which point they heard a tape of a girl saying 'I'm not really much of a dancer', and had to take it from there. The experimenter's idea of a good answer was 'Nor am I, let's go outside', whereas a poor answer might be 'Oh er' — accepting the rebuff. The two groups of men also did some personality tests of self-confidence and anxiousness, and gave the names of two male and two female friends who would be prepared to rate the man's dating frequency, ways with women, and 'social skill'. This battery of tests turned up some interesting results, and in particular showed that fluency — saying the right thing and saying it quickly — was what counted most. The successful men were much quicker to reply in the 'taped situations test' and came out with much longer answers, while in the live conversation they rarely paused compared with the tongue-tied unsuccessful men. Ratings of social skill by the girls in the test situations and by the male and female friends also largely depended on speed and fluency. Smiling often, looking at the girl more, agreeing with her, and nodding a lot did not reliably distinguish the successful and unsuccessful men. Results like this, which need, of course, to be repeated with a larger number of more varied men, are very valuable to people planning programmes of therapy, guidance, social skill training, and the like.

Other cultures have their own, quite different ways of paying court. When a Hottentot man decides which girl to court — she must, however, be a cross-cousin of his — he asks her parents for her hand and is traditionally refused it. He thereupon watches her hut and learns where she sleeps, then slips in one night and lies down beside her, at which point she gets up and moves. He returns the next night and keeps returning until she either decides against him by not being there when he arrives, or decides to marry him, in which case she stays there all night and the marriage is consummated. By contrast, animal courtship methods are generally quite direct — the frog, for example, mounts any object of the appropriate size and only lets go if it struggles. Humans have the capacity to be equally direct by word as well as by deed, but direct invitation is rare and usually prohibited with a few exceptions. Balinese and Lepcha men can simply ask a girl to have intercourse by pronouncing the name of the sex organs. Siriono men can ask directly but must whisper. On Bali, the women can also ask the men to have intercourse, and Lepcha women, while they are not supposed to, often do the same. In a very few societies women can invite intercourse by exposing their genitals to the man, but this is usually strictly forbidden [1]. It is far commoner for most invitations to courtship or seduction to be vague or symbolic, and often not made verbally at all; an exchange of glances, a smile, the choice of who to sit next to or how close to sit, constitute an unspoken invitation to go further. A special type of indirect invitation is found in some societies — 'love magic' [13]. The man tells the girl he is interested in her by casting a spell on her, the point being that he does it *in her presence, or to her knowledge,* using methods that seem rather odd by Western standards — blowing ashes in the girl's face, splitting a special substance on her, flashing a mirror at her. The significant point is the girl knows what the man means, but does not have to admit it if she is not interested.

It seems odd that humans, having the gift of language to express their thoughts and intentions, should use the same sorts of signals as animals — signals which are vague, liable to be misunderstood, hard to describe. In fact this very feature of vagueness is a great advantage in courtship, for direct verbal invitations require direct replies which either commit the speaker, or offend the one who asked. Invitations given in a vague way, by 'non-verbal communication' or in indirect or symbolic ways, are not binding on either party and can be withdrawn or refused without causing a direct affront. Thus one common approach in the West is for the man to invite the woman to a particular film, not primarily because he wants to see that film, nor even because he supposes she particularly wants to, but because this is a standard and socially approved way of striking up a relationship.

Naturally those conventions can only work if certain other rules are observed as well. When a man is refused a date to see a certain film he should not really press the point too far, by suggesting alternative days or films for fear of making the rejection personal, although some persistence is often expected, depending on the circumstances. One of the rules of the game is to take a symbolic or indirect rejection as final. Another and much stronger rule forbids one to comment on non-verbal behaviour in particular, nor on the interaction in general. A piece of behaviour, a smile, or moving away, may often be just about as clear as the spoken word, but the rules forbid one to mention it. It is not done to say, 'But you smiled at me when we met, which meant you were interested' or 'Why have you moved away, don't you like me?' This rule exists to safeguard the essential features of non-verbal interchanges — their vagueness, lack of commitment, the fact that they cannot be 'taken down and used in evidence'. Perhaps one reason for subdued lighting at parties, dances, and the like is to allow a rejected man or woman to 'escape' without everyone being able to see clearly that he or she has been reject. Actually a recent study [14] shows just what a large effect being in the dark makes on people's behaviour. Groups of eight students, four men and four women, were left in a totally dark room for an hour with rather dramatic effects. Groups of strangers — or pairs of strangers for that matter — would not be expected to hold hands, kiss, and cuddle on a first meeting if they were in a lighted room, but most of the men and women in the dark room did just that. The authors of the study argue that physical contact is 'natural' behaviour, i.e. allowed to appear when the social conventions are removed by darkness and anonymity; this is perhaps going too far, especially since we have learned to be suspicious of theories about 'natural' or 'instinctive' behavour, but the results are striking even so.

The 'non-commitment' principle holds particularly true for 'deviant' sexual groups, like homosexuals or wife-swappers, where elaborate sequences of signals are exchanged to avoid any naive people getting involved by mistake. For example, couples seeking wife-swapping or group sex experiences start by advertising in special papers using a special jargon — 'Attractive refined professional marrieds would like to hear from similar liberal minded marrieds' — or by going to a special bar or club. An advertisement is followed up by a phone call or letter, enclosing a photograph which, often being nude, must tend to make sexual intentions clearer. Next comes a first 'date' between the two couples, when no sexual contact is made but the couples sum each other up and refer to sexual activities by a 'secret' code in which 'TV' means transvestism, or 'Roman culture' means holding orgies. Only after these preliminaries might the couples arrange an actual sexual encounter [15].

The use of sequences of neutral or insignificant signals to establish contact, while avoiding involving the innocent, reaches its most elaborate form in public contacts between male homosexuals and also reaches its most compressed form, for the whole sequence from sighting to sexual contact may take only minutes. One sequence, in London 20 years ago, started by asking for a light and giving a smile, continued by remarks about marriage and why the man was out at that time of night, and the offer of a drink, and ended its first stage by noting the pub lacked a friendly atmosphere and naming one that did not — a known homosexual pub of course — and noting that 'some pretty queer' people went there [16]. Obviously the details change with different times and places — partly because the meaning of words like 'queer' or 'gay' becomes public sooner or later. A more recent American account has looked at homosexual liaisons in public lavatories or 'rest rooms', where the whole sequence of events is even more compressed [17]. Again, the first essential is to know where to go, for only a minority of lavatories are used by homosexuals (and it is worth noting that they are only used by a particular type of homosexual man, many of whom are married but do not enjoy satisfying sex lives at home). Once in the lavatory the man has to make it clear he is interested in sex — not urination — and whether he wants to be at the giving or receiving end of fellatio. Interest is expressed partly by gaze, partly by standing well back from the urinal, but most unequivocally by displaying an erect penis,* while role in fellatio depends on whether the man stands at the urinal, or sits in one of the (generally doorless) cubicles. No words are exchanged before during, or after. Even this highly compressed and unusual type of sexual encounter shows the basic features — a reliance on custom, the use of symbolic acts, looks and gestures, rather than words, and sequence of events that allows one to back out at any stage without explanation or apology right up to the late minute.

A considerable amount of research and observation on non-verbal communication or 'silent language' in courtship has been reported. For example, men who are about to start courting show a characteristic pattern of 'courtship readiness', involving increase in muscle tone, a general stiffening of the muscles which results in a more upright position,

---

*The 'exception that proves the rule' that genital displays do not feature in human courtship.

pulling back the shoulders and pulling in the stomach, possibly extending to the face, smoothing out double chins and bags under the eyes [18]. These resemble rather the characteristic changes in animals when confronted by another animal or a predator — the 'fight or flight' reaction, which is a generalized readiness for action. While exposure of the genitals is definitely not permitted behaviour in most societies, including the West, some people have suggested that symbolic versions of such exposure are widely used. Certainly, nearly all women go to great trouble to present their sexual characteristics to their best advantage, using make-up and carefully choosing clothes to make the most of their figures, adopting postures when sitting or standing that show off their figures. Convention still limits the male's self-presentation; make-up is largely taboo and dyed hair considered eccentric. So, too, is exposing large areas of skin; off the shoulder fashions have never been the thing for men, perhaps because male flesh's tendency to hairiness makes it less attractive. The male, now and in the past, seems to aim at an attractive appearance by slimness and tight-fitting clothes.

Desmond Morris [19] has suggested that some men and women get round the prohibition on nudity by wearing such tight trousers that the genitals are clearly outlined; certainly some men and women do wear clothes that have this effect but may not mean it to. Some women go further and sit or stand in ways that emphasize their breasts or which expose their thighs to a greater or lesser extent, but this behaviour is not all that common and it is not certain that women who behave like this are really courting. For one thing, these diaplays tend to broadcast rather than give to a particular person, and, even when they are given to one man, are often not followed through, making the behaviour flirting rather than a genuine invitation. Posture can show how a women feels towards a man in a less blatant but more reliable way, for it has been shown that women sitting talking to men they like adopt a more 'open' posture, with arms and legs not crossed [20]. Other research has shown that standing with arms uncrossed was seen as more friendly than standing with arms crossed, but this only works for women, however, for 'open' postures have no special significance in men [21].

There are certain characteristic gestures made by men when they see a pretty girl, which vary from culture to culture. Arabs stroke their beards, and Italians pull their earlobes, while the English, perhaps characteristically, look away over-casually. The sight of the girl and the intention to court her are also often announced by preening — unnecessary adjustments to tie, hair, or socks. Women can also betray their interest in men in similar ways — smoothing hair, straightening seams, occasionally by blushing. These cues can be very noticeable and often give people away, so to this extent they are an effective form of communication but they are not deliberate, and in fact often people would prefer not to communicate by them. It has been suggested that non-verbal behaviour of this type is a form of 'leakage', an involuntary betrayal of what the person really thinks or feels but does not want to show [22]. When a person tries to suppress something, to disguise his or her feelings, or to lie, the pattern of behaviour associated with the true feeling tends to slip out in fragmentary form, particularly through those forms of non-verbal behaviour that are least subject to voluntary control, and in those parts of the body least subject to voluntary control. Thus people betray their true feelings by gesture rather than facial expression, by hesitation rather than in words, and in the extremities of the body (such as the feet rather than in the face). Some time ago Freud made a similar point that repressed wishes will manifest themselves in surreptitious ways, such as slips of the tongue. It has been claimed that presenting the palm outwards or stroking the wrist can be a very reliable sign of readiness to court, when performed by American women. Again, this is an example of 'leakage' without awareness.

So far reference has been made to communication of sexual interest by more or less involuntary non-verbal behaviour. However, while posture and gestures may give people away, other forms of non-verbal behaviour are used more deliberately to express interest. In the opening stages of courtship, angle and distance between man and woman are among the most important of these. Courting couples generally sit side by side in bars and restaurants, and it has been noted that sitting next to someone can by itself produce feelings of intimacy, strong enough to make some patients in therapy groups anxious. Some interesting observations have been made on the significance of the postures people adopt when sitting side by side. Usually the couple will turn inwards towards each other, thereby closing off other people present, but sometimes this closing off is not complete so that one person will be oriented towards the other from the waist up, while the lower half of his or her body is oriented towards a third person, possibly showing that the person is not wholeheartedly committed to the person he or she is apparently courting [18].

Gaze is one of the most important cues, especially in the very early stages before any words are spoken, for a glance can convey interest, and the holding of a gaze is even more significant. Normally two strangers who have not spoken, and who do not want to, will avoid or cut off any accidental 'eye-contact', and 'eye contacts' — meeting the other's eye — are very short, averaging from 1 to 2 seconds even between friends conversing [23]. Gaze met or held can signal sexual interest, as can gaze held for a moment and then broken; gaze which breaks off, to wander down the other's body, is a more frankly sexual invitation. In a larger group of three or more people talking, gaze can be used in subtler ways to indicate the direction of a peron's interest. In such a group it is usual to look at the speaker, so gaze directed at someone else for any length of time acquires some significance.

So far looking at someone has been considered as a deliberate signal, which it often is, but not looking at someone is often an unintended signal meaning the same thing. Many suitors, especially inexperienced ones, find it too embarrassing to look at the girl they are interested in, which can be revealing to their friends if not to the girl herself. Experiments [24] filming the eye movement of people looking at photographs which include a nude woman have shown that some people have a remarkable ability to look everywhere on the photography but never at the nude woman, raising the interesting question how they know the nude is there at all. In fact, once something has been perceived peripherally, in the corner of the eye, it is easy to continue 'not to see it'.

Recent psychological explanations of the fascination of the eyes have emphasized the important of 'eye-spot' and 'eye-ring' patterns. It has been demonstrated that two horizontally placed circles (eye patterns) will excite animals and humans much more than two circles placed in any other configuration (such as vertically, like traffic lights, or diagonally). In animals, like mice and dogs, this seems to be an instinctive response to the eye patterns, for the young of the species reacted to the 'eyes' even though they had been reared in isolation since birth. It may also be that human infants have a similar predisposition to notice the eyes rather than any other facial feature. In further studies it has been shown that if the horizontally placed circles are ringed by one or two outer circles then this configuration produced a proportionately greater response, especially in men. Of course, in a sense these facts have been known for some time. It was customary for women in Egyptian, Greek, and Roman times to enhance their eyes in just the way an 'eye ring' does. Greek women used antimony ore, burnt and pulverized, to paint under their eyes, and to darken the brows and eyelashes, and most cosmetic techniques today still involve emphasizing the eyes or creating eye-rings [23].

Another investigator [25] has made two interesting further discoveries about the eye. The first is that the pupils of a person's eyes expand when they see an erotic or attractive stimulus. In general, men's pupils expand when they are looking at pictures of an attractive woman but not when looking at pictures of men or babies. Women's pupils, on the other hand, dilate to pictures of good-looking men and to pictures of babies, but not to pictures of women. To the careful observer this could be a valuable clue provided he or she bore in mind that pupil dilation signifies interest in general, rather than sexual interest in particular. The same investigator went on to show a series of pictures to a group of 20 men; the series included two photographs of an attractive young woman, identical except that one had been retouched to make the pupils look larger, while the other had been similarly treated to make them look smaller. The average response to the picture with the large pupils (measured by noting the change in size of the man's pupils as he looked at the photograph) was more than twice as great as the response to the picture with small pupils, yet few of the men taking part in the study noticed that the photos were not identical, so it seems that they may have been attracted to the large pupils without knowing the reason. The experiment has been repeated with women reacting to large and small pupils on a photograph of a man, and the same results were obtained. The appeal of large pupils, for a person of the opposite sex, probably lies in the fact, demonstrated in the first series of experiments, that enlarged pupils imply an extraordinary interest in whatever the individual is looking at, an interest which could be sexual.

The significance of pupil dilation has also been known at least to a few people for a long time. Chinese jade merchants were said to gauge a customer's interest in different pieces by his pupil dilation. In the

Middle Ages women enlarged their pupils with the drug *belladonna* (which means in Italian 'beautiful woman') in the belief — now scientifically verified — it would make them more attractive. Pupil dilation effects may have something to do with preferences for different eye-colours curiously enough. It is known that the pupil dilates — and contracts — more readily in blue-eyed people than in brown-eyed people; furthermore, changes in pupil size can be seen much more easily in a blue-eyed person. In other words a man or woman with blue eyes gives stronger and easily seen pupil responses to someone he or she likes than a brown-eyed person.

The decisive moment in courtship is, of course, the first physical contact, which in Western society definitely turns the relationship from social to sexual. Indeed, it is this transition that many men find very difficult. There are various non-committing ways of doing it, helping across the road, up the stairs, or the like, being one, but the best is dancing, which allows couples to touch and to keep touching if they want, or to break off if they do not take to each other. Dancing plays a big role in courtship in many societies, but generally, according to one anthropological survey, only in societies where young people are free to choose their own mates, whereas societies that rely on arranged marriage do not encourage the sexes to mix and especially not to touch each other.

Lester Kirkendall's interviews with 200 American college men yielded some interesting insights into how they try to seduce girls. Some rely on verbal arguments, persuading the girl she really has no grounds for refusing, telling her that 'all the college girls are doing it', or accusing her of letting her parents think for her. Others claim to be in love or say that intercourse 'will strengthen the relationship' or plead special cases, like impending call up, and many, of course, try to allay the girl's fear of pregnancy or exposure. Some try to set the right mood by referring to sex in a general or indirect way, while others report that girls they had met did the same, and took it as cue to willingness. The most experienced and successful seducer in Kirkendall's sample favoured this method, commenting on love scenes in films, or drawing attention to the activities of other couples; perhaps he was working on the Kingsley Amis principle 'that every minute a girl is allowed to spend in official ignorance of a man's intentions means two minutes extra build-up when the time comes'.

A rather elaborate experiment has recently been reported to see if men use sexual humour to convey sexual interest to girls [26]. It found that a man who was sexually aroused by talking to an attractive and flirtatious girl rated dirty jokes higher and was more likely to tell her his ratings than if the girl he talked to were sober and formal. It does not follow, of course, that the girl would be impressed by this tactic in this experiment or a real life meeting. Other men use a radically different approach, summed up by one who said: 'If you begin by talking you'll talk yourself right out of it. I never talk . . . I just work slowly, but always go a little further each time.' Often couples had intercourse regularly without ever referring to the fact before or after. In Kirkendall's sample the 'gropers' outnumbered the 'talkers' 3 to 1, but Kirkendall's survey includes no data on their relative success.

Yet another group of men prefer even more direct tactics, documented by 10 years' research on 'sex aggression', [27] which showed that 1 in 4 American college men had tried to get their way by force, while 2 in 3 of women had experienced assaults, ranging from unwelcome attempts to neck or kiss to violent rape. Men become aggressive not for the most part because they are disturbed or abnormal, but because they moved in circles where sexual conquests were expected, many being fraternity men, sometimes because they thought the girl 'deserved' it because she had shown herself to be a 'teaser' or a 'gold digger', sometimes because they misunderstood a girl from a different social class. The same men also tried to get girls drunk, or professed love falsely, or threatened to ditch the girl unless she obliged. In most cases the couple had already reached some stage of sexual intimacy, mostly 'deep petting', but in a quarter of cases no physical contact had been made, so the attack came 'out of the blue', indicating that the man had dangerously wrong ideas about courtship and the girl's state of mind. Most surprising — to men at least — are the girls' reactions, for only 3 of 163 girls complained to police or authority, and only 30% broke off the relationship regardless of the severity of the assault; evidently most American girls are hardened to this sort of approach, which is perhaps just as well because it is made as often in engaged or steady couples as in pickup dates. Indeed, attempts at intercourse are more frequent in engaged and steady couples, because they obviously neck and pet voluntarily for the most part.

Subtler tactics of self-presentation or ingratiation can be used in place of the 'smash and grab' approach of sexual aggression. A well-known basic premise is that people like others who agree with them, or who seem to like them or to approve of them as people; this principle is correct but only so long as the agreement or approval is seen to have the right motive. Blatant flattery or sycophancy is not generally very welcome, so to say how much one agrees with someone is better done before they expressed their own opinion, to give the impression of independence. This is, of course, difficult, unless one already knows their opinion somehow or can make an accurate inference about it. A less well-known tactic is the 'uncertainty reduction principle'. People are not much impressed by being told about their known good points, because they know all about them already, nor are they likely to believe compliments about known bad points; it is better to reassure them by complimenting them on the points that they are not certain about themselves, if one knows or can guess what these are. Compliments can be made more convincing still by criticizing – not too heavily – a few of the person's known weak points, so that he or she thinks the critic is an accurate and impartial observer. It is also psychologically sound to make a few carefully selected criticisms because they make compliments more plausible and valuable, for if someone is always nice, niceness is expected and so not valued. An alternative way of getting compliments across is through a third party who is likely to repeat them making them seem much more convincing.

Recently some interesting research has been done on the phenomenon of 'playing hard to get', which soon disproved the initial theory that men like girls who are hard to get, as the study showed that they consistently preferred women who were easy to get. Men rang up girls they had been given as computer dates and the girls hesitated when asked for a date or said they could not manage that day. The men were not impressed and did not rate the girls any more highly. Men were similarly unfavourably disposed towards a prostitute – a real one apparently with real customers – who said she did not accept anyone as a client, only the ones she liked. It eventually turned out that men only liked girls who were selectively hard to get – hard for everyone else but easy for them [28,29].

There are other even more Machiavellian ways of charming and impressing others, such as the tactic derived from what psychologists usually refer to as the 'pratfall' experiment [30]. The reasoning of this study ran as follows: people prefer others of superior ability and accomplishments, but are also a little wary of them because of the fear that they are perhaps too perfect and may show them up. If a near perfect person were humanized a little by being seen to make a clumsy blunder, he would become more acceptable. This was contrived by making a near perfect person appear to commit a clumsy blunder or 'pratfall' and spill a cup of coffee over himself in front of the judges. The experiment worked in that the clumsy but highly accomplished person was seen more favourably, but a person of only average accomplishments lost esteem as a result of his 'pratfall'.

A similarly ingenious laboratory experiment [31] has examined the role of self-esteem in courtship, based on the reasonable theory that the higher someone's opinion of himself or herself the more confident a man will be about asking the girl for a date or the more choosy a confident girl will be when asked. Men with low self-confidence are in fact more reluctant to ask for dates for fear of being refused — 'fear of failure' — and this low self-esteem is a more or less enduring aspect of the individual, shaped by his experience with other people in general and with the opposite sex in particular. Supposing, however, the experimenter temporarily lowered someone's self-esteem by devising a rebuff for him or her; would this then affect his or her response to the opposite sex? This experiment looked at the effect in girls of 'failing' a test on their reaction to being asked for a date by an attractive male stranger a few minutes later, and found far more of the 'failed' group accepted the invitation than of the control group. These results suggest that an approach to a girl will have a greater chance of success if timed to follow a failure or humiliation of some sort; indeed, recognition of this fact probably underlies the popular notion of 'catching someone on the rebound' after failure of an earlier relationship.

A phrase much in vogue over the last few years has been 'altered states of consciousness' and it has suggested recently that love or sex are such a state, or can be reinforced by them. If a state of generalized internal tension, called 'arousal', can be induced in someone, they will behave differently and in particular will become strongly attracted to someone of the opposite sex, but only in appropriate circumstances. The two vital questions become, therefore, How can this state be induced?

and What is meant by 'appropriate circumstances'? According to the theory, the state really is generalized and can be induced by a great variety of things, one of which is sexual contact. Hence if a boy and girl have some sexual contact they will be drawn to each other much more, particularly if it is their first experience. So far this sounds like a statement of the blindingly obvious, but the interest lies in the fact that the state of arousal is generalized or undifferentiated, so the same state can be produced not just by sexual contact but by fear, or anger, or loud noises, or, as in a famous demonstration, by adrenaline. Again, because the state is generalized and undifferentiated, the person himself or herself must identify it in the light of 'appropriate circumstances'. In the adrenaline experiment, [32] different 'appropriate circumstances' were manufactured by the experimenter, producing different strong emotions in the subject; if someone got at him and criticized him and the experiment, he became angry, whereas if someone behaved in a jolly happy-go-lucky manner, the subject fell in with this mood, but only if he had been given adrenaline, for the subjects who did not get it remained unmoved. If sexual excitement or love do fit into his theory and are a form of 'arousal', all sorts of interesting possibilities are opened. A man or woman will be made more susceptible to advances and more likely to fall in love if he or she can be put into a state of tension while with a suitable partner, whether the tension is fear, anger, or whatever. Recent experiments [33] have actually found a link between fear, anger, and sex arousal, showing that frightened men produced more sexually significant stories, and that angry men had a higher concentration of acid phosphatase in their urine, a sign again of sexual arousal. Of course, attempts to get someone in the right mood by making them angry or afraid would backfire if he or she saw the would-be seducer as the cause for anger or the source of the fear. Further research [34] has shown that the interrelation of sex, anxiety, and aggression is complex; for example, women who saw a threatening film, then a sex film, were more aroused by the sex film than they were when they saw it after a neutral film. Evidently the anxiety carries over and increases sexual arousal, but only when it precedes the sexual experience. When the women saw the sex film first, then the threatening or neutral film, the threatening film damped down their sexual arousal more sharply and rapidly than the neutral film. Sexual arousal was measured by vaginal blood flow.

An interesting variation on the 'general arousal' theme comes from a study on the confusion of physical exertion and sexual arousal [35]. Physical exercise makes the heart beat faster and increases blood pressure, as well as making the person doing the exercise feel hot and bothered; the significant point is that the subjective feelings wear off before heart rate and blood pressure return to normal, so there is a period lasting several minutes when the person is still 'aroused' but does not realize it. In the particular experiment being described, which used a bicycle-type exercise machine, the in-between phase started about 5 minutes after the exercise stopped and lasted several minutes. During these 3 or 4 minutes the experimental volunteers saw an erotic film, which they found significantly more exciting than people who saw it after they had completely recovered from the exercise, or people who saw it just after stopping exercise, when they were still aware of its effects. The people who saw the film when still aware of being 'hot and bothered' knew why they felt aroused, or thought they did, whereas the people who did not realize they were still physically experiencing the effects of exercise 'mis-attributed' their excitement to the sexual stimulus. This experiment throws a new light on the role of dancing in courtship or seduction; some 5 minutes or so after a moderately energetic dance the couple will feel sexually aroused through a transmutation of the effects of exercise. Other forms of exercise should in theory produce the same effects, although the exact timing of the 'in-between' phase will depend on how strenuous the exercise is; in the static bicycle experiment it did not depend much on the individual, unusually for a generalization about behaviour. An alternation of fast and slow dances should make for the best effects, allowing the couples to be in each others' arms — during the slow dance — the crucial 5 minutes or so after the fast one. Driving fast is another method, occasionally recommended for producing the right frame of mind, but is rather risky; if it frightens the passenger, he or she will naturally blame the driver, and will not 'mis-attribute' the excitement to a sexual stimulus or to any other.

Heterosexual relations are rather like the young of some species of fish — the great majority of them do not survive very long. Many do not get beyond the first date, many more do not last more than a few weeks. In Western society, even formalization by engagement or marriage is no guarantee of survival, for the relationship can break up at any time, although statistically some relationships are more vulnerable than others — e.g. marriages between couples under 21.

The most obvious cause, or at least occasion, of breaking up, is a third person coming on the scene and winning the affections of one of the original couple, and this was found in a survey of American students to account for about a quarter of broken romances. The survey found a large sex difference, for women were twice as likely as men to break off a relationship in order to start a new one (with someone already on the scene), which probably follows from the custom of male initiative, if it is assumed that (other) men are less respectful of existing relationships than (other) women. Many relationships do not break up because someone new appears on the scene, but suffer a more insidious and depressing fate — 'progressive mutual loss of interest'. The decline of the relationship is not marked by external intervention, or even by the discovery of mutual incompatibilities of personality or attitude, but by a simple cooling towards each other, and in a survey of American students accounted for nearly a half of all terminated courtships.

'Aronson's law of marital infidelity' [36] has been formulated to account for loss of interest between couples. Aronson found that compliments from strangers were much more valuable than compliments from friends and spouses, while, conversely, insults or unfriendly comments from friends and spouses were much more damaging than those received from strangers, so that any newcomer can make him/herself pleasant more easily than an established partner can, whereas the latter retains only the capacity to hurt or offend. This is a 'frame of reference effect' meaning that one judges all events by what one is used to, so that pleasantness, compliments, etc., from a partner being the usual thing are just an average, rather uninteresting occurrence, and a newcomer always has a built-in advantage over the established partner. The tendency for engaged or married couples to fall into a routine can only increase the effect — hence perhaps the frequent suggestions in advice columns to wear/cook/do something different. Then, again, everyone has irritating habits which do not lose their effect with time, unlike smiles and compliments, but seem to get more irritating still.

REFERENCES

1. C. B. Ford and F. A. Beach (1952) *Patterns of sexual behaviour*, Methuen, London.

2. K. Amis (1969) *The green man*, Cape, London.
3. K. S. Larsen (1971) An investigation of sexual behaviour among Norwegian college students: a motivational study. *J. Marr. Fam.* **33**, 219—27.
4. M. Argyle and A. Kendon (1967) The experimental analysis of social performance. *Adv. exp. soc. Psychol.* **3**, 55—98.
5. C. Symonds (1972) A vocabulary of sexual enticement. *J. Sex Res.* **8**, 136—9.
6. J. W. Thibaut and H. H. Kelley (1959) *The social psychology of groups*, Wiley, New York.
7. H. L. Zetterberg (1966) The secret ranking. *J. Marr. Fam.* **28**, 134—42.
8. C. T. Twentyman and R. M. McFall (1975) Behavioural training of social skills in shy males. *J. cons. clin. Psychol.* **43**, 384—95.
9. J. P. Curran (1977) Skills training as an approach to the treatment of heterosexual-social anxiety: a review. *Psych. Bull.* **85**, 140—57.
10. A. Russell and R. Winkler (1977) Evaluation of assertive training and homosexual guidance service groups designed to improve homosexual functioning. *J. cons. clin. Psychol.* **45**, 1—13.
11. L. A. Kirkendall (1961) *Premarital intercourse and interpersonal relationships*, Julian Press, New York.
12. H. Arkowitz, E. Lichtenstein, K. McGovern, and P. Hines (1975) The behavioural assessment of social competence in males. *Beh. Ther.* **6**, 3—13.
13. P. C. Rosenblatt (1971) Communication in the practice of love magic. *Soc. For.* **49**, 482—7.
14. K. Gergen, M. M. Gergen, and W. H. Barton (1973) Deviance in the dark. *Psychol. Today* **7**, 129—33, 143.
15. G. D. Barthell (1970) Group sex among the Mid-Americans. *J. Sex Res.* **6**, 113—30.
16. P. Wildeblood (1956) *A way of life*. Weidenfeld & Nicolson, London.
17. R. A. L. Humphreys (1970) *Tearoom trade: impersonal sex in public places*, Aldine, Chicago.
18. A. E. Scheflen (1965) Quasi-courtship behaviour in psychotherapy. *Psychiatry* **28**, 245—57.
19. D. Morris (1971) *Intimate behaviour*, Cape, London.
20. A. Mehrabian (1972) *Nonverbal communication*, Aldine, Chicago.
21. P. Machotka (1965) Body movement as communication. *Beh. Sci. Res.* **2**, 33—66.
22. P. Ekman and W. V. Friesen (1969) Nonverbal leakage and cues to deception. *Psychiatry* **32**, 88—106.
23. M. Argyle and M. Cook (1976) *Gaze and mutual gaze*, Cambridge University Press.
24. L. Luborsky, B. Blinder, and N. Mackworth (1963) Eye fixation and recall of pictures as a function of GSR responsivity. *Perc. Mot. Skills* **16**, 469—83.
25. E. H. Hess (1965) Attitude and pupil size. *Am. Sci.* **212**, 46—54.
26. J. M. Davis and A. Farina (1970 Humour appreciation as social communication *J. pers. soc. Psychol.* **15**, 175—8.
27. C. Kirkpatrick and E. Kanin (1957) Male sex aggression on a university campus. *Am. sociol. Rev.* **22**, 52—8.
28. E. J. Kanin (1969) Selected dyadic aspects of male sex aggression. *J. Sex Res.* **5**, 12—28.
29. E. Walster *et al.* (1973) 'Playing hard to get'; understanding an elusive phenomenon. *J. pers. soc. Psychol.* **26**, 113—21.

30. D. R. Mettee and P. C. Wilkins (1972) When similarity 'hurts': effects of perceived ability and a humorous blunder on interpersonal attractiveness. *J. pers. soc. Psych.* **22** 246—58.

31. E. Walster (1965) The effect of self-esteem on romantic liking. *J. exp. soc. Psychol.* **1**, 184—97.

32. S. Schachter and J. Singer (1962) Cognitive, social and physiological determinants of emotional states. *Psych. Rev.* **69**, 379—99.

33. A. M. Barclay (1971) Linking sexual and aggressive motives: contributions of 'irrelevant' arousals. *J. Pers.* **39**, 481—92.

34. P. W. Hoon, J. P. Wincze, and E. F. Hoon (1977) A test of reciprocal inhibition: are anxiety and sexual arousal in women mutually inhibitory? *J. abnorm. Psychol.* **86**, 65—76.

35. J. Cavior *et al.* (1975) Enhancement of experienced sexual arousal in response to erotic stimuli through misattribution of unrelated residual excitation. *J. pers. soc. Psychol.* **32**, 69—75.

36. E. Aronson (1970) Some antecedents of interpersonal attraction. *Nebraska Symp. on Motivation*, vol. 17.

Chapter 6

FOR BETTER, FOR WORSE

People who are sexually attracted to each other and have a lasting and successful relationship may be said to be 'well matched'. However, it has proved very difficult for psychologists to decide in exactly which ways such couples are matched. This chapter surveys data on the role of personality and behaviour in attraction. These may be divided up into theories such as similarity which states that attraction between couples follows if their personalities — intelligence, adjustment, etc. — are similar. Complementary needs theories suggest that attraction depends on the matching of opposite personalities, so that dominant women marry submissive men, etc. This theory is intuitively plausible but the evidence is poor. Then there are the more recent filter theories which suggest that different factors — living or working close to someone, similar attitudes, etc. — work at different stages in the relationship. We can thus see the forming of a relationship between two people as involving a series of filters; each filter works to reject unsuitable partners. The chapter also contains a discussion of the illusions many 'well matched' couples have of each other. People tend to assume that their partners share their feelings about many matters but research shows that surprisingly often there is a tendency to think that your partner agrees when, in fact, he/she does not.

In short-term sexual encounters all that really matters is what the other person looks like and whether they are willing — both things that can be discovered fairly quickly. There is not the time nor any need to find out what the other person is 'really like'. Long-term relationships and marriage, on the other hand, mean more than 'four legs in a bed', so partners will be chosen more carefully. In particular the whole process takes much longer; there are always the people who write to magazines saying they married within a week of meeting, but most engagements last a year or more. What goes on during this time has fascinated psychologists, sociologists, as well as demographers and even biologists, who all want to know why some engagements last, and some do not, to discover in fact what determines people's choice of a mate.

The research on attraction and 'mate selection' begins at the beginning by looking at where the couple live, and establishing what might seem rather trivial, that people choose mates — and friends for that matter — who are close at hand. Much of the research in this area has been done by biologists who are interested in 'gene pools' and inbreeding effects, or by demographers who simply want to trace population movements or study social class mobility. In 1932 an American sociologist, James Bossard [1] noted the addresses on 5000 marriage licences in Philadelphia and found that people tended to marry someone living near them; 17% of couples had been living within one block of each other and 31% within four blocks. Only a fifth of the couples lived in different cities before marriage. This statement about proximity, known as 'Bossard's law', has been studied at length by American sociologists and a special index of distance — the 'Standard City Block', one-eighth of a mile long — has been devised. Bossard's discovery may seem trivial at first glance, but on further analysis the effect turns out to be surprisingly powerful. The vast majority of potential partners live *outside* one's immediate neighbourhood. It is this fact that makes the proximity effect much more striking. The first American sociologists [2] to realize this developed their argument by the ingenious method of plotting all 'available brides' — actually all those women who got married during the period of the study — on a town plan and looking at the number of brides available to each man getting married that year, within circles of differing sizes. They found that within a half-mile radius — and 3 in every 10 of Bossard's sample married someone that close — there was an average of only 5 'available brides', so the man who marries the 'girl next door' is choosing from a very limited number of possible mates.

The 'Bossard effect' is not limited to urban America, but has been observed in London also; in 51 of 94 couples studied, [3] both husband

and wife came from the same borough (Camden). It has been documented in the English countryside, in Oxfordshire, and Northumberland, although the distances are naturally greater all round, and looking further afield in France, Sweden, Finland, India, and French West Africa. The effect is weakening, however, because people can move further and more freely, as neatly demonstrated by the data of the Oxfordshire study [4] where the coming of the railway in the 1850s doubled average husband–wife distances. Mobility may also explain why men, especially in their twenties, marry further afield than women. There are some striking exceptions to the rule, for in some societies taboos and social customs rule out most local mates, forcing men to look further afield. The explanation for Bossard's law that immediately springs to mind is that it is easier to find someone close at hand and easier to keep seeing them. Why suffer the miseries of long journeys right across London or New York when there are plenty of partners who live nearby? This is a rather cynical argument in many ways, for it implies, firstly, that all possible dates or mates are much of a muchness, and, secondly, that someone is going to have to be very special to merit a 2-hour bus or train journey. If there is a 'Mr. Right' or 'Miss Right', surely people would spare no trouble to be with him or her, but the sad fact is that people are most unlikely to meet their Mr. or Miss Right at all if they are at the other side of a big city. Although, having met by chance, many couples do put up with geographical separation as some of Bossard's additional data showed.

A subtler explanation of Bossard's law emerges, however, from some recent research on what psychologists call 'mere exposure' [5]. Consider the example of a man who regularly sees a girl at work but only from a distance, so he does not get a chance to talk to her and does not know anything about her. What will his feelings be towards her after a year? The proverb says 'familiarity breeds contempt', while common sense might say that he will feel just the same as he felt at the beginning of the year. Some remarkable studies suggest that the man will feel much friendlier, simply because he has seen the girl frequently. 'Mere exposure', in the absence of anything else, makes people more favourably inclined to each other. In one study the experimenter arranged for names to be put in the college newspaper varying numbers of times during a term, and subsequently found the more often people saw the name the more they liked it. In another study it was contrived that people should meet others varying numbers of times, ostensibly to undergo experiments on taste, and it emerged that although the people had no chance to speak, repeated encounters fostered friendly feelings between them. A further study showed the effect did not, contrary again to common-sense expectations, have a point of diminishing returns; people did not start to sicken of the sight of a stranger even after 96 encounters. These results can be taken to show that a man and a girl who see each other every day for a year will come to like each other, *other things being equal.* Other things that may not be equal include the appearance of the couple, for a very plain man might rise in the esteem of a very attractive girl, but nowhere near enough to become an acceptable partner. One might also speculate that if the girl dislikes something about the man's appearance — perhaps he is black and she is a racist — 'mere exposure' would lead to hostility (but common sense might be wrong and their initial hostility might lessen). The main limitation is that people do not meet regularly without interacting at all, and once they meet and talk to each other, all the influences like attitude similarity, personality, and background come into play. 'Mere exposure' only sets the scene for the first encounter.

People choose their marriage partners from the limited number of people who are close at hand, but within the 'field of eligibles' more personal factors must operate. (Assuming there is a 'field'. Men and women often complain — often with justice — that they simply do not know anyone eligible or, more rarely, experience a feeling of being trapped, because there is only one eligible mate in their social circle). One of the earliest ideas in the history of modern psychology, and one of the most popular, is that men and women are looking for a replacement opposite sex parent; the man will marry someone who reminds him of his mother, while the woman wants a father figure. This theme achieves its most elaborate form, of course, in psychoanalytic theory, and forms part of the central core of Freudian theory. One's choice of a marriage partner, according to psychoanalysis, is determined, like nearly everything of any significance, by the age of 5. The explanations offered often seem involved, improbable, and frequently disgusting, and are likely to be repudiated by the people about whom they are made, which, paradoxically, strengthens the Freudian's certainty in the truth of the explanation. Memory of the events involved is 'repressed' because it is too threatening to be allowed into consciousness.

Much of the evidence for psychoanalytic explanations comes from case studies. Why, for example, should a girl of beauty, intelligence, and charm' marry 'an ill-favoured, homely, poorly equipped neurotic and dependent man'? Because according to one typical account, [6] she wanted to 'hide herself'. 'In her choice of husband, she was saying to the world "This is all that I am, and all that I am good for". Or why should a girl marry one of her 'charming, alcoholic wastrel' brothers' friends but in an 'unconscious effort to wipe away the pain that these brothers had caused her through so many years.' He, on the other hand, 'married her out of an unconscious homosexual attachment to her brothers'. Academic psychologists have little time for this sort of material. Not merely can the analyst select cases to fit his theory, ignoring all those that do not, but the information itself is very dubious. The analyst does not determine personality by tests or questionnaires which have some elements of objectivity, but uses his own subjective judgement. Furthermore, he claims to be able to see things that no one but another analyst can see, such as anxiety in a seemingly self-confident person, or a murderous hatred for an apparently well-liked spouse or parent. It is impossible to refute the psychoanalytic explanation by any form of counter-evidence, which makes it in the eyes of many psychologists a meaningless and unscientific account.

Nevertheless, there may be some 'hard' data relevant to psycho-dynamic theories. For example, if men are really seeking to marry their mother when they select a wife they will presumably choose a wife who resembles their mother in some way, while women should select a husband who reminds them of their fathers.* There is, in fact, little or no evidence that spouses are chosen because they physically resemble the opposite sex parent. One early study applied some complicated and not very plausible reasoning to age of marriage and the search for a substitute mother. Searching through Who's Who?, the researcher [7]

*Freudian theory could fairly be called 'sexist' in as much as the theory pays less attention to women, giving, for example, rather a perfunctory account of the 'Electra' complex which is the female version of the Oedipus complex, and also because it shows women in an even worse light than men.

found that oldest sons marry on average nearly 2 years younger than second and subsequent born sons, which could be relevant to the Oedipus complex, so long as two assumptions are granted: firstly, the oldest sons, by marrying younger, marry younger wives; and, secondly, that, being oldest sons, their own mothers were also younger during the son's infancy. They are thus apparently choosing a girl who resembles their mother in age. In fact, even if the assumptions are granted, the results do not demonstrate a search for a mother-substitute, for the result could be an effect of primogeniture.

'Post-Freudian' theories pay more attention to the rest of the family than Freud so the resemblance of chosen partners to brothers or sisters becomes relevant. Most studies of this sort have found no significant trends, but one more recent study has uncovered something. An analysis [8] of 246 couples found, as did previous researchers, no matching of number, age, or sex of siblings between husband and wife, but when happiness of the marriage was included in the analysis something did emerge. Men who had younger sisters and had married women with older brothers were happier than men with older sisters who had married women with younger brothers, findings interpreted — tentatively — in terms of male dominance. The women with older brothers were used to being dominated by men, and the men who had the younger sisters were used to dominating. Obviously this explanation makes a lot of assumptions that would need to be tested: that men dominate married life, and that interlocking dominance-submission patterns are conducive to happy marriage.

It is evidently difficult to demonstrate Oedipal or Electral patterns of mate choice in terms of physique or family structure; perhaps personality traits themselves will show a resemblance, so that people choose mates who have personalities like their opposite sex parent. Unfortunately, no one has compared the personality of cross-sex parent with that of spouse; instead, research [9] has been limited to a variation on the 'ideal mate' theme. Six hundred college women were asked to describe their ideal husband, their father, a male relative, and current male companion; none of the three real people resembled the ideal mate much, but current boyfriend beat father by a small head. In any case, striking similarity of personality, whether rated or measured by tests, would not prove the Freudian theory, for almost any theory of personality would account for such an effect. Perhaps the surprising thing is that parental characteristics seem to have *so little* effect on mate choice. Even this is not so surprising to those familiar with research on child rearing and personality, who know that despite what most people think, the way children are brought up seems to have rather little consistent, measurable effect on their behaviour then or later in life.

It may be difficult for psycho-dynamic theorists to show that parents or the family determine who the person marries, but it is very easy to show that they determine who the person shall *not* marry. Virtually every society in the world, past and present, has a very strong taboo against incest; sexual relations between parent and child, and between siblings, are universally prohibited and generally punishable by death. The Freudian explains the incest taboo by pointing out first that there are rarely dire and terrible prohibitions against things no one wants to do. The small boy strongly desires his mother and begins to express an interest, but he is frightened off by the father and the threat of castration by him. The whole episode is so frightening that the child represses it; he forgets it and can only remember it with great difficulty during psychoanalysis. The little girl similarly desires her father, and is frightened off by her mother, but not by the threat of castration for she thinks that has already happened. (Hence, according to Freud, the inferior moral character of women.) Shorn of its wilder extravagances, this is a plausible theory, for it is quite likely that the child will form an attachment to the parents — especially the boy for the mother, fathers playing a less prominent role in bringing up small children and that discouraging or redirecting this interest will cause friction. As a result the child's and later the adult's interest in the opposite sex will be channelled either away from the same sex parent altogether, or, as Freudians argue, into a search for a father or mother substitute.

Of course, the existence of the incest taboo does not actually 'prove' Freudian theory. In fact, some well-documented facts go against its predictions. For example, father—daughter incest is the commonest form, which does not quite fit Freudian theory, especially as the father takes the initiative, not the daughter. The Freudian could, of course, argue that the infrequency of mother—son incest only goes to show how strong the taboo is and how well repressed the memories, and also that the father only *seems* to take the initiative in father—daughter incest. In these circumstances, the only way to disprove such a theory is to show that another one better fits the facts of the case.

Some people explain incest prohibitions in terms of rules and social customs, while others prefer a 'biological' explanation, i.e. one that talks of the 'survival value' of the taboo, its long-term evolutionary benefit to mankind. Sociologists tend to say that incest is forbidden because it would upset the family structure. It very likely would, but so would lots of other things that are not punishable by death and universally reviled. Biologists offer a biological explanation; incest leads to inbreeding which causes a marked deterioration in subsequent generations, so that a society that permitted it would tend to die out. There is ample evidence that inbreeding leads to physical and intellectual deterioration, but it is still necessary to explain how the prohibition is actually maintained in a given society; there must be some disposition in the individual that discourages incest. In fact, one of Freud's basic ideas — that people want to commit incest — is partly correct, for several surveys have shown that it is more common than most people think. For example, a recent survey [10] in Northern Ireland found that about 4% of patients in psychiatric hospitals, guidance clinics, and remand homes reported incestuous experience.

There are some remarkable studies done on Israeli *kibbutzim* which showed that the children reared together — in a sort of perpetual mixed sex boarding school from birth — showed no sexual interest in each other, and did not choose each other as dates or spouses, whereas a similar group of English or American students would date and marry within the group quite a lot. In 125 couples there was not one exception of the rule [11]. More recently another study [12] looked at 2769 marriages by *kibbutz* members, and found *not one* marriage between 'peer group members', i.e. between children raised together. These are remarkable findings because it is so rare in social psychology to be able to find an absolute law. Most researchers would be excited if the rate of within-peer group marriages had been even 10% lower, but then, of course, the incest taboo seems to be an exceptional phenomenon. The *kibbutz* 'pseudo-incest' taboo is definitely not a cultural prohibition, for no one would have objected if peer group members intermarried. (In fact people would have welcomed it as one of the problems in *kibbutzim* is that young people marry outsiders or foreigners and leave the *kibbutz*.) One researcher [12] argued that the critical period in developing the psuedo-incest taboo is early in childhood — the first 5 years in fact — but this evidence is not very convincing; 12 apparent exceptions to his rule were peer group members who married but had not been together right throughout infancy. The suggestion is that the intense physical contact with siblings or peers leads to 'negative imprinting' — an irreversible life-long aversion to sexual relations with them. This theory is plausible, and would in fact neatly account for the evidence on actual incest rates. Fathers have less to do with their small children and often do not handle them much, so would have less 'negative imprinting' which would explain why father—daughter incest is the usual case. Mothers, of course, do handle their children a lot, so negative imprinting would occur, just as in siblings.

Further evidence for the 'negative imprinting' theory comes from 'Sim-pua' marriages in Taiwan (Formosa) [13]. The bride enters the future husband's home as a child aged 3 at the most, and often less than a year, and is brought up with the husband as if they were siblings. When they marry, the marriages are not a success; the couples are often reluctant to consummate the marriage, have fewer children, divorce often, and have affairs frequently.

It always used to be said that animals show no signs of anything like an incest taboo, and this is doubtless true for many species. However, careful observation [14] of monkeys has revealed a virtually total avoidance of mother—son copulations in some species. In baboons mother—son copulations and inbreeding are avoided by a simple expedient: the young male baboon always leaves his home troop, whereas young females rarely do. Thus exogamy is assured by a process that bears an interesting resemblance to customs found in some human village societies (but not in many others), which require men to seek brides outside the village.

The earlier discussion of Bossard's law of proximity in fact left out a third explanation of the fact. Besides convenience and mere exposure there is the theory that the effect is not really of proximity at all but rather of social custom. Society's unwritten rules require a person to marry someone of the same age, religion, race, class, etc.; since the people living in a particular district tend to be of the same class, race, religion (but not the same age), it is not surprising that a high proportion of marriages are between people living close together. Obviously this theory can explain Bossard's results only to the extent that people are segregated by class, race, religion, etc.

These restrictions on choice of date or mate all define what is sometimes called the 'field of eligibles'. Western society, like all others, lays down certain rules about the age, class, and background of the partners, which further limit choice of partners, already limited by physical opportunity. Many of these who are close at hand simply do not exist as marriage partners — or as friends — because custom forbids it. The individual cannot associate with someone of different religion, class, race, because he or she would be censured, ostracized, occasionally even run the risk of murder, or because the norms have been so well learnt that he or she would not want to, would not even contemplate it. The artificial barriers to social relations are probably higher and more numerous in a country like the United States, which has many minorities, than in a more homogeneous country like Britain. Some barriers exist in all societies however, one example being age; in the West it is customary for husband and wife to be approximately the same age. Although men marry younger women more often than women marry younger men, marriages with an age difference of more than 10 years are rare. In some cultures it is not usual to marry someone of the same or similar age, and where large age differences are customary it is generally the man who is older; an example is East Pakistan (now Bangladesh) where in 1961 men married on average at 23 years and girls at 14 years.

Earlier surveys on choice of partner in the United States found white—black marriages very rare; indeed, in one survey [15] of 523 couples in New Haven, not one marriage was inter-racial, probably because at that time mixed marriages were generally frowned on and were illegal in many states. Since then the rate of inter-racial marriages has increased threefold, so that in one study [16] in 1965, 15% of black American males married white women and 5% of black American women married white men. Of course, if marriage took no regard of race, these figures would be virtually reversed, with only a small minority of blacks marrying blacks. Besides the obvious reason that inter-racial marriages are unpopular if not illegal, there is a more subtle reason for their rarity that emerges from the discussion of stereotypes in an earlier chapter. It is impossible to get to know everybody one meets, and in fact most other people are simply slotted into a pigeon hole and dismissed.

Obviously the easiest of pigeon holes of all to put someone in is a 'colour-coded' one, from which it follows that stereotyping of Negroes will be particularly marked, and perhaps the likelihood of getting to know one properly correspondingly reduced. The same early surveys, in New Haven, also showed that ethnic origin and religion created substantial barriers in the selection of partners, and that 9 in every 10 marriages stayed within religious/ethnic boundaries. The effect was strongest for Jews, 97% of whom married Jews, and was almost as strong for Roman Catholics (94%) but rather weaker for Protestants (74.4%). There was in fact little sign that America was a 'melting pot' in which former identities were being lost and everyone was becoming 100% American. Integration was occurring within religious boundaries to some extent, so that East European Jewish Americans were marrying Russian Jewish Americans, although Italian Americans did not marry even across ethnic boundaries. The author of one survey aptly described New Haven as a 'triple melting pot' rather than a single one. Another large survey [17] of 1000 couples produced similar results — religion was the most potent single factor in choosing a partner. 'Ethnicity' is not quite as readily visible as race, but requires knowledge of surnames. It has actually been demonstrated experimentally that one cannot tell Protestants from Catholics just by their appearance, although Jews can be identified with better than chance accuracy.

Most religions discourage or forbid marriages outside the faith, so religious 'cleavages' will be widespread, but ethnic boundaries are a different matter. In Britain there is no data on intermarriage of English, Welsh, Irish, and Scottish, nor on people's reactions to it, while Asian and West Indian minorities have not been in Britain long enough for the issue to arise on any scale, although press reports suggest some Asian parents want to maintain Asian customs, including arranged marriages, often with partners still in the home country. Looking further afield, a recent report [18] suggests that Singapore, sometimes cited as a harmonious 'multi-racial' society, has low intermarriage rates. Australia appears to be developing patterns of 'ethnic' intermarriage not unlike those of the United States, for Greek marries Greek, Italian marries

Italian, but British immigrants mostly marry into established 'old Australian' families [19].

People may tolerate 'them' at work, in public places, and as fellow-citizens, but they still do not want their daughters to marry one. 'They' are not just foreigners, immigrants, ethnic minorities; 'they' are also members of other social classes. Several surveys have shown that people marry within their own social class. A large study [17] of 1000 American couples some time ago showed that people marry generally someone from the same class and income bracket, and a recent survey [20] of men and women who graduated from British universities in 1960 got the same results — marriage within social classes and a tendency for men to marry 'down' more often than women. The explanation seems clear enough: a cynical and unromantic observer will argue that women marry for money, or to maintain the 'style to which they are accustomed', whereas men marry women not for money but for something else, such as 'looks'. More generally there are several compelling reasons for marrying within one's own social circle, starting with the fact that the people nearest at hand are likely to share one's religion, race, and social status. The similar people close at hand are likely to be the ones that are differentiated as individuals, whereas the larger numbers of different people further afield present a problem of 'cognitive overloading' — there are too many to cope with so they are 'pigeonholed' and never really understood. However, there is more to the effect of class in mate choice than mere opportunity, for social custom often dictates choice of someone with similar background. Informants who contributed the data in early studies also said they definitely disapproved of an older man marrying a much younger girl. Similarly, men and women are subject to considerable family pressure to marry within their religions, especially if they are Jewish or Roman Catholic. People speak unfavourably of men or women marrying 'below themselves', i.e. into a lower social class, and formerly spoke of 'fortune hunters' and 'adventurers', meaning people who sought to marry into a higher social class. Social norms like these usually have some reason behind them. Marriages between people of different religions create problems for the children. Marriages between people of different income groups may mean a painful change in standards of living for the 'descending' person, while marriages between people of widely different ages can lead to a variety of problems. (Curiously enough, however, one famous study [21] of marital compatibility found that age differences did not affect the success of the marriage much, and that the happiest groups were wives whose husbands were from 4 to 10 years younger than themselves — a most unusual group. Similarly, attempts to link divorce rate and interreligious marriages have been inconclusive.)

Age, race, religion, social class, as well as physical proximity, may all be seen to play a major part in determining whether or not two people get together and ultimately marry. It is interesting to notice how the rules associated with these factors are widely accepted even though they are rarely made explicit. It is also interesting to see how little difference apparent relaxation of these rules by modern, 'tolerant' Western societies has made to actual behaviour. Most girls marry a man a little older than themselves who is similar in the important social attributes, and this familiar social matrix has become a firmly established patterning of the various biological pieces. One wonders how much scope is left for choice based on individual personal characteristics. The constraints do become noticeable when someone in a big city realizes he or she has no acceptable partner — or perhaps one and only one — despite the thousands of unmarried people around him or her. Taking for the moment a more optimistic approach and considering a person who has a good 'field of eligibles' to choose from, what determines his or her choice — besides physical appearance? A lucky boy or girl at college or in a large office may have dozens of partners to choose from, so personal factors can influence his or her choice. Research divides itself neatly into two fields: attitudes and personality.

Just as people tend to marry or make friends with other people like them in income, background, etc., so they also choose partners whose opinions resemble their own. Couples' views on every issue from birth control to Communism, or aesthetics to smoking, are similar. This finding — not in itself very remarkable — might be described as one of the fundamental laws of social attraction. However, it is not enough to show that married or otherwise established couples have similar opinions to show that similarity leads to attraction, for the couple may have had different ideas when they met, and grown similar, perhaps by the dominant partner imposing his or her opinions on the other. They could have similar attitudes because they come from the same background.

College couples may match each others' liberal outlooks, not because they liked the others' views particularly but simply because everyone at college thinks the same. A series of laboratory studies has demonstrated that similarity of attitude has a true causal relationship with attraction. In these studies [22], subjects were given a list of opinions held by what they took to be another subject, and asked on some pretext to say what they thought of him or her; it emerged that they liked similar others and were more attracted to them, and also thought them more intelligent, of better moral character, better informed on current affairs, and 'well adjusted'. These opinions about the other person were entirely dependent on the other's outlook, for the subjects have no other information (and could not, for the other person does not really exist). An obvious objection to these results occurs to everyone who reads the account of the study, that the method is very 'artificial' or 'unrealistic' and can one be sure the findings apply to actual encounters between real people? A more sophisticated version of the same criticism queries whether people might realize something of the purpose of the study and co-operate by saying what they think the researcher wants to hear, and also argues that the experimenter only gives subjects one piece of information about someone, so it is not all that surprising that people base their evaluation on it. These criticisms were partly met by a second study [23], using 'computer dates', in which the couples had varying degrees of shared outlook, and showing that couples with similar attitudes were more attracted to each other, sexually as well as generally and thought the other a more desirable marriage partner. The effect went beyond mere words, and was lasting, for the similar couples stood much closer to each other after the date, and a follow-up some weeks later showed that similar couples could remember each other's names more often, had spoken to each other more often since the arranged meeting, and in a few cases had made further dates, whereas none of the dissimilar couples had.

The effect is often really rather modest, however, for while high similarity of husband and wife's attitudes about Communism or birth control (in 1936) have been reported, the similarity can often be much less and sometimes non-existent. One study [24] found similarity of outlook − or lack of it − seems to make no difference at all to couples' relationship over a 6-month period. Another [25] found similarity of attitude only at the level of least involvement — 'most preferred date' — with steady couples, engaged couples, and married couples showing no agreement at all. Most surprising of all was a definite disagreement, represented by a correlation of −0.67, between couples living together: as the author of the study put it: 'a funny thing happened to the agreement effect on the way to the bedroom.' It would evidently be a grave mistake to infer attraction or compatibility from perfectly matching political and social outlook, or, indeed to infer the lack of either from mismatch.

Some attempts have been made to refine the 'similarity law' to improve its predictive power. The most obvious limiting condition is the importance of the attitude for the person holding it. A committed party member will presumably scrutinize the opinions of a prospective mate more carefully than someone who votes — if they vote at all — for the more personable leader, or because their family always votes that way. Many attitudes are of such minor importance to most people that they seem unlikely to affect their opinion of others; for example, views on fluoridation of water, the relative merits of different makes of car, or the independence of Nagaland. Generally only cranks, or people with delusions of grandeur, exact conformity to trivial opinions, as a condition of acceptance. However, not all social psychologists would agree with this proposition, and it has been argued that agreement is what counts, regardless of importance or content; a study, using the 'imaginary stranger' method, obtained results showing that importance of topic made no difference. A subsequent study [26] showed that what counts is the individual's interest in the topic rather than his assessment of its importance in general. An avid stamp collector would agree that philately was less 'important' than 'world peace' but would choose stamp collectors for friends and not be particularly concerned about their views on pacifist issues. A survey [27] of draft-card burners reported that they tended to drift away from their former friends and dates and to judge new acquaintances by whether they shared anti-war views. Other studies have concentrated on the extent of agreement rather than content. 'Extent' can mean simply the number of shared opinions or can mean the proportion of total opinion held in common. It has been shown quite clearly that attraction to someone increases steadily the more opinions are held in common, which may appear obvious with the benefit of hindsight, but it could plausibly be argued that the effect should be all or none, so that any disagreement would make someone unacceptable, or else that any further disagreement beyond a certain point would have no effect because the other has already been 'written off'.

While the actual extent of similarity in couples was limited, there is a marked tendency for couples to think they are more similar than they really are when predicting each other's attitudes and personality. The effect tends to be greater the vaguer or less important the issue involved, for it is easier not to realize what someone thinks about religion in general than to fail to discover they are a practising Roman Catholic. Indeed, none of the voluminous literature on demographic similarity looks at the couple's *perceptions* of each other at all. Class is defined by income or occupation − not by what people say about themselves. Perhaps − indeed almost certainly − imagined similarity of class will be greater than objectively determined similarity, so that the girl from an upper middle-class family sees her husband as a business man rather than a shopkeeper, while he sees her father as a middle grade civil servant when he is in fact very much at the top of the ladder. Pursuing this line of thought further, it would be interesting to see if couples misperceive each others' ages, ethnic origins, or education, or even think they live closer to each other than they really do.

Why should people marry or choose as sexual partners those who are like themselves? There are several reasons why they should not. Dissimilar people are likely to be more interesting, to tell one things one does not already know, to 'make a change'. There are also likely to be social and political benefits in breaking down sub-cultural barriers. But in fact people do not go out of their way to interact with people unlike themselves but cling to circles of like-minded others, of the same income, religion, class, etc., as has already been seen.

One favourite approach to explaining the effect of similarity has been 'balance' or 'cognitive consistency' theories. These take various forms, but essentially all start with a triangle consisting of two people and an opinion; if one person likes the other, or approves of the opinion, a positive relation exists, whereas dislike or disapproval constitute 'negative' relations. According to balance theories some situations are balanced and some are not. The situation where both man and woman like each other and both approve of foxhunting is balanced; if the two people like each other, but one approves of foxhunting and one does not, the situation is unbalanced. 'Imbalance' causes a 'strain to symmetry', a sort of mental discomfort that can be relieved only by changing something. The man can stop liking the girl, can try to change her mind about foxhunting, can change his own mind, or, as noted, can delude himself that the girl's opinions match his own. The 'opinion' part of the triangle need not be a political one, it can be one person's opinion of another, so if a man dislikes his girlfriend's friends, 'imbalance' or 'strain' results. People want their friends to like their other friends or to dislike their enemies. ('Like', but nothing stronger of course — balance theory obviously does not apply to sexual relations.)

As explained so far, balance theory amounts to little more than a roundabout way of making the familiar point that pairs of friends and lovers share opinions to some extent. Balance theory needs to be able to say more than this; in fact it goes on to analyse not just the simple case of similarity of opinion and attraction, but to consider all other possible relations, e.g. the situation where a person dislikes two other people and to derive the prediction that he will expect the two to like each other. It further yields the general principle that any triangular relationship containing two positive relations is unbalanced, as is any with none, whereas triangles with one positive relation or three are 'balanced'. Unfortunately these interesting predictions do not work out, for if a man dislikes a girl he does not tend to reject anything she believes in, nor to want her to dislike his friends or her friends to dislike him. Rather, he remains indifferent to what she thinks. Even the predictions about simple situations are vague, for any one of four things may resolve 'strain', and the theory also tends to be circular, for it has an escape clause that the opinion must be 'relevant'. Finally, it is quite often simply incorrect, for people can and do tolerate obvious and important differences of opinion with friends and lovers. It is uninformative for it does not say why some situations are 'balanced' and others are not, nor why people experience 'strain' when a friend does not accept their view [28].

'Reinforcement theory' [23] gives a different and simpler explanation of similarity effects, reasoning that people like similar others because they are more rewarding than dissimilar, an argument already applied to similarity of income or education. For one thing people usually air their opinions, often at length, and it is tedious to be told about fluoridation of water, or football, if one is not interested in either. This would be a 'costly' or 'unrewarding' — in psychological jargon — encounter for the listener because he would be thinking of all the more interesting things he might be doing with more interesting people. Talking to someone who positively disagrees can also be 'costly' because of the risk of argument, anger, and ridicule. However, there is another more complicated reason why people with shared opinions find each other 'rewarding', and this depends on the notion of 'social reality' and 'social comparison'. Most opinions are precisely opinions; they are not objectively verifiable. They cannot be proved correct by any test or investigation, but can only seem right if other people hold them also, which constitutes 'social reality'. If other people disagree with cherished opinions, the opinions lose 'social reality' and the holder loses self-confidence, from which it follows that people seek out and prefer the company of others who 'reinforce' their desire for social reality, and reject those who threaten their view of things. Hence religion, because it involves the least verifiable propositions that have the greatest need of social reality, has been the centre of the fiercest struggle to exact conformity of belief. People are most attracted to others who share their *unverifiable* opinions; the way to someone's heart is not to agree with them about who won the World Cup but about who *ought* to have won it. 'Social comparison' theory takes the explanation of similarity and attraction a stage further. People want reassurance not just about their opinions, but about themselves, their abilities, and behaviour in general. They prefer friends who are in the same range of ability as themselves, because they can make meaningful comparisons with them, whereas they can form no precise ideas of their athletic prowess in the company of Olympic athletes, on the one hand, or of cripples, on the other. People also like to be with similar others, to be able to compare others' behaviour with their own, and to satisfy themselves that they are doing the right things — using the right knife at dinner for example.

The explanations of why similarity is rewarding and similar people attractive so far seem to take a rather limited view of social life, showing men and women as constantly on the defensive — afraid of dissimilar people because they might be boring, embarrassing, or might undermine a person's self-confidence. These narrow and timid considerations prevent people widening their horizons and meeting with the interesting new people there are in the world. Actually, of course, the preference for similarity is limited and several recent pieces of research have studied these limitations, showing that people choose similar others because they are afraid dissimilar others may eject them. The fear of rejection gets weaker over time so the effect of similarity on attraction has largely disappeared after people have known each other for a year or more. Some people do not need to wait a year or more and have so much self-confidence that they are not afraid of a rebuff. If the fear of rejection is eliminated by assuring people that others are bound to like them, most people will choose dissimilar others.

The methods used to study the social influences on attraction discussed in this chapter have been indirect, involving the scrutiny of public records or the setting up of disguised experiments. The reader may wonder why a more straightforward, 'common-sense' method has not been used, like asking men and women about the kinds of people they would like to go out with and/or marry, and what sort of person they particularly avoid. Indeed, this kind of research has been done but the results are rarely enlightening. It is one of the limitations of the method that people give plenty of reasons which could well be rationalizations or cultural stereotypes. Equally, much of the information that is given is very vague and tends to reflect widely held cultural values. For example, when asked what they look for in a partner many American men say they want a wife who is affectionate, romantic, physically attractive, and a good home-maker, whereas women want a husband with conventional sex standards, good financial prospects, ambition, industry, and who is considerate and sociable. [29] Other recurring themes are an avoidance of bad habits (such as smoking) in spouses generally. The latter is an old theme, for a survey [30] of the nineteenth-century popular books on mate selection shows that drinking, swearing, and gambling were frequently mentioned as things to guard against. (Another Victorian theme was health and the avoidance of inherited defects, but this is rarely mentioned in modern surveys.)

Researchers are often impatient with the poor results of the direct method. A British survey [31] asked 'ordinary' working-class people why they chose their marriage partners and was surprised by the 'apparent irrelevancy and triviality' of the reasons they gave. Many people simply said it was because of his or her ways, or 'he wasn't like the others', or if they were more specific they mentioned apparently minor details like the partner's voice, manners, or resemblance to a film star.

Thus opinion polls about the 'ideal mate' are suspect because people play down or are unaware of the very important influences of social class, age, religion, proximity, familiarity, and similarity. Yet, as may be seen, a combination of all these factors yields a prediction about mating that account for most of the pairings in any large sample of married couples taken at random. It may be that people overlook or play down these influences because to acknowledge them would be unromantic or unworthy, and they feel that choice of a partner, or friends for that matter, ought to be based on higher considerations.

The other favourite approach to explaining how people choose their mates was in terms of personality. Certainly most couples like to think that even if they have not found their soul mate, they have at least something in common. The question is: What is that something, over and above the similarity of background and outlook already documented? Research [32] early established that couples do *not* have similar personalities; these studies typically proceeded by finding groups of married, engaged, or dating couples giving them personality tests, and then looking for significant similarities or differences. A typical study of this type in the 1930s gave the 42-item 'Thurstone Neuroticism Inventory' to 80 couples (the more questions like 'Do you daydream a lot?' the man or women answers with 'yes', the more neurotic he or she is) and found a modest and positive relationship between the scores of husband and wife. Other early studies of this sort obtained similar results: modest, very modest, or non-existent similarities of personality test scores. Such personality traits as dominance, introversion, self-sufficiency, measured by the Bernreuter Personality Inventory, and 'Mental Hygiene', measured by Woodworth's questionnaire, were more or less unrelated in husband and wife, although the same experimenters sometimes studied similarity of attitude or outlook and found greater similarities. Later studies [33] using more recent questionnaires like the Minnesota Multiphasic Personality Inventory (MMPI) or Cattell's '16PF' have fared no better, a slight tendency to match on neurotic personality occasionally emerges [34] but is too slight to be of more than theoretical interest.

If similarity of personality does not exist in fact, it does exist in the 'eye of the beholder'. As with attitudes and intentions, couples assume a similarity of personality far greater than actually emerges. Perhaps the tendency to distort reality — in line with wishful thinking — is strong enough, and personality as a concept vague enough, that men and women never really see each other as they really are, at least before they marry, hence the dissimilarity when their characters are objectively measured. In fact, some of the largest similarities between partners lie in narrow and specific pieces of behaviour. For example, one study [35] found that similarity of drinking habits was very important and came second only to religion in choosing a mate. Another survey [36] claims that the quality of someone's voice and their readiness to use it are important, so that if 'speech thresholds' differed in couples, they did not get on; some marriages suffered because one spouse had a harsh or otherwise unpleasant voice. These are things likely to be important to the courting couple because they are also more 'visible'. It is easy to observe someone's drinking habits or talkativeness, whereas it is obviously going to be more difficult to decide if they believe they daydream a lot, and have nightmares, and indigestion, and any of the self-impressions that a professional psychologist can sum together to give an index of neuroticism. This is particularly so since people put on their best front during courtship. Indeed, one could take seriously the personality theorist's claim to give a complete exhaustive account of personality, and a complete exhaustive measure of it but still point out that the layman or woman is unlikely to do as well in the limited time before marriage, and with a limited, doctored sample of the other's behaviour to work on, so it is not surprising, therefore, that questionnaires find only a limited similarity for there is only a limited similarity to find, reflecting the fact that the couple really do not know each other that well.

If personality tests are not much use for predicting compatibility in marriage, why do computer-dating services use them? They do not, to be sure, use the ones like the 16PF or the MMPI, for the excellent reason that these tests can only be used by qualified psychologists and are not allowed to be reproduced in newspapers and magazines or to be used in postal surveys. Computer-dating organizations use tests apparently of their own devising and of unknown but dubious value. One typical example includes a 'colour preference test' which works on the assumption that people who prefer yellow to blue or red, etc., will have something in common. They may do, of course, but it is rather unlikely, for colour preferences have rarely been demonstrated to have much to do with personality, and even if they had, it would not follow that colour preference predicts compatibility. To be fair, other points of the advertisement include questions on leisure activities, income, race, religion, and also are not afraid to ask the person what sort of partner they would like, something the old school of psychologists would never dream of doing.

One piece of behaviour, important to lasting relationships but ignored by many personality inventories, is sexual behaviour. There are large individual differences in sex drive as Kinsey and others since have documented at great length; married couples, in their early twenties, have intercourse on average 2–3 times a week, but the range of frequencies is staggering, from never to four times a day every day of the week.

Perhaps couples might select each other for similarity of sex drive. Two studies [37] have found high husband–wife correlation for EPPs 'heterosexuality' scores — the highest correlations discovered with the inventory — based on items like 'I like to become sexually aroused.'

One study [37] obtained some more direct evidence by asking 99 courting couples to estimate the strength of their sex drive and to report how recently they had had an orgasm, finding some evidence of matching.* This survey also found that couples where the man had a high sex drive fared less well and were less likely to have 'progressed' towards marriage 6 months later, perhaps because the man's sex demands led to the girl seeing herself as being 'used for her body', as well as to impatience and frustration in the man. There is more to sex than frequency since many couples, especially in college circles, set store on expertise, so perhaps a couple whose view on 'bedroom gymnastics' differ would break up sooner. A recent survey [38] found that men set great

---

*The 'recency of orgasm' finding may on first reflection appear rather obvious, like the 'discovery' that husband and wife tend to have the same number of children, but the report goes on to mention that men had a higher rate of orgasm than women, which implies that the analysis includes masturbation, and presumably the odd infidelity. The data would be more impressive if results were presented separately for couples that had intercourse and those that did not.

store on 'erotic ability' in their fiancées, and that their estimates of their own ability and that of their mates related highly,* whereas girls' estimates of the similarity of their own and their fiancé's ability were much lower.† Of course, peoples' estimates of their 'erotic ability' may be biased, but it would be a trifle unfair to expect the researchers to provide more objective data.

Even if people do not marry someone whose personality closely resembles their own, perhaps they ought to because it would lead to happier marriages, and some large investigations of happy and unhappy marriages have looked into this possibility, with mixed results. Several studies found no relation between similarity and happiness, although one [33] found unstably married couples differed on four traits whereas stably married couples' personalities tended to match. These traits were 'affectothymia' (which means approximately outgoing and warm-hearted), 'surgency' (happy-go-lucky, enthusiastic), 'protension' (suspicious and self-opinionated), and self-sufficiency. It has also been shown that couples whose relationship progressed over a month period resembled each other more in extent of neurotic tendencies.

Research based on personality questionnaires has had very modest success and the same holds for research on similarity of mental health in couples. A recent review [39] of a dozen or so surveys of this sort found that husband and wife tend to share mental illness to some extent and even had the same type of illness, but the effect is quite small; for example, one study found that in 9 couples out of 84 studied in a Canadian clinic, both husband and wife were neurotic, whereas one would have expected only 4 or 5 'concordant' pairs, given the rate of neurosis in the whole sample. A comparable survey, in Croydon, covered 500 established marriages, and found that couples showed some similarity of neurotic tendency, but incidence of actual neurosis was too low for any significant results to emerge. Interestingly enough there was a highly significant similarity of physical health between husband and wife, for women married to men in ill health were twice as likely to have had a physical illness themselves over the last year. Another study of 74 married couples at a psychiatric hospital near Chichester found that in

*A correlation of +0.71; the highest in the study.
†A correlation of +0.43.

31 couples husband and wife had the same diagnosis, twice as many as would be expected by chance. Results like this may be evidence of 'contagion' (one partner 'driving the other mad') or may be a genuine case of like choosing like. The Canadian survey, since it used clinical records, could answer this question by looking back to before the marriage; there was not the slightest similarity of symptoms before the couple came together, which supports the 'contagion' theory. Several surveys made the same point, using an ingenious method based on the reasoning that schizophrenia, especially its severer forms, is partly inherited or, to be precise, a predisposition to it is. If shared schizophrenia draws couples together, there would be similar histories of schizophrenia in both families, whereas if one spouse develops the illness because of the behaviour of the other, it would not occur frequently in both families.

These studies produced little convincing evidence that people choose partners because they share the same psychiatric symptoms. It would be surprising if this did happen actually, for most psychiatric symptoms by their very nature make life difficult for the individual or those around him or her, and neither circumstance is likely to make the person very attractive to others. Similarity of symptoms would only follow from a 'scrap-heap' principle that such people gravitate to each other, because they cannot attract anyone nicer, or perhaps because they meet in psychiatric hospitals and clinics. In fact severe psychiatric illness, like severe mental retardation, tends to prevent men and women getting together at all, as documented in a recent survey [40] of an English psychiatric hospital, where only 18% of the patients showed any sexual interest in each other. It is not surprising, therefore, that marriage rates for schizophrenic patients are low, being 77% of normal rates for women in their early twenties and only 17% for male patients, although men 'catch up' and achieve something nearer normal rates by the age of 40.

The influence of intelligence and ability on choice of a partner are much greater and more in line with those for attitudes. Several early studies [32] found fairly high similarities between the IQs of both partners, and similar results have been obtained in one or two more recent studies. However, it is difficult to identify cause and effect for it is uncertain whether people choose partners on the basis of intelligence, or whether they choose them for some other reason which happens to correlate with it. For example, social class and intelligence correlate to some extent, so the person who conforms with social custom and marries someone of the same social background is incidentally likely to marry someone in the same range of intelligence. Again it might well be a proximity effect, for many marriages are arranged while the couple are at college, which produces an incidental matching of intelligence. Indeed, it is often said patronizingly that American girls go to college to find a husband. Marrying someone met at work is likely again to imply a general similarity of intellect. In fact there is some anecdotal evidence that the intelligence effect is also a proximity effect; for it has been reported [41] that American women, working on the assumption that men do not like clever women, play 'dumb' by, for example, deliberately mis-spelling simple words.* Obviously, if the girl conceals her true character it cannot form a basis for choosing her.

However, there is some evidence that intelligence does play a more positive role in choosing mates, for one early study [42] found a fairly good relationship between the scores of actual couples for reasoning ability,† but a weaker and negative relationship†† for random pairs drawn from the same sample. If the similarity between real pairs were really just a proximity or social class effect, the relationship for random pairs would have been fairly good also. It is in any case obvious that very large differences in intelligence would tend to cause friction and to make communication difficult. There is also evidence of assortative mating at the other end of the spectrum of intelligence, in a study [43] showing that mentally retarded people tended to pair off three times as often as chance would dictate. They also found that where there was a large difference in intelligence — more than thirty points between husband and wife — it was usually the wife who was the more intelligent, and had married 'down'. The opposite was true of social class; men married 'down' and women did not.

One of the popular sayings about mate choice is 'birds of a feather flock together', while the other is 'opposites attract'. A lot of effort has gone into trying to find some empirical evidence for the latter view,

---

*This report dates from 1946 and it may no longer be true. It does not seem to the authors to have much truth in British universities.
†A correlation of +0.34.
††A correlation of −0.11.

associated with the American sociologist Robert Winch [44]. Winch argued, quite plausibly, that people do not always want or need similar mates, or friends for that matter, for surely a dominant man will get on better with a submissive woman, and vice versa, and a 'nurturant' (motherly) woman will get on better with and be appreciated more by a 'succorant' (dependent) man. In an intensive study of 25 newly married couples, Winch found some support for his ideas and claimed his couples tended to have 'complementary needs'. Unfortunately no one else could repeat Winch's findings, although at least a dozen investigations have tried [45]. One study found slight evidence for 'complementary needs' on 4 of the 15 EPPS scales, but only for happily married couples. It has been suggested that Winch's investigation was, in fact, too intensive, because he took so many measures of the couples' needs that, merely on the 'monkeys-and-typewriters' principle, some were bound to show 'complementarity', or as one commentator [45] drily noted: 'Almost any set of data, if sufficiently badgered, can be exhausted into submission.' This eminently sensible theory seems to have been proved wrong, or at least to have failed to have been proved right, for the same reasons that such modest effects of personality similarity have been found, namely the over-general nature of personality trait and measures. What matters in a relationship is not 'dominance' in general but dominance in particular. A dominant wife might want the man to submit to her, but not presumably to everyone else too, nor in fact is she likely to want the man to submit to her on every occasion. She will have rather more specific explanations, which are so far too specific to be detected by the wide trawl of a personality test. This line of reasoning had led to 'role' theories of mate selection which argues that everyone has certain ideas about marriage and about the sort of husband or wife they would like, and that they tend to marry someone who fits this picture. A man who has 'conventional' 'sexist' ideas about marriage will (or should) marry a girl who in turn expects to stay at home, not know what the family income is, take the subordinate role in most decisions and so on. Some interesting illustrative data on 'role' in marriage emerged in an early study [35], where couples agreed on whether the wife should work after marriage and on how many children to have, more closely than on anything else. There is not a lot to be said about this approach, except that it obviously has some truth, that it can supplement approaches based on personality, but also that it is far from invariably true. Many marriages are unsuccessul precisely because the couple do not find out what they expect of each other, or, having realized they differ, suppose that love will see them through. It is not difficult to find what people think about working wives, children, or housework, but it seems to be something that couples do not talk about until the later stages of courtship, if then. Indeed, discussing children and housework is traditionally one of the best ways of discouraging men who are less than wholly enthusiastic about the responsibilities entailed in this side of marriage.

There are all sorts of influences on peoples' choice of partners — proximity, similarity of background, attitudes, and values, as well as personality and ability; obviously they do not all affect peoples' choice at the same time. Closeness affects choice initially, while class, religion, or race often affect choice before the couples meet at all by determining who shall live near or work with whom, while attitudes and personality will come into prominence later and start weeding out relationships that will not last much longer. They will not have an immediate effect, for real encounters are not like most experiments, in that men and women are not presented with a completed attitude inventory or a personality profile of each other before their first date. It takes time to find what someone thinks about a wide range of social and political issues, and there is ample scope for misunderstanding. By the same token it takes still longer to get to know someone's personality, and the possibility of error and distortion is greater still. (Curiously enough all the vast literature on personality and group psychology contains little or nothing on the length of time it takes to get to know someone.) One recent attempt to pull together diverse findings in this field has resulted in the SVR theory of choice, [37] where S stands for 'stimulus', which includes dress, age, occupation, status, and looks, the things one sees before and during the first encounter. Supposing the couple pass through the net of the 'stimulus' filter, they enter the 'value' stage, where they compare attitudes and outlook and should they survive this, the final stage is 'role', where ideas about what to do on their dates, about sexual intimacy match sufficiently, and life-styles in general and married life are compared. This theory is quite sound but could be elaborated somewhat because it seems to omit something included in a 'rival' stage theory [46] — the 'four-spoke wheel' theory in which the first stage is 'rapport'. Appearance, status, and the like are important, but so is what happens on the first date. If the couple do not 'hit it off' or establish 'rapport' they are unlikely to meet again. While 'rapport' no doubt depends a lot on shared similarity of background, it depends ultimately on the social competence of the people involved, for some men and women find it harder to get on with others, often through ignorance of social ritual. The 'role' stage of the SVR theory also seems rather all-embracing, for in some relationships 'role definition' is limited to deciding whether to sleep together or not, and if so 'your place or mine', while in others the whole future of the marriage is mapped out in detail. The rival 'wheel' theory has two later stages — following a 'self-relevation' stage that corresponds roughly to the SVR theory's 'value' stage — namely 'mutual dependency' and 'personality need fulfilment'. The latter becomes relevant only in a longer, more serious relationship.

The most compelling evidence for 'filtering' and the differing importance of different influences at different stages of courtship comes from a study [47] in the early sixties. This study is also interesting because it is one of the few to discover any evidence supporting the principle that 'opposites attract'. The authors of this study looked at couples who had been engaged for either less than 18 months or more than 18 and looked at them twice, initially to give them tests of attitudes and personality, and 6 months later to find out how many now felt 'closer' than before. Value consensus predicted a developing relationship in the group who had known each other less than 18 months, for 78% of those who agreed on standards of 'family success' felt closer, opposed to only 35% of those who agreed less well, but 'value consensus' did not predict increasing closeness for the other group who had known each other for more than 18 months. Instead possession of opposite personality types was found to matter, and a greater proportion of couples who complemented each other's interpersonal needs of dominance or 'inclusion' had drawn closer 6 months later — a relationship that did not hold for the short-term group. This finding is very interesting and has been extensively quoted, for it suggests personality factors will not become important in the first year or even 2 years of a relationship, and that when they do, complementary needs will lead to attraction. Unfortunately, a recent study [48] using a larger sample failed to find any evidence of a dividing line at 1½ year's acquaintance, although they did find some limited evidence that couples opposed in personality prospered.

Early investigations of attraction looked for 'the personality of the popular person', just as early research on leadership searched for 'the personality of the leader'. Modest and unreliable relationships resulted, followed by a change of approach, based on the argument that it was wrong to look for general correlates of popularity or influence. An 'interaction' approach was better because a given person might be popular with some people but not with others, which makes it pointless to look at a person's character in isolation. All depended on the other person, hence the emphasis on similarity and 'complementarity', which still dominates thinking in the area. However, it now looks that the similarity and complementarity approaches are themselves over-simplified.

Thus a recent study [49] obtained data on intimacy and attraction, which appeared to have yielded a typically weak proof on the similarity theory, but on closer inspection it turned out that what was really happening was that people who had low scores for intimacy were unpopular, but that there were enough cases of highly 'intimate' people choosing − as everyone tended to − other 'intimate'* people, to make it look on a superficial analysis that choices were based on similarity. Actually several other studies [50] around the same time rebelled against the similarity approach, and produced similar evidence. It is not surprising to learn that everyone, regardless of his or her own character, wants friends who are sincere, trustworthy, and honest. Another study showed that people who are 'cognitively simple' − who see others in simple 'black and white' terms − like others who do the same, whereas 'cognitively complex' people do not insist on 'complex' friends; as one might expect from people who have more detailed and elaborated sets of ideas about other people and the social world generally, they accept people as friends regardless of their 'complexity'. Perhaps the most important experiments are two [51] using the Eysenck Personality Inventory, which measures only two very general aspects of behaviour − 'extroversion', which is a mixture of sociability and impulsiveness, and

---

*The author of the study does not explain what he means by 'intimate' apart from saying that low scorers are 'cold fish'.

'neuroticism', meaning roughly anxiousness, or personal (instability). One study found that everyone, including introverts, tended to like extroverted people, while the other [52] found that everyone tended to avoid people with neurotic tendencies, even other neurotics.

What is the significance of these results? One can say things like, 'neurotic and introverts are less popular than stable and extroverted people' while bearing in mind, of course, that correlations are quite modest. Most psychologists would tend to shy away from saying anything of the sort, from a feeling that it is somehow unfair to the unpopular people, and in fact some of the appeal of the 'interaction' approach to attraction was undoubtedly the idea that there is a suitable mate or friend for everyone. This may be true, but unfortunately it seems that there are rather more potential mates, dates, or friends for some people than for others.

People are attractive because they have pleasant personalities, opinions in common, have the same background, are physically presentable, live nearby, and, as George Orwell said, have the warm inner glow only *money* gives. The more people lack these assets, the less attractive they are, a proposition that is the basis of *social exchange theory* [53]. People want as dates and mates the most 'rewarding' others they can get, not in itself a very profound or original thought; the interest of social exchange theory is that it argues that all the miscellaneous factors leading to or detracting from attractiveness can be brought together under a single heading of rewards and costs, reduced to a single coinage and hence compared in the same scales. A very unattractive man can compensate for his appearance by a nice personality or by being rich. One can explain why a man *does* cross New York or London to meet a girl, by pointing out that she is an exceptionally attractive girl who, moreover, dispenses sexual favours not available locally. It is possible in effect to draw up a balance sheet for every relationship and predict if it will last; if not who will break it off, and who else they will choose instead. However, there are one or two snags or complications in this apparently neat scheme. It is often said 'Beauty is in the eye of the beholder', and while this is not entirely true and there is considerable agreement on who is and is not nice looking, there is also a lot of room for idiosyncrasies. Thus one cannot say with absolute certainty that a beautiful girl is equally 'rewarding' to every man, and the same goes for the other entries on the balance sheet. Similarity of opinions matters less to people with great self-confidence, or — probably — to those with no opinions much of their own.

All this boils down to saying that rewards are subjective and exist in the eye of the beholder and hence vary from person to person. This in turn makes it difficult to draw up the sort of social balance sheets envisaged by the theory, and in fact no one has devised a way of actually measuring rewards and costs in a relationship so as to make predictions about its future course. Evidence for the theory derives from wisdom after the event, saying, for example, that a relationship that broke up had ceased to be sufficiently rewarding to one or both of those involved, whereas one that is flourishing is still in the black. Critics rightly consider this is unimpressive as support for the theory.

There is another, subtler limitation to social exchange theory. It draws a simple analogy between economics and social life, which falls down precisely because people do not usually see their social relations that way. A businessman who tells A that he will buy B's services because they are cheaper and better than A's is simply doing his job, but what would people think of a man who told a girl that he would stop going out with her and take up with her friend who was more interesting, nicer looking, and more likely to have intercourse with him? And what would his new girl friend think of this explanation? Of course some men (and women) do *think* this way, but they do not usually say so. People who ditch their friends and lovers as soon as they cease to be 'useful' get a bad reputation, because while we may in fact order our relations in a quasi-economic manner, it is bad manners to be seen too obviously to do so. There is an element of commitment in friendship and dating that is ignored in the economic analogy. In social exchange terms it may be costly to terminate a relationship, even if it has ceased to be rewarding, because of the upset involved and because it gets the person concerned a bad name.

R E F E R E N C E S

1. J. H. S. Bossard (1932) Residential propinquity as a factor in marriage selection. *Am. J. Sociol.* **38**, 219–24.
2. W. R. Cotton and R. Smircich (1964) A comparison of mathematical models for the effect of residential propinquity on mate selection. *Am. sociol. Rev.* **29**, 522–9.

3. D. A. Pond, A. Ryle and M. Hamilton (1963) Marriage and neurosis in a working class population. *Br. J. Psychiat.* **109**, 592–8.
4. G. A. Harrison, R. W. Hiorns and C. F. Kuchemann (1971) Social class and marriage patterns in some Oxfordshire populations. *J. biosoc. Sci.* **3**, 1–12.
5. R. B. Zajonc (1970) Brainwash: familiarity breeds contempt. *Psychol. Today.*
6. L. S. Kubie (1956) Psychoanalysis and marriage, in V. W. Eisenstein (ed.), *Neurotic interaction in marriage*, Basic Books, New York.
7. W. D. Commins (1932) Marriage age of eldest sons. *J. soc. Psychol.* **3**, 487–90.
8. T. D. Kemper (1966) Mate selection and marital satisfaction according to sibling type of husband and wife. *J. Marr. Fam.* **28**, 346–9.
9. A. Mangus (1936) Relation between the young woman's conceptions of her intimate male associates and of her ideal husband. *J. soc. Psychol.* **7**, 403–20.
10. N. Lukianowicz (1972) Incest. *Br. J. Psychiat.* **120**, 301–13, and D. Lester (1972) Incest. *J. sex Res.* **8**, 268–85.
11. Y. Talmon (1964) Mate selection in collective settlements. *Am. sociol. Rev.* **29**, 491–508.
12. J. Shepher (1971) Mate selection among second generation kibbutz adolescents and adults: incest avoidance and negative imprinting. *Arch. sex Beh.* **1**, 293–307
13. A. P. Wolf (1968) Adopt a daughter-in-law, marry a sister: a Chinese solution to the problem of the incest taboo. *Am. Anthropol.* **70**, 864–74.
14. D. S. Sade (1968) Inhibition of son–mother mating among free-ranging rhesus monkeys. *Sci. Psychoanal.* **7**, 18–35.
15. R. J. Kennedy (1944) Single or triple melting pot? Intermarriage trends in New Haven 1870–1940. *Am. J. Sociol.* **39**, 331–9.
16. T. P. Monaghan (1969) Are interracial marriages really less stable? *Soc. For.* **48**, 461–7.
17. E. W. Burgess and P. Wallin (1953) *Engagement and marriage*, Lippincott, Chicago.
18. R. Hassan and G. Benjamin (1973) Ethnic outmarriage rates in Singapore. *J. Marr. Fam.* **35**, 731–8.
19. C. A. Price and J. Zubrzycki (1962) Immigrant marriage patterns in *Australia. Pop. Stud.* **16**, 123–33.
20. R. K. Kelsall, A. Poole and A. Kahn (1971) Marriage and family building patterns of university graduates. *J. biosoc. Sci.* **3**, 281–7.
21. L. Terman (1938) *Psychological factors in marital happiness*, McGraw-Hill, New York.
22. D. Byrne (1969) Attitudes and attraction, in L. Berkowitz (ed.), *Advances in Experimental Social Psychology*, vol. 4, Academic, New York.
23. D. Byrne *et al.* (1970) Continuity between the experimental study of attraction and 'real life' computer dating. *J. pers. soc. Psychol.* **16**, 57–65.
24. G. Levinger (1972) Little sand box and big quarry: comments on Byrne's paradigmatic spade for research on interpersonal attraction. *Rep res. soc. Psychol.* **3**, 3–18.
25. R. Centers (1975) Attitude similarity–dissimilarity as a correlate of heterosexual attraction and love. *J. Marr. Fam.* **37**, 305–14.
26. G. L. Clore and B. Baldridge (1968) Interpersonal attraction: the role of agreement and topic agreement. *J. pers. soc. Psychol.* **9**, 340–6.

27. M. Useem (1972) Ideological and interpersonal change in the Radical Protest Movement. *Soc. Prob.* **19**, 451–9.
28. R. B. Zajonc (1968) Cognitive theories in social psychology, in G. Lindzey and E. Aronson (eds.), *Handbook of social psychology*, vol. 1, Addison-Wesley, Reading, Mass.
29. L. E. Hewitt (1958) Student perceptions of traits desired in themselves as dating and marriage partners. *Marr. Fam. Liv.* **20**, 344–9.
30. M. Gordon and M. C. Bernstein (1970) Mate choice and domestic life in the nineteenth century marriage manual. *J. Marr. Fam.* **32**, 665–74.
31. E. Slater and M. Woodside (1951) *Patterns of marriage*, Cassell, London.
32. H. N. Richardson (1939) Studies of mental resemblance between husbands and wives and between friends. *Psychol. Bull.* **36**, 104–20.
33. R. B. Cattell and J. R. Nesselroade (1967) Likeness and completeness theories examined by sixteen personality factor measures on stably and unstably married couples. *J. pers. soc. Psychol.* **4**, 351–61.
34. B. I. Murstein (1967) The relationship of mental health to marital choice and courtship progress. *J. Marr. Fam.* **29**, 447–51, and B. H. Yom, I. A. Kraft, P. E. Bradley, J. A. Wakefield, E. B. Doughtie and J. A. Cox (1975) A common factor in the MMPI scales of married couples. *J. Pers. Ass.* **39**, 64–9.
35. E. W. Burgess and P. Wallin (1953) *Engagement and marriage*, Lippincott, Philadelphia.
36. G. Shipman (1960) Speech thresholds and voice tolerance in marital interaction. *Marr. Fam. Liv.* **22**, 203–9.
37. B. I. Murstein (1970) Stimulus–value–role: a theory of marital choice. *J. Marr. Fam.* **32**, 465–81.
38. R. Centers (1972) The completion hypothesis and the compensatory dynamic in intersexual attraction and love. *J. Psychol.* **82**, 111–26.
39. M. A. Crago (1972) Psychopathology in married couples. *Psychol. Bull.* **77**, 114–28
40. R. Morgan and J. Rogers (1971) Some results of the policy of integrating men and women patients in a mental hospital. *Soc. Psychiat.* **6**, 113–16.
41. M. Komarovsky (1946) Cultural contradictions in sex roles. *Am. J. Sociol.* **52**, 184–7.
42. B. Schiller (1932) A quantitative analysis of marriage selection in a small group. *J. soc. Psychol.* **3**, 297–319.
43. E. W. Reed and S. C. Reed (1965) *Mental retardation: a family study*, Saunders, Philadelphia.
44. R. F. Winch (1958) *Mate selection*, Harper, New York.
45. R. G. Tharp (1963) Psychological patterning in marriage. *Psychol. Bull.* **60**, 97–117.
46. I. L. Reiss (1960) Towards a sociology of the heterosexual love relationship. *Marr. Fam. Liv.* **22**, 139–45.
47. A. C. Kerckhoff and K. E. Davis (1962) Value consensus and need complementarity and in mate selection. *Am. sociol. Rev.* **27**, 295–303.
48. G. Levinger *et al.* (1970) Progress towards permanence in courtship: a test of the Kerckhoff–Davis hypothesis. *Sociometry*, **33**, 427–43.
49. P. H. Wright (1968) Need similarity, need complementarity and the place of personality in interpersonal attraction. *J. exp. pers. Res.* **3**, 126–35.

50. S. Johnston and R. Centers (1973) Cognitive systematization and interpersonal attraction. *J. soc. Psychol.* **90**, 95–104.
51. C. Hendrick and S. R. Brown (1971) Introversion, extraversion and interpersonal attraction. *J. pers. soc. Psychol.* **20**, 31–5.
52. P. G. Banikiotes *et al.* (1972) Interpersonal attraction in simulated and real interactions. *J. pers. soc. Psychol.* **23**, 1–7.
53. J. W. Thibaut and H. H. Kelley (1959) *The social psychology of groups*, Wiley, New York.

Chapter 7

TAKE A LOOK AT YOURSELF

The attitudes of modern consumer societies to a person's physical appearance are creating more and more problems for those who feel they cannot compete with those who are better endowed physically. Because looks are so prized (see chapters 2 and 3), many people tend to place the blame on their physical appearance when their sexual and social lives begin to go wrong. A whole new field of psychiatry has grown up to cope with people whose image of their own bodies prevents them from leading normal, happy lives. Many people with this condition seek expensive plastic surgery to help them. The idea that such people are weak-willed or seriously disturbed in psychiatric terms is treated at some length by examining various real-life case histories. The conclusions is that there is little evidence of personality disturbance in such people; plastic surgery is often an immediate and lasting solution to their problems. They are simply victims of the tendency to glamorize physical appearance and to encourage people to believe that it is eminently desirable.

Appearance is important in our everyday social lives and no one should underestimate the value of good looks. But general awareness of their significance causes problems for many people who do not possess them (or feel that they do not). They can become depressed, display bizarre nervous symptoms, and often they seek physical remedies such as plastic surgery. This chapter is about such people and about how the general preoccupation of our society with outward appearance can drive an underprivileged section quietly mad.

It goes without saying that we do not see ourselves quite as others see us. We have an image of ourselves ('self-image') and of our bodies ('body image'), and these two affect each other in a curious way. Sometimes we can become aware of the interplay when we dress up or have our hair cut in a way that suits us. In these cases it is easy to understand the old advertising maxim of 'look good — feel good'. At other times, it is possible to notice the reversal 'Feel good — look good' when being in a good mood can alter our perception of even our own most crooked facial feature. Kathrin Perutz expresses both these feelings in her book *Beyond the looking glass* [1]. Commenting on her own image in the mirror she says:

> 'On a good day, I can see dark brown eyes, long lashes, a sensual mouth, smooth skin and an endearing nose. On a bad day these are eclipsed and only the bags under my eyes, wrinkles, kinky hair, fat lips and pug nose are visible. On a terrible day, there's almost nothing to see at all except a blur of indefensible humanity as I avert my gaze. And on a glorious day, the beautiful eyes hold me, full of love, humour and intelligence' [p. 173].

Oscar Wilde said that 'To love oneself is the beginning of a life-long romance', but it would appear the courting of our own appearance is a turbulent affair. Many people are quite admiring of their own intelligence, flair, and lack of prejudice, but it seems that most of us display extraordinary modesty when listing the worth of our physical attributes. It may be that under constant pressure from advertisers to look better, there is a tendency for people to set their sights too high. There can be little doubt, as argued in Chapter 2, that there is a general awareness of what the ideal physical appearance should be. However, most people will state that unfortunately the ideal and the appearance they are aware of having are very far apart. Perhaps it is this apparent discrepancy that can make many people certain that those possessing the ideal appearance are also endowed with personal qualities which presumably they themselves would like to have. Thus, when groups of overweight, underweight, and normal weight men were shown silhouettes of fat, thin, and normal male bodies, all of them wanted to look like the normal [2]. All the men, regardless of their own weight, saw such a body as belonging to someone who is active, energetic, and dominant as opposed to the fat and thin silhouettes which they imagined belonged to men who were withdrawn, shy, and dependent. Even children seem to think in the same way.

Satisfaction with our bodies can be defined as the extent to which our perceived actual body deviates from our personal ideal. This was seen when men and women were given a list of body characteristics and asked to rate what they thought of the appearance of these characteristics of their own body; they were also asked to put the characteristics in the order they felt was important for determining how physically attractive they themselves were [3]. The list of characteristics is given in Table 7.1. Finally, all the men and women were required to describe themselves by choosing appropriate adjectives from a list. From this

TABLE 7.1. THE 24 BODY CHARACTERISTICS SELECTED FOR A STUDY OF BODY SATISFACTION AMONG MEN AND WOMEN

Facial complexion	Hips
Ears	Shoulder width
Chest	Mouth
Profile	Neck
Weight distribution	Teeth
Eyes	Nose
Height	Chin
Ankles	Hair texture
Waist	Body build
Arms	Hair colour
Shape of legs	Thighs
General appearance	Face

investigation it was seen that the ways in which people described themselves were related directly to the satisfaction they had with their appearance. Thus, those who had a more favourable image of themselves showed also that they were more satisfied with their bodies. The relationship was slightly greater for women than for men. It was also found that satisfaction with certain body characteristics was more important for self-image than satisfaction with other characteristics. Again, there were slight differences between men and women in this respect, and the two lists of the most important body characteristics in producing favourable self-image are reproduced in Table 7.2.

TABLE 7.2. THE MOST IMPORTANT BODY
CHARACTERISTICS FOR DETERMINING
SELF IMAGE IN MEN AND WOMEN GIVEN
IN THEIR ORDER OF SIGNIFICANCE

Men	Women
Facial complexion	Body build
Hair texture	General appearance
Nose	Profile
Face	Hips
Shape of legs	Thighs
Distribution of weight	Ankles
Body build	Face
Teeth	Distribution of weight
Waist	Chest
Thighs	Waist
	Eyes
	Hair colour
	Facial complexion
	Chin
	Height
	Nose

The study just reported suggested that those having the greater satisfactions with their bodies had the more favourable image of their personalities. The satisfaction that people have with their bodies comes to a great extent from how they imagine other people see them as physical beings. But is this latter information likely to be correct in most people's minds, do we really have an accurate picture of how others see us? Recent work suggests we do not and, most interestingly, it points out that deep down we may be far from optimistic about the favourableness of others' opinions about us. Children and adolescents were asked to rank photographs of their classmates separately by sex from most to least physically attractive [4]. Every photograph was 5 inches by 7 inches, black and white, showing the whole body, and all the raters were also asked to rank a photograph of themselves which was included with those of classmates of their own sex. Each person was then asked how he thought his classmates as a group would rank his picture. From this it was clear that a person's own estimate of how he ranks physically was closely related to how he expected his classmates to rate him. This was true for both sexes. However, neither the self-ranking nor the estimate were related to a significant degree with the *actual* rankings given by classmates. Estimates were almost always lower, and among fifth-grade girls, for instance, three-quarters ranked themselves as the least physically attractive girl in their class. According to the author the girls when interviewed claimed that their self-ratings were not due to modesty. It appears that although they were attractive by others' standards they emphasized deficiencies in their appearance which others did not. It could be that they do so because they judge themselves more than they judge others around them by the ideal standards set in films and advertisements. There is evidence, too, that this tendency affects women more than men. Another investigation [5] explored the discrepancy between a group of American women's real size and what they each considered ideal size. It was found here that the self-rated ideal size for body weight, waist, and hips was significantly *smaller* than the average measured size of those parts, whereas the ideal bust measurement was larger than the average bust measurement of all the women. A man's weak spot, in the same respect, would appear to be his height. Men who were surveyed believed in general that the ideal male height was taller than their own. Many men who mentioned this fact also felt that willpower, intellectual distance, sexual strength, and protectiveness were the ideal qualities in a husband. A good number of these seemed to seek symbolic expression of their ideal by choosing to be engaged or married to partners who were a great deal smaller than the partners other men of their height chose. The conclusions must be that many men and women have a clear image of an ideal physical appearance which is beyond reach of their own and it would not be surprising if, in some cases, anxiety and insecurity were to develop as a result of this.

A straightforward expectation might be that those whose appearance deviated most from what is regarded as ideal, would be prone to the greatest anxiety and insecurity feelings. It would be wrong to believe this, however, because society seems willing to excuse the physical appearance of certain categories of people on condition that they will pay the price of being typecast according to their attributes. Erving Goffman has dealt sympathetically with many such examples in his book *Stigma* [6] which looks at physically and otherwise unattractive people who are 'disqualified from full social acceptance'. Clear cases of such stigma are men who are well below average height. As a result of society's general admiration for male height and the expectation that a man should be taller than his partner, such men are almost always prevented from enjoying normal lives. They need not be outcasts, however, for it is open to them to play the traditional roles of 'jesters' and 'favourites of well-to-do ladies'. Goffman sees this as small men impersonating small men. It is no wonder that short persons choose an alternative when they can and it has been noted that the sequence of a short person meeting a short person of the opposite sex — dating, going steady, getting engaged, and marrying — is often urgently accelerated. In fact, three or more of these steps may occur in the span of a 5-day 'Little People's Association' convention period [7]. Short people marry other short people because they find an opportunity at last, but also because they are expected to. A recent German survey [8] found that healthy people supposed that people disfigured by skin complaints would be as attracted to someone with such a complaint as to someone without, although of course the healthy people generally expressed themselves as feeling repelled by skin diseases. Their attitude seemed to be 'I don't care for it myself, but of course it's different for them'.

Others may also be forced to play clear roles as a result of their physical appearance. For example, men with a genetic condition, known as Klinefelter's syndrome, have bodies which do not show signs of normal male development. The onset of puberty is late, they have small penises, small sterile testes, and may even grow breasts. Although such men often do not feel they are women, their unattractiveness to that sex and their rejection by men usually forces them to adopt exhibitionistic effeminate roles and even to become overt homosexuals.

These three examples have been deliberately chosen because they illustrate clearly how very unusual physical appearance can prevent people from leading normal happy lives and how the individuals concerned can usually cope with this situation by living out expected roles. Those for whom no clear roles are prescribed are the ones most in danger of lapsing into depression and even psychosis as a result of their physical appearance. A study of a typical American State College has revealed just how common this problem is. There the dominant campus values appear to be social and recreational similar to those of the high school the students have just left. The first and foremost value is reported to be physical attractiveness followed by 'sophistication', demonstrated ability to date high-prestige members of the opposite sex, membership of a fraternity or seniority, holding elective student positions, and being able to dance well. In such circumstances, physical attractiveness seems to be the basic determinant both of campus success and of the self-image which the students carry with them in their interactions with others. When those students developing the most severe emotional disturbances are examined, they are found to have certain characteristics in common. Many of them earn high grades but they also tend to be physically unattractive, 'repulsive in some cases', and 'lacking any social grace'.

Here are examples of case reports of students listing their attractiveness and their reasons for interview [9].

Case A. Male.
Complexion red and irritated.
Inferiority feelings. Cannot bear criticism. Has withdrawn from social life.

Case B. Male.
Small, slight, unprepossessing. Hesitant, awkward gait.
Butt of campus jokes. Has contemplated suicide.

Case C. Male.
Long history of being overweight. Gross, ungainly appearance.
Absolute reject in courtship competition. Indulges in constant self-disparagement.

Case D. Male.
Short, rotund. Wears glasses. Feminine walk. Extreme neurotic.
Marked inferiority feelings. Depressed. Has contemplated suicide.

Case E. Male.
Tall, thin. Acne. Worn glasses since childhood. Stammers.
Extreme withdrawal during depressions. Doubts own masculinity.
Has severe inferiority feelings. Believes girls ridicule him.

Case F. Female.
Thyroid condition. Gross, lumpy features.
Feels unwanted. Looks over shoulder when walking to make sure no one is talking about her. Cannot concentrate or sleep. Regards self as abject failure — constantly refers to self as 'a drip'. Suicidal.

Case G. Female.
Overweight. Weak eyes. Unprepossessing appearance.
Extremely sensitive about size. 'If I could lose thirty or forty pounds, I would be acceptable socially'. Cries to excess. Lacks confidence. Marked suicidal trend.

It will be noticed how in each of these cases a damaged self-image is central. There is a tendency for most of the neurotic boys' conflicts to be channelled into despair of not being handsome and virile; the girls are mortified because they are not beautiful, shapely, and charming. In such cases any orthodox form of treatment such as psychotherapy is of little use for the dominant value of physical attractiveness is overpowering. 'When one's personal conviction of inferiority and worthlessness are being constantly *and objectively* reaffirmed in social interaction', say the authors of this study, 'steps should be taken to change that specific area of interaction as far as possible.' In other words, put the students in an environment where other values are more important than physical attractiveness. But where might such an environment easily be found, for the campus is surely a microcosm of the world outside?

The conduct of the very short, the effeminate, and the very ugly is perhaps easy to understand. The image they have of their own bodies is not greatly distorted they *are* disqualified from full social acceptance and discriminated against by reason of their appearance. Less obvious are cases where people of normal appearance misperceive their own bodies to such an extent that they may take drastic steps to alter their looks. Clear examples of this are certain teenage girls who suffer from a condition termed *anorexia nervosa*. In anorexia the refusal to eat is so absolute that the girl (19 out of 20 cases are girls) eventually wastes away to skin and bone, and if treatment is unsuccessful she may die. Of course, anorexia is a label describing symptoms which may have different causes in different girls. One explanation is that, initially, anorexia is rooted in a desire the girl has to be attractive — in fact, one of its symptoms is that cases of anorexia often believe that by starving themselves they will become more appealing. The affliction takes a fairly predictable course. A girl sustains a strenuous diet, often not eating anything during the course of several days, but she is able to hide her thinness by wearing loose-fitting clothes. Many girls who develop anorexia in their teens were generally plump children who began sexual maturation as young as 9, 10, or 11. According to some theories, teasing about their fatness which they experienced in late childhood becomes linked in their minds with the emotional stresses of early adolescence. They imagine that if they become thin these stresses will be eased and at the same time they will become attractive to the opposite sex. However, what tends to happen is that by losing weight a girl with anorexia loses also the signs of her sexual maturity; her breasts disappear and her menstrual periods cease. Recent research has shown that the hormonal make-up of a girl who is severely afflicted by anorexia reverts to that of a pre-adolescent girl. Thus the girl who starves herself eventually solves her problems of attractiveness by diminishing her appeal to men but at the same time attaining a state of a sexuality in which she may be aware of this but ceases to care.

While many adolescent girls become pathologically concerned about their weight, adolescent men often focus their personal dissatisfactions on another part of their body — their penis. Real or imagined smallness of the penis is an important and rarely discussed feature of male body-image. As a result of a mistaken but common supposition (primarily among men) that the larger a man's penis the better he is as a lover, many men blame the unhappiness of their sexual and emotional lives on the inadequacy of their own genitals. Thus, psychiatric case histories contain notes such as the following.

Case 6. A married woman, aged 23 years, complained of marked depression. She explained that her husband was angered by a frigidity from which she had suffered since marrying at the age of 16 years. He attributed her present frigidity to the supposed small size of his penis, about which he complained bitterly. He had rendered her life a misery by his extreme sexual jealously. He had purchased an Alsatian dog to keep other men away from the house. The dog was so savage that it eventually throttled itself by its own lead as it attempted to jump over a fence to attack a passer-by. The husband insisted on doing all the shopping himself to prevent her having a clandestine meeting with a paramour. She stated that they had both had extra-marital liaisons. The patient did not herself complain that her husband's penis was too small [10].

This is clearly an instance where a man had developed a morbid sexual jealousy because of his conviction that he had a small penis and was therefore an incompetent lover. Many men say they developed such a (mistaken) conviction as a result of teasing by others in the showers after a football match, or by noting the size of sex organs illustrated in pornographic magazines. The point to note is that their body-image then becomes a focus for the dissatisfaction they feel in their self-image. This is an important point and it will be returned to many times in the remainder of the present chapter.

The $64 question for these professionally concerned with correcting a distorted body-image is how to deal with a discontent that has clearly become so great that the sufferer is forced to ask for professional advice. Will it help the man who is convinced of the smallness of his penis to be told that he is wrong and be offered analysis of his emotional problems? Would it be better to offer him a silicone implant in his sex organ so that he has the confidence that he is as well endowed physically as any other man? It is important to appreciate the stark contrast of these two positions when evaluating the modern trend to cosmetic surgery as a therapy for afflictions that seem to be based on appearance. Might it be that when men and women ask for their noses to be straightened or their faces to be reshaped, they, too, are focusing their discontentments on a feature of their body and magnifying its significance out of all proportion? Let us look at the evidence.

Modern advertising methods often put pressure on men and women to demand alterations in their appearance, and in recent years the public have come to accept all kinds of aids to doing so and all kinds of claims for their success. The back pages of women's magazines are filled with advertisements for pills, hormone creams and exercises to enlarge the breasts; men's magazines contain advertisements offering antidotes to falling hair. Even if these are ignored few can have failed to notice that the most admired women are rarely flat-chested even if a few well-liked men are bald. (The two most famous bald film stars are *totally* bald, making it obvious that some of the hair loss is voluntary, and possibly leaving people with the idea they could grow it back if they chose.) As a result of such pressure, it is not surprising that many of the flat-chested and the balding join others with crooked noses, scars, or other deformities in seeking surgical help. But not everyone who suffers in these ways does come forward, and it would be interesting to know if those who do constitute a special group whose inability to cope with their unattractiveness represents a deeper psychiatric disturbance.

There have been a number of psychiatric studies made of those who seek plastic surgery, but two in particular will be examined here. These two are interesting because they were conducted on different sides of the Atlantic, in Britain and America, and because both of them involved a scrutiny of patients who had minimal deformities (or, in certain opinions, no deformity at all). The American study [11] indicates that the great majority of patients are women (83 out of 98 people interviewed) and that 77% of the patients were 40 years of age or under. The great majority are in the age group 20—40 year age groups. Both reports agree on the same fact. Most of the patients are severely psychiatrically disturbed; 70% of the American patients were assigned a psychiatric diagnosis even by conservative criteria, and all of the British sample were said to be psychologically disturbed. It is easy to see this if one reads the following abbreviated case history of one of the British patients [12].

Case 56. Mr. N, a painter and decorator aged 23, complained about the appearance of his mouth and requested cosmetic surgery. When he was 17 he dressed up to go out one evening and his younger sister commented: 'You look very nice but you have got a small mouth.' This comment triggered off much rumination and self-examination. He studied himself in the mirror and agreed his mouth was small. He kept comparing himself with other people and became more and more preoccupied. 'I thought of nothing else.' He became self-conscious and embarrassed meeting people, particularly girls . . . . 'I held my mouth so that it might look wider, tried to pull my ears back and my mouth up at the corners.' Eventually he took an overdose and was admitted to hospital.

Diagnosis: sensitive personality disorder . . . . His concern about himself was an overvalued idea and he could not be reassured.

If the majority of plastic surgery patients are suffering from psychiatric disturbances as these studies suggest, there is also a uniformity in the choices they make for alteration. Certain parts of the body, such as eyes, nose, breasts, and genitalia, have cropped up over and over again and also those seeking alterations to one area rather than another have been studied to see if they are uniform in age, background, or any other respect. Two examples, plastic surgery of the nose and enlargement of the female breasts, will be selected here for particular attention.

The nose is God's gift to psychoanalysts for it is extraordinarily useful as an example of phallic symbolism. In one way it can be seen as a surrogate of the male penis and in another it can be taken as resembling the vagina. The fact that it drips, and be touched, picked, and blown into a handkerchief has given rise to no end of speculation in psychoanalytic literature. Thus:

'At no time within her memory has she indulged in either clitorial or vaginal masturbation. She experienced pleasurable general bodily sensations but these never included the genital area. Her nose picking, always done in secret, was accompanied by pleasurable sensations and a 'feeling of gratification'. On occasions she attempted to suppress or limit her 'urge' to pick . . . . Evidently nose-picking was a masturbatory equivalent.' [13]

Because of this background, many psychiatrists have paid special attention to those seeking attention to their noses. An American investigation [14] of 26 adolescent cases reports that 22 of these were girls and 12 were Jewish. In 10 of the 26 cases the father was separated from the family (by death, divorce, or legal separation). In the cases where the father was still at home he was often described as distant and cold. Mothers were frequently seen as overprotective and unstable. There was some evidence that the girls identified with their fathers' personalities and temperaments. A British investigation [15] of 44 people who sought plastic surgery to the nose notes that 20 of them were men and 24 were women; 34 of them were under 30 and 11 were over 30. This study also remarks that there was no evidence to show that the less disfigured men and women suffered from the greatest disturbances. There were no differences between the sexes either on the psychological tests they were given or with regard to the psychiatric diagnosis made of them. Because of the emphasis often given to identification with one or other parent as playing an important role in unconscious reasons behind requests for nasal operations, note was taken of this in the 45 patients interviewed. Here, 28 of the patients had no conscious identification, 7 identified with their mother, 8 with their father, and 2 with other members of their family.

In the opinion of many psychiatrists, to offer surgery to most of the cases mentioned in these two studies would be quite wrong. The dissatisfaction with the nose is seen as symbolizing a greater psychological disturbance on the part of the patient; it is regarded as a symptom of his affliction and not as a cause of it. Yet when many of the patients are asked how they feel about the operation at intervals afterwards (and for periods up to 10 years) their replies are almost always favourable [16]. They nearly all say, (1) they would seek surgery again, (2) they felt less inhibited after surgery, (3) they gained social confidence. It would seem that such markedly sensitive people as come forward will be helped in their total adjustment and their interpersonal relationships by removal of the source of an over-valued idea about their appearance; even surgery on a minimally disfigured patient can be strikingly beneficial. The moral is that many psychiatrists miss the most obvious reasons why the nose should be so important to such people. No matter its size or shape, it is in full view, ever present and cannot be covered or obscured. A person obsessed with the size and shape of the nose is particularly vulnerable because of its conspicuousness and its importance in determining the appearance of the face frontally and in profile. Cultural expectations are that men should have large noses and women small, thus there is added to the consideration of beauty one of sexual identification. There is no unconscious mystery about either of these two facts. This opinion is supported if case histories of men and woman seeking nasal cosmetic operations are examined. Physical and sexual attraction appear as dominant reasons again and again, thus:

'   . . . Two years previously, he had become seriously interested in a girl who apparently liked him. He contemplated asking her to marry him; but felt he would be unacceptable on account of his nose. He broke off with the girl and retreated to a lonely solitary life' [16].

In other cases where sexual and physical reasons are not given other equally valid ones are. Many Jewish patients wish to alter their noses in an attempt to be considered as individuals and not as members of an ethnic group.

Even more than has been written about the psychological significance of noses has been written about the female breasts and the desire of many women to have their own enlarged. Again, it is the psychoanalytically oriented theorists who have had most to say. A commonly expressed view is that women who seek breast enlargement in adulthood have had their early relationships with their mothers disrupted in some way and the psychological work of identification normally done in childhood was not accomplished. Insufficiencies in the completion of this identification contributed to lifelong doubts about their own feminity and the ability to become a whole woman. By seeking to enlarge their breasts they are seeking a reunion with their mother through narcissistic identification because the full breast is a symbol of their mother. Their own breasts, previously insufficient, are now able to give them the feminine self-esteem their mothers had not.

Studies of women who do seek to have their breasts enlarged do support the above analysis in certain respects. Most reports agree that the woman who comes forward tends to be aged around 33 years, white, Protestant, middle class, and married with one or more children. Some accounts stress that these women are going through a period of adjustment at the time when they present themselves as candidates for surgery. They frequently are seen just prior to, or subsequent to, divorce or separation from their husbands, and it is not unusual for a woman to request the procedure immediately prior to marriage. In terms of psychoanalytic theory, these adjustments might bring to a head the lifelong doubts referred to above about their abilities to become a whole woman. One account [17] examines the childhood history of 26 patients and reveals that 'only 1 patient of 26 was evaluated by both psychiatrists to have a reasonably secure and happy childhood experience'. This is supported by evidence that in 3 cases their mother had died before they were 10, in 5 cases their parents had been divorced before or around adolescence, in 16 cases they had alcoholic, paranoid, or otherwise grossly disturbed fathers, and in 16 cases they had anxious depressed mothers who overtly or subtly rejected them. However, even in the light of these facts, the psychiatrists and plastic surgeons are faced by a dilemma. As two of those directly involved have said:

> 'Partly as a result of exposure to advertising propaganda and questionable publicity, many physically normal women develop an almost paralysing self-consciousness focused on the feeling that they do not have the correct sized bosom. Whether one views them as the victims of the attitudes of a cross society, or as uniquely distorted character problems in a psychiatric sense, none the less, their lives and often the lives of their husbands and families are made miserable by the development of such conflicts' [Ref 17, 279].

Under the circumstances most surgeons will operate if they can be sure that the women really wants to have the enlargement for herself and not just because her husband or a friend advised her so. Follow-up studies made of women who do have breast enlargements are uniformly encouraging. Many women report that their sex lives are happier, their interpersonal and marital relationships improve, and they feel generally less inhibited. One account mentions that: 'Even in cases where the psychiatrist was highly sceptical at first that any physical procedure could provide even temporary help, to say nothing of more lasting personality changes, excellent results were observed' [18].

Once more it is possible to see a patient's physical aberrations as causes of the disorder and not as symptoms of a deep underlying conscious need, for when the 'symptoms' (small breasts) are treated the course of the individual's life is often changed. Again the moral is that one can be 'too clever' in trying to deal with personal problems. It is probable that well-dressed young middle-class women turn up for surgery because they can both afford it and because they also feel that if large-breasted women are desirable as the magazines say, now is the time to inject some extra physical attraction when their other charms are fading slightly. This latter consideration would be particularly important for women recently divorced who presumably wanted to marry again soon. Some psychiatrists make a lot of the fact that it is women who have had children who request breast enlargement. They mention here that large breasts may be an attempt by such women to maintain the femine-fulfilling role of pregnancy because their new breasts will remind them of milk-filled ones. But it would be simpler to say here that women at this age often feel for the first time self-assured enough to go to a surgeon with their lifelong problem. It is mentioned that many adult women would have preferred to have their breasts enlarged as adolescents but were too embarrassed to request it, or had fears that they might be admonished by their families.

These two examples, the nose and the female breast, have been deliberately chosen here because they are cases where the psychoanalyst feels he is on the safest ground. Yet as may be seen, the extravagant ideas the analyst has about why people should want plastic surgery can be plausibly replaced by much simpler ones. There is a widespread appreciation in our Society of people who are physically and sexually attractive. Notions of attraction are centred on the body and the face, and anyone who wishes to feel more attractive will obviously attempt to improve him or herself in one of these places. All this is supported when, as can be seen, those who do have such changes made almost always feel happier, more attractive, and often enjoy better sex lives. If such simple explanations may be substituted, it may be asked why psychiatric explanations, particularly of the psychoanalytic kind, are ever taken seriously at all. There seem to be two reasons for this. For one thing, they are sometimes correct in the sense that a small number of people given cosmetic surgery do not enjoy better lives and some become even more disturbed because the main 'excuse' for their failure has been removed and they have nothing to fall back upon for blame. However, the main reasons psychoanalytic and similar theories still dominate this area is that a strong Puritan streak runs through our culture. Although most of us are preoccupied with physical appearance, we disapprove of narcissism and vanity. Thus, while sometimes on the brink of doing so ourselves, we disapprove strongly of people who are willing to go to great lengths and to suffer physical pain in order to improve their appearance: we like to believe such people are mentally disturbed. This stigma is in many people's minds when they seek surgery, and it adds an element of guilt to an already disturbed personality. It is surely often just this guilt that helps convince the unwary psychiatrist that something deeper is being shielded. The convenience of psychiatric explanations goes further than this, too, for by focusing attention on those weaker individuals who 'give in' we can conveniently forget the strength of the convention about attractiveness to which we all meekly subscribe.

If plastic surgery can so easily improve the self-image and social relationships of patients who ask for it and can afford it, it might well do the same for others with specific disfigurements. This idea prompted some research with disfigured prisoners in New York City — with very promising results [19]. The research was part of a 3-year investigation carried out to evaluate the effect of plastic surgery administered with and without social and vocational services to male prison inmates. The prisoners chosen were mainly from the most disadvantaged areas of New York City: 47% of them were Negro, 33% were Whites, and 20% were Puerto Ricans. Eighty per cent of the prisoners had not completed high school and all of them has suffered disfigurements ranging from knife and burn scars to lop-ears, needle tracks from drug usage, and tattoos. The idea was that the removal of these disfigurements by plastic surgery would reduce recidivism (return to prison), increase job success (previously poor), and improve psychological adjustment. The 168 individuals chosen for the study were split at random into four groups. The first group received surgery only, the second received surgery plus social and vocational help, the third received social and vocational help, and the fourth no treatment at all. In this way it was possible to evaluate the effect of surgery and of social and vocational help and of their combination.

The plastic surgery procedures were carried out in civilian hospitals following an inmate's release from prison and follow-ups were conducted one year following surgery or release from prison. During this one-year period those prisoners receiving surgery and who were not drug addicts offended again 36% less often than those who received no treatment at all, whereas those receiving only social and vocational services offended at a rate 33% higher. This latter group also showed poorer social relations during the one-year follow-up period. However, plastic surgery did not appear to benefit prisoners who were drug addicts who showed an 8% reduction following surgery while with those addicts receiving social and vocational services alone, there was a 33% reduction in recidivism. It was also noted that plastic surgery appeared to help those with facial disfigurements to a greater extent than those with disfigurements on their bodies. The authors suggest that plastic surgery may act as a catalyst in making the offender change other aspects of himself in addition to his appearance. And after all, as they say: 'The cost of plastic surgery, although relatively high, can be considered negligible if the offender is helped to remain out of prison for even one year.'

Of course, there must be a limit to the use of plastic surgery, and its current popularity is in itself witness to the idea that our culture values appearance so much that forces many people to go to great lengths to improve theirs. If the numbers of those presenting themselves for surgical techniques is the tip of an iceberg of unhappiness created by this preoccupation for good looks, then it must be time for us to examine our values once more.

As someone once said, it is not a person's sexual relations that cause his disturbances, it is his social relations. If we heed this we shift the blame, for 'social relations' involve us all.

REFERENCES

1. K. Perutz (1972) *Beyond the looking glass*, Penguin, Harmondsworth.
2. W. J. Dibiase and L. A. Hjelle (1968) Body image stereotype preferences among male college students. *Perc. Mot. Skills* 27, 1143—6.
3. R. M. Lerner *et al.* (1973) Relations among physical attractiveness, body attitudes and self-concept in male and female college students. *J. Psychol.* 85, 119—30.
4. N. Cavior (1970) Physical attractiveness self-concept: a test of Mead's hypothesis. *Proc. 79th Ann. Conf. Am. Psychol. Assoc.* 6, 319—20.
5. S. M. Jourard and P. F. Secord (1955) Body cathexis and the ideal female figure. *J. abnorm. soc. Psychol.* 50, 243—6.
6. E. Goffman (1963) *Stigma*. Prentice Hall, New Jersey.
7. M. S. Weinberg (1963) The problems of midgets and dwarfs and organizational remedies: a study of Little People of America. *J. Health soc. Behav.* 9, 65—71
8. K. Bosse *et al.* (1976) Social situation of persons with dermatoses as a phenomenon of interpersonal perception. *Z. psychosom. Med. Psychanal.* 22, 3—61.
9. A. W. Green and S. Loomis (1947) Pattern of mental conflict in a typical state university. *J. abnorm. soc. Psychol.* , 342—55.
10. J. Todd *et al.* (1971) Real or imaginary hypophallism: a cause of inferiority feelings and morbid sexual jealousy. *Br. J. Psychiat.* 119, 315—18.
11. M. T. Edgerton *et al.* (1960) Surgical—psychiatric study of patients seeking plastic (cosmetic) surgery. *Br. J. plast. Surg.* 13, 136—45.
12. G. G. Hay (1970) Dysmorphophobia. *Br. J. Psychiat.* 116, 399—406.
13. M. H. Hollender (1956) Observations on nasal symptoms: relationship of anatomical structure of the nose to psychological symptoms. *Psychiat. Quart.* 30, 1—12.
14. N. J. Knorr *et al.* (1968) Psychiatric—surgical approach to adolescent disturbance to self-image. *Plast. recon. Surg.* 41, 248—53.

15. G. G. Hay (1970) Psychiatric aspects of cosmetic nasal operations *Br. J. Psychiat.* **116**, 35—97.
16. W. E. Jacobsen *et al.* (1960) Psychiatric evaluation of male patients seeking cosmetic surgery. *Plast. vecon. Surg.* **26**, 356—72.
17. M. T. Edgerton *et al.* (1961) Augmentation mammaplasty: II, further surgical and psychiatric evaluation. *Plast. recon. Surg.* **27**, 279—302.
18. M. T. Edgerton and A. R. McClary (1958) Augmentation mammaplasty: psychiatric implications and surgical indications. *Plast. recon. Surg.* **21**, 279—305.
19. R. L. Kurtzberg *et al.* (1968) Surgical and social rehabilitation of adult offenders. *Proc. 76th Ann. Conf. Am. Psych. Assoc.* **3**, 649—50.

Chapter 8

FUTURE APPEARANCES

This short chapter considers how physical attractiveness might be separated in people's minds from sexual attractiveness and social success. It might be possible to introduce new laws banning discrimination on the grounds of physical unacceptability and improve selection procedures such as those used to screen job applicants. Some recent attempts to train unattractive people in ways which make them more confident are also considered. The ultimate solution to this modern problem which causes much personal unhappiness for those less attractive would be to change urban life as we now know it and to create small, stable communities. Only then does sexual attraction have a chance of becoming rooted in knowledge of individuals as they are rather than as they look.

Modern society's preoccupation with physical appearance and its admiration of those who are desirable to the opposite sex is not novel. Every society has talked and written about, painted and photographed its more beautiful people. Of course, there is nothing wrong with this. The beautiful body deserves appreciation just as much as any other exquisite natural or manmade physical form. However, many modern societies are going beyond the point of simply admiring the physical form and are tending more and more to forge a link between beauty and behaviour, between appearance and ability. Outer beauty is being taken to imply inner beauty, and good physical appearance is becoming an important precursor to success. In such an atmosphere more and more people are feeling, as we saw in the last chapter, that their lack of physical beauty is associated with a deficiency of character; a physical deformity is felt as a personal defect. On the other hand, the physically and sexually attractive enjoy privilege and status. We all acknowledge that beauty is only skin deep, but, on the other hand, we refuse to act as if it were true. Facial discrimination is just as widespread as racial discrimination but much less well publicized.

A good part of the blame for this state of affairs must be shared equally between our own readiness to accept simple and rapid ways of judging people and the mass media, who shape our expectations and standardize our taste. These two effects reinforce each other and it is interesting to see how they do so. It all starts during socialization of children. It has always been normal for parents to hand on their experience about the world to their children as they grow up. A good part of this experience concerns information about people: 'Don't trust men who offer lifts'; 'Don't play with boys from the next street'; 'Follow Jim's example, he's a nice boy'. Information handed on to children by their parents consists partly of personal and quite idiosyncratic judgements and partly of opinions shared by a majority of people in society ('Foreigners are not to be trusted'; 'Men from Boston are always well mannered'). When communications were relatively poor and cultural transmission of information about people was difficult, the proportion of idiosyncratic to personal information given to children must have been higher. Parents had no easy access to predigested images of people so they had to rely on their own experience and judgements. Equally, there must have been such less certainty about what the culturally shared information was supposed to be. This meant that opinions about people were probably more varied from one class and community to another. With an increase in the efficiency of communications, as well as the growth of predominantly visual modes like still photography, films, and television, two things have happened. The same standard information about people is being transmitted more widely and at the same time emphasis has been placed more and more on what people look like. In this situation, not only have certain physical preferences become more firmly and universally established over others (see, for example, the agreement reached by British and American people over facial beauty: Chapter 2), but physical appearance itself has become the most widely used medium through which judgements are made. We are encouraged directly to compare for their looks the people we meet with those we have been taught to admire in films and on television, and who daily smile at us from posters, magazines, and newspapers.

Once physical appearance has been established in this way as of prime importance when we are judging others, it becomes easy to convince people, by repetition of the message, that certain characteristics are almost always to be found with good looks. Open any popular magazine and look at the advertisements. When people are portrayed, they are almost all tall, well-groomed models with excellent physiques. They sit at ease in fast expensive cars and we are given the impression that they are wealthy, well-bred and discriminating. Often we are expected to believe that if we buy the product they endorse we are similar to them — and we do not take much convincing. In many advertisements a figure of one sex will stand surrounded by several members of the opposite sex who clearly cannot wait to get their hands on him or her. This is the way the connection between physical attractiveness, sexual attractiveness, and personality is reinforced, and little by little we accept it as reality.

It is difficult for us not to be caught up in all this admiration for the beautiful for it has become so much a part of our everyday lives. Most of us want to have some appeal for others, particularly for our sex partners, so we envy people who are consistently revered as sexually attractive and do our best to be like them. Beauty has become more than a physical description when applied to others. The stereotype of 'beautiful people' encourages us all to make the often mistaken generalization which connects fine appearance with good character. We have seen in Chapter 3 how impossible it is for us to avoid making generalizations about other people. In the first place we simply do not have the mental capacity to think of the majority of people we meet as individuals. Secondly, even if we were capable of individualizing others, there is rarely any time allowed for delay in making judgements of others, particularly strangers. The ability to form an impression quickly is indispensable in everyday life. It helps us to address others in the right way; it helps us to decide whether a stranger may be trusted or not. It would be as absurd to ask people to stop stereo typing others as it would be to ask them to stop breathing. Yet stereotypes are very often wrong. Faced with this situation, it ought to be possible to teach people, when their stereotypes are poor ones, to form better stereotypes. By 'better' is not necessarily meant 'nicer'. Terms like mercenary, happy-go-lucky, shrewd, conservative, stolid, very religious, which are frequently included in opinions of ethnic and social class groups, may not be complimentary but they could quite genuinely express a likely difference between one *group* and another. Many of these differences are due to parental child-rearing attitudes, and it would be foolish to ignore such variations in upbringing as shapers of adult personality. Someone has used the term 'verotype' to describe these 'better' stereotypes, although this is misleading as it has its root in the Latin word for truth (and there is nothing absolutely true about any stereotype). In Chapter 4 of this book an attempt was made to set out some 'verotypes' to replace the stereotypes commonly associated with sexual attraction. In the immediate case, a replacement of the beautiful/good and ugly/bad stereotype with something less powerful would seem to be both necessary and very difficult.

It ought to be possible also to minimize the inevitable effects of stereotyping, by making people aware of why other people's behaviour takes the form that it does. A person's behaviour, as we saw in Chapter 3, can be shaped and modified by what others expect and how they behave towards him or her. A widely held stereotype becomes a social conspiracy aimed at making as certain as possible that people behave in predicted ways. If you firmly believe that someone is stupid and treat them as if they are, it is very difficult for them to perform well. If several people believe the same thing of them, the temptation to give in to consensus opinion can be too great for an individual and he or she eventually loses the will to believe otherwise. If we all become aware that expecting different behaviours of the beautiful and the ugly, the tall and athletic, and the short and fat becomes a self-fulfilling prophesy, then we will go some way towards balancing the injustice of our current stereotypes.

In some situations a knowledge of our personal biases may help us make more informed judgements of other people. It is difficult to find out how much we as individuals are taken in by appearance. The best way to identify bias is to discuss with someone else the people one likes and the reasons why one likes them. By this method it is often possible to discover consistencies in preferences and expectations. Consciousness-raising groups can help but even this is not a foolproof method for many prejudices are shared in our culture – in particular by friends and work colleagues. This would mean that many judgements could go unquestioned if two or three like-minded people sit down to compare notes. Nevertheless, such a system is better than nothing and many of those selecting people for jobs, for example, ought to bear it in mind. Most job interview systems in current use could be greatly improved if two or three selectors saw people independently in a one-to-one situation, wrote a report so that they were committed to paper, and then met with their fellow interviewers to discuss the candidates they had seen. At such a meeting, which is commonly called a selectors' conference, many interviewers are unpleasantly surprised to discover how wide ranging their own prejudice is. Many may also have been prevented through such a procedure from hiring the pretty girl who could not type in favour of the plain one who could. One of the present authors has shown in a study [2] that selectors are capable of recognizing and using information about their biases even if their personal prejudices have never been pointed out to them. Indeed, in the case of interviewees who were sexually attractive, their reaction was to over-compensate and mark the better looking worse than they deserved *if they knew their judgements were under scrutiny and were going to have to be justified afterwards.* Over-compensation of this kind can easily be corrected. The main thing to notice is that such a reverse prejudice indicates that selectors (and presumably the rest of us too) can fight biases when judgements are made under certain conditions.

Of course, even if all the methods mentioned here were used a change in attitude to physical appearance would come about slowly, if at all. It is worth noting that even a national propaganda campaign (like the recent 'black is beautiful') can have little effect, probably because the virtues of tolerance cannot be advertised and sold to the public like cigarettes or washing machines. Just as government counter-smoking propaganda competes with the tobacco industries' pro-smoking advertising and does not win, so propaganda minimizing the importance of appearance would compete with advertising paid for with the larger budgets of cosmetic and clothing industries to name but two.

What else can be done on a grand scale and what will be the consequences if we do not bother to do anything? Taking the latter question first; some writers have suggested that we are in real danger of creating a stratified society in which the physically attractive will rise to the top, like cream in a glass. For example, one author, Sorokin [1] says:

> ' . . . in the present society in various ways there goes on permanent recruiting of beautiful women into the higher social strata. The same process in different ways seems to have proceeded in past societies. If such is the case, the beauty and handsomeness of the mother, being transmitted to her children facilitate an accumulation of comeliness in the higher classes. Through this process of social selection — a variety of Darwin's sexual selection — the higher social layers come to be more handsome than the lower ones. [p.246].

Sorokin clearly sees ugliness as a very great obstacle to social climbing and goes on to argue that the kind of selection mentioned above, as well as lack of physical work, better hygiene, better food, and more time for body care, are likely to lead to a greater degree of handsomeness among the upper classes. This is a fascinating theory but it is rather unlikely. For one thing, an improvement in social and economic conditions has steadily reduced the work, hygiene, and food gaps he mentions even though it has not eliminated them entirely. He is right about the transmission of facial beauty. The parental determination of such erphological characteristics, as they are called, is fairly high, and people rarely imagine it when they say that children look like their parents. Nevertheless, there is not, as was shown in Chapter 2, one criterion for facial beauty and, even if there were, preferences change slowly but surely from one generation to the next. This could mean that in many cases parents were once considered beautiful yet their children who resemble them strongly are not considered so. But facial structure is not the only feature that attracts, and Sorokin's theory may still hold for other features. Reference has been made in this book to height and body weight, just to take two examples. The amount that parental height determines their offspring's height is at least as great as for facial characteristics. Some have argued that a general increase in diet and healthiness will reduce the difference between the smallest and largest in present and future generations. The facts go against this. The material benefits enjoyed by our own Western societies have indeed increased the average height of our generation over the one living 100 years ago. But this increase (about 1–1½ inches in Britain and 2½–3½ inches in some other countries) seems to have been spread uniformly across social classes so that there is practically the same variation in height now as there ever was. Thus, if in a settled population all men started to marry women equivalent in height, then one aspect of Sorokin's theory could be taken seriously. Under such conditions people would remain segregated sexually and therefore socially from one generation to the next. However, as there are no clear signs that this is happening, Sorokin's idea as applied even to this characteristic seems unduly alarmist.

The concept of sexual and physical attraction therefore only seems to penalize or greatly favour elements in any one generation, but the same prejudices may not, largely due to changes in preference, affect their offspring in the next. On the assumption that society's intolerance will not be dealt with easily or quickly, some psychologists are applying the sort of measures that lend themselves to dealing with deficiencies in an individual's attractiveness. These measures are known as social skills training programmes and they are, as yet, at an early stage of development [3]. Social skills training is designed to deal with individual difficulties in social behaviour and appearance in a highly practical way. If a person is shy in the company of the opposite sex or finds it difficult to make friends, then they are made to practise under controlled conditions the kind of things that ought to increase their personal effectiveness in company. Here is an actual case history which illustrates the method very well.

'Ann.' Female, aged 23, graduate student. *Diagnosis*: depression and depersonalization. Described as 'always having done well academically but badly socially. Appeared rather young for her age, and dressed in rather staid attire; speaks in extremely polished, formal English, not able to mix with people.'

Ann, despite a very successful academic career, felt herself a social failure. She saw herself as fat and unattractive, and thought she gave the impression of the stereotype academic female, pedantic and abrupt. 'I recognize that I talk in an elaborate and stylized fashion', she said. She had difficulty in talking about herself and her feelings in conversation and she did not like parties because she could not do the dances in fashion. Ann was seen seven times by the psychologists who carried out the social skills training. The first of these was an assessment session at which she adopted a 'superior' facial expression and a clipped and superior style of speaking. The psychologists report her conversation as very intellectual during this session with long words and formal phrases. At the first of the subsequent training sessions she was shown that by changing one's tone of voice, facial expressions, gesture, and posture, how different attitudes and feelings can be conveyed, and she was encouraged to practise these variations. At the second session she had an informal talk with some people of her own age, which lasted 15 minutes and was videotaped. With only Ann, the clinical psychologist and an electronics technician present, this tape was played back in stages and Ann could see and criticize her own performance. She also received gentle and constructive criticism from the psychologist present. At the fifth session, Ann was asked to talk to a young man and to try and control the conversation. She did not do well, so after a break for 'rehearsal' she was asked to try again. This time she showed more interest, more initiative, and gave 'a more attractive performance'. In addition, her appearance had been discussed with her at the previous session and she arrived at this one with her hair done and dressed in more colourful and flattering clothes. She vowed now that she was going to slim and to take more exercise. At final sessions she was encouraged to be more personal in her conversation and after more rehearsals she showed (in conversation with a woman) that she could be more intimate, show more interest, and appear more friendly than she had done ever before. After this, Ann's depression symptoms greatly improved. She continued to look smarter in appearance and seemed much more lively and composed. After 20 months she still found it hard to believe that she could be accepted as a person who might become a friend. Her mother, however, reported that she was a much happier and pleasanter individual to be with.

Social skills training can only nibble at the great social problem of unattractiveness. The problem is that even if it becomes an established form of therapy, it will be expensive to carry out because it demands so much professional time. Investigations are currently being made to discover the feasibility of group training. In this, similarly troubled people would get together under the eye of a psychologist and co-operate in practice sessions, etc., in an attempt to help each other out. If this is successful it would reduce the cost of training somewhat.

Social skills training, like plastic surgery, can only tackle some of the *symptoms* of our society's preoccupation with sexual and physical attraction, but fails to reach the *cause*. Legislation is being used in a small way to do this but its role will always be limited. For example, it is being made more difficult to discriminate according to appearance in employee selection. In many American states it is already illegal to demand photographs with job applications — although this is primarily to avoid racial discrimination. In areas where it is more difficult and even less desirable to legislate — television, films, and advertising — it might be made clear that a responsibility exists to show homely people more frequently to be leading normal, happy, and successful lives. A good amount of the world we see through these media is inhabited by 'beautiful' people, and this can only have the effect of heightening awareness of appearance, on the one hand, and making us discontented with our friends, dates, spouses, and even ourselves, on the other.

In the last analysis, efforts to relieve the causes underlying the problems and injustices must be based on some theory about why things are going wrong. It is clear that some of the blame can be attributed to the effects of big city life and of failure to adapt to it. Man lives 'naturally' in relatively small groups to dozens, hundreds, thousands possibly, but not millions. As most of even our recent ancestors lived in such groups it is probable that many of our present courtship rules and customs originated there. In effect, we are using small town and village social habits in the large city without realizing how badly they fit. Consider first the emphasis on physical appearance. In a small community the range of attractiveness will be far less on the simple principle that while there are likely to be 2000 girls and boys with a 'face-in-a-thousand' in a city of 2 million, there is not likely to be more than one in a village of 800. People will therefore be more equal in appearance, and as they vary less on this dimension this will matter less in their interpersonal relations. Equally, in a small stable community people know each other better and this has several important consequences. Less reliance is placed on appearance because more time is available to find out how others think and feel and what their characteristic behaviour patterns are. Because they know each other well and form part of a stable community, behaviour by one individual towards another is expected to be more responsible. Word spreads quickly in small villages and towns, and exploitation of another person is quickly noticed and criticized.

By contrast, interpersonal relationships in large communities and cities are often much briefer, and much more opportunity exists for one person to exploit another. A feature of life in big cities is the great number of short meetings that take place between strangers or between people who see each other regularly but always in the same setting — shopkeepers, bus conductors, traffic wardens, work colleagues. In a large organization especially, one knows hundreds of people by sight. It is impossible to get to know all these people individually so we pigeon-hole them in a set of boxes designed more for our convenience — and protection — than for an accurate representation of what they are really like. A superficial assessment of someone enables us to put them in the 'thick athlete' box or the 'dumb blonde' box or whatever, and such rapid, almost dismissive, assessments naturally rely very largely on appearance.

The variability of urban life has also forced us to construct semi-rigid systems of social rules which restrict our individual behaviour and penalize those who cannot easily learn them. In smaller communities the social rules can be simpler. There is likely to be a recognized place for meeting the opposite sex and a known and acceptable way of building up a relationship. The uncertainty and confusion characteristic of meetings between young people of both sexes is reduced.

Of course, this is an exceptionally rosy view of village and small town life. It might be said that the prying, gossiping, and spitefulness that can exist side by side with the benefits of small community life are being overlooked. This is true, but the essential principle that social relations in a small community will differ from those in a city still seems to hold. So does the idea argued in Chapter 3 that we are psychologically incapable of getting to know well more than a small handful of people. Even then we will be unsuccessful unless we spend a lot of time with them in order to build up an acquaintance with the greater part of their behaviour. All this seems to point to the establishment of smaller communities in our society as a way of overcoming the dangers of overstretching man's ability to deal with the social world. A return to an idyllic rural past is obviously impossible. But the social engineer who can recreate the features of small community existence within urban life is likely also to create an atmosphere of better social and sexual relations.

R E F E R E N C E S

1. P. A. Sorokin (1964) *Social and cultural mobility*, Free Press, New York.
2. R. E. McHenry (1972) An analysis of the ability to form impressions of other persons, D.Phil thesis, University of Oxford.
3. M. Argyle *et al.* (1974) Explorations in the treatment of personality disorders and neuroses by social skills training. *Br. J. med. Psychol.* **47**, 163–72.

AUTHOR INDEX

Kephart, W. M.   104
Kerckhoff, A. C.   164
Kinsey, A.   4, 16, 20, 82, 84, 85, 86,
  87, 101, 103, 121, 153
Kirkendall, L. A.   83, 95, 103, 114, 123,
  130
Kirkpatrick, C.   131
Kleck, R. E.   49
Knorr, N. J.   183
Komarovsky, M.   164
Kraft, I. A.   164
Krebs, D.   48, 49
Kubie, L. S.   163
Kuchemann, C. F.   163
Kurtzberg, R. L.   184

Landy, D.   48
Larsen, K. S.   107, 130
Lavoie, J. C.   75
Lavrakas, P. J.   20
Lawson, E. D.   74
Lerner, R. M.   47, 49, 183
Lester, D.   163
Levin, S. M.   20
Levinger, G.   163, 164
Lewis, J. R.   49
Lewis, S. A.   48
Lichtenstein, E.   130
Lindzey, G.   164
Logan, T. G.   21
Lombardi, D. A.   49
Loomis, S.   183
Luborsky, L.   130
Luce, C. B.   49
Luckey, E. B.   103
Lukianowicz, N.   163
Luschen, M. E.   20

McClary, A. R.   184
McClear, P. M.   20
McClelland, D. C.   104
McDavid, J.   75
McFall, R. M.   130
McGarry, M. S.   75
McGovern, K.   130
McGuire, R. J.   20
McHenry, R. E.   195
McKeachie, W. J.   74
Machotka, P.   130

Mackworth, N.   130
Mangus, A.   163
Maslow, A. H.   103
Masters, F. W.   49
Masters, W.   12, 18, 20
Mathes, E. W.   48, 49
Mathews, A. M.   20
Mehrabian, A.   130
Mettee, D. R.   131
Miller, A. G.   74
Miller, H. L.   49
Mills, J.   47
Mirande, A. M.   103
Monaghan, T. P.   163
Morgan, R.   164
Morris, D.   12, 20, 94, 104, 119, 130
Morris, N. M.   20
Mosher, D. L.   103
Murstein, B. I.   48, 164

Nass, G.   74, 103
Nesselroade, J. R.   164

Oskamp, S.   20
Ostrove, N.   75

Parrott, G. L.   49
Patterson, E. W. J.   48
Paulhus, D. L.   104
Perlman, D.   49
Perrin, F. A. C.   48
Perutz, K.   167, 183
Petrullo, L.   102
Pierce, D. M.   20
Pond, D. A.   163
Poole, A.   163
Potkay, C. R.   102
Price, C. A.   163

Reed, E. W.   164
Reed, S. C.   164
Reiling, A. M.   49
Reiss, I.   102
Richardson, H. N.   164
Richardson, S. A.   49
Risso, M.   104
Riverbark, W. H.   49
Roff, M.   104
Rogers, J.   164

200

AUTHOR INDEX

Roll, S.   74
Rosenblatt, P. C.   104, 130
Russell, A.   130
Ryle, A.   163

Sade, D. S.   163
Schachter, S.   131
Scheflen, A.   130
Schiavo, R. S.   47
Schiller, B.   164
Schmidt, G.   21
Schofield, M.   103
Schroder, C.   49
Secord, P. F.   183
Seligman, C.   75
Shepher, J.   163
Shepherd, J. W.   49
Shipman, G.   164
Sigall, H.   48, 75
Sigusch, V.   21
Simon, W.   103
Singer, J.   131
Skipper, J. K.   74
Slater, E.   164
Smircich, R.   164
Sobrero, A.   20
Sorokin, P. A.   195
Stephan, W.   75
Swanson, D. W.   104
Symonds, C.   130

Tagiuri, R.   102
Talmon, V.   163
Teevan, J. J.   103
Terman, L.   163
Tesser, A.   49
Tharp, R. G.   164
Thibaut, J. W.   130, 165
Thiel, D. L.   47

Thumin, F. J.   48
Todd, J.   183
Touhey, J. C.   74
Twentyman, C. T.   130

Udry, J. R.   20, 47, 102
Useem, M.   164

Vener, A. M.   103

Wakefield, J. A.   164
Waller, W.   48
Wallin, P.   163, 164
Walster, E.   48, 49, 75, 103, 131
Ward, C. D.   48
Ward-Hull, C. I.   20
Weinberg, M. S.   183
Wells, B. W. P.   103
West, G. G.   75
Wiggins, J. S.   20
Wildeblood, P.   130
Wilkins, P. C.   131
Wilson, P. P.   48
Wilson, R. R.   103
Winch, R. F.   164
Wincze, J. P.   21, 131
Winkler, R.   130
Wolf, A. P.   163
Worral, N.   20
Wright, P. H.   165

Yorburg, B.   103

Zajonc, R. B.   49, 163, 164
Zelnick, M.   103
Zetterberg, H. L.   130
Zubrzycki, J.   163
Zuckerman, M.   20

SUBJECT INDEX